A History *of* *the* Church *in* 100 Objects

"My heart was stirred. A beautiful book about how God works through real stuff in the Incarnation to bring the mysteries of the spiritual realm into this phenomenal world. As usual, Mike Aquilina uses words with real craft and art to take us beyond words and into the mysteries of God in Christ."

John Michael Talbot
Catholic musician, author, and founder of the Brothers and Sisters of Charity

"This stunning new book shows how much grace can be found in everyday objects. Through the ordinary matter of desks and stones, tunics and textbooks, bottles and parchment, the Aquilinas weave together a beautiful picture of God at work. For lovers of history, faith, and matter, *A History of the Church in 100 Objects* is a delight."

Emily Stimpson
Coauthor of *The Catholic Almanac*

"Richly entertaining and highly informative, *A History of the Church in 100 Objects* is a journey through two millennia of Catholic history in the company of gracious and knowledgeable guides. A gem to enliven faith while shedding fresh light on the Church's long pilgrimage through the centuries. I recommend it with pleasure."

Russell Shaw
Author of *American Church: The Remarkable Rise, Meteoric Fall, and Uncertain Future of Catholicism in America*

"A thoroughly enjoyable book by an author who is always inspiring, stimulating, and thoroughly enjoyable! I can't think of a more captivating way to follow Cardinal John Henry Newman's challenge to become 'deep in history.'"

Marcus Grodi
Founder and president of The Coming Home Network International

"Mike Aquilina demonstrates once again a profound ability to impart vital teachings about the Catholic faith in a way that can be appreciated by anyone. A collection of objects, seemingly unrelated and spread across the globe, demonstrate poignantly both the universality of the Church and her relevance to every era. Aquilina truly is one of American Catholicism's most gifted, articulate, and clever writers."

Matthew Bunson
Senior fellow of the St. Paul Center for Biblical Theology
Coauthor of *Encyclopedia of Saints* and *The 35 Doctors of the Church*

"Catholicism means 'stuff counts,' because God chose the stuff of this world to bring his people to salvation—a process that begins with creation, reaches its apex in the life and ministry of Jesus, and continues today with the sacraments, in which the stuff of this world becomes a vehicle for sanctifying grace. Mike Aquilina tells the story of the Church through some very important stuff in an engaging and thought-provoking contribution to the New Evangelization."

George Weigel
Distinguished senior fellow and William E. Simon chair in Catholic Studies
Ethics and Public Policy Center

"A picture is worth a thousand words. Mike Aquilina, with skill and encyclopedic knowledge, gives new meaning to this old maxim. In *A History of the Church in 100 Objects*, we discover the rich story of our faith uniquely told through great pictures and explanations really worth knowing. Everyone should have this book."

Cardinal Donald Wuerl
Archbishop of Washington, DC

"A fascinating, unique spiritual feast."

Rodney Stark
Distinguished professor of the social sciences at Baylor University
Author of *Bearing False Witness: Debunking Centuries of Anti-Catholic History*

A History *of* *the* Church *in* 100 Objects

MIKE AQUILINA
WITH GRACE AQUILINA

AVE MARIA PRESS AVE Notre Dame, Indiana

© 2017 by Mike Aquilina and Grace Aquilina

All rights reserved. No part of this book may be used or reproduced in any manner whatsoever, except in the case of reprints in the context of reviews, without written permission from Ave Maria Press®, Inc., P.O. Box 428, Notre Dame, IN 46556, 1-800-282-1865.

Founded in 1865, Ave Maria Press is a ministry of the United States Province of Holy Cross.

www.avemariapress.com

Paperback: ISBN-13 978-1-59471-750-5

E-book: ISBN-13 978-1-59471-751-2

Cover image of Pope Benedict XV's pen © John Latour; image of wrench © Rosemary Aquilina.

Cover and text design by Andy Wagoner.

Printed and bound in the United States of America.

Library of Congress Cataloging-in-Publication Data is available.

For Sue

Contents

Introduction

It was Palm Sunday, and for once our family had arrived early for Mass—so early, in fact, that we saw our pastor as he was leaving the rectory. We exchanged our hellos and made small talk. I marveled that the parking lot was already full.

"Everybody comes to church on Palm Sunday and Ash Wednesday," he replied drily. "It's the two days they get free stuff."

Catholicism is indeed the religion of "stuff." Ours is the church of ashes and incense, icons and statues, bread and wine, water and oil, incorrupt bodies, and bones encased in glass.

None of this is incidental to the faith. We're not just about spiritual life. We're about the whole person. So matter matters, too. To an amazing degree, matter *makes* the faith as we live it day to day.

And it's always been this way. In the year AD 383, St. Gregory of Nyssa noted that all through the Old Testament God had saved his people by means of *stuff*:

> Moses' rod was a hazel switch—common wood that any hands might cut and carry and use as they please before tossing it into the fire. But God purposed to work miracles through that rod—great miracles beyond the power of words to express [see Ex 4–14]. . . . Likewise, the mantle of one of the prophets, a simple goatskin, made Elisha famous throughout the whole world [see 2 Kgs 2:8]. . . . A bramble bush showed the presence of God to Moses [see Ex 3:2]. The remains of Elisha raised a dead man to life [see 2 Kgs 13:21]. (St. Gregory of Nyssa, *On the Baptism of Christ*)

The God of Jesus Christ is the God of Israel—the God of Abraham and Isaac and Jacob. And it is his custom to get mixed up in the lives and history of his people. In the ancient world, Jews and Christians were unique in having no patience with myth. God appeared to Israel at specific times—datable by genealogy and dynastic charts—and in specific places. Biblical religion dares us to check its facts.

If the Israelites had a religious claim to make, they provided the provenance along with it. Within the Ark of the Covenant they kept the tablets of the law along with Aaron's staff and some samplings of manna. The early Christians, in their turn, kept St. Peter's bones hidden in plain sight in Rome and gradually accumulated a shrine around their treasure.

Others may call us a "religion of the book," but we're not. We're a religion of the Word, the divine Word, who is utterly unlike our spoken or written words (see *Catechism of the Catholic Church*, n. 108). Words are made of warmed-up breeze and most of them pass away as soon as they're let loose. But God the Word is "living and active, sharper than a two-edged sword" (Heb 4:12); and God the Word has assumed the material of our world by taking flesh. He has dwelt among us. We call that fact the *Incarnation*.

The Incarnation is the heart of the Christian creed and the point of every Mass. It is the definitive revelation of God. When the Son took flesh by the power of the Holy Spirit, he revealed God's eternal fatherhood. This is how the world came to know God as a Trinity of divine persons and share the inner life of the Trinity through the sacraments.

In Jesus Christ, God "worked out my salvation through matter," said St. John of Damascus in the eighth century. "Never will I cease honoring the matter which wrought my salvation! . . . God has filled it with his grace and power" (St. John of Damascus, *On Holy Images* 1.16).

The earliest Christians thought of salvation as something tangible and historical:

> What was from the beginning,
>   what we have heard,
>   what we have seen with our eyes,
>   what we looked upon
>   and touched with our hands
>   concerns the Word of life—
> for the life was made visible;

we have seen it and testify to it
and proclaim to you the eternal life
that was with the Father and was made visible to us.
 (1 Jn 1:1–2, NABRE)

In fact, the "incarnational principle" extends through all of history as individual Christians—and entire nations—come to share divine life through the sacraments. The life that is invisible is "made visible" for us to see. Our Christian forebears give testimony in the things—the material culture, the "stuff"—they left behind.

So when we Christians tell our story, we don't just write it up in books. We preserve the memory in memorials, monuments, and museums. We build grand basilicas to house tiny relics.

This book attempts to tell the Christian story in an incarnational way—through the examination of one hundred objects. Some of these are ordinary household items, and some are priceless works of art. Some are worthless by earthly standards, while others have become industries in themselves, tourist destinations drawing pilgrims by the thousands every year.

Salvation history is history, not myth. It doesn't occur in moments shrouded in mists before time. It doesn't take place on the heights of Mount Olympus, invisible to us mere mortals who live at sea level.

Salvation history is the story of God entering our world, sometimes with flash and dazzle, but most often through ordinary stuff amid the mess of centuries. And salvation history did not end with the close of the biblical narrative. It's not even over yet. The end of the Bible opens out onto the beginning of our age.

God makes himself known and accessible through material things, always accommodating himself to our condition. It is, after all, the condition he created for us—spiritual and material—and the condition he assumed for our salvation.

 ～

Since most people tend to think of history in eras, we have divided the chapters of this book into seven groups.

The Church of the Apostles and Martyrs
The Church and the Empire
The Dark Ages
The Middle Ages
Renaissance and Reformations
The Age of Revolutions
The Global Village

We recognize the problems inherent in chopping history up this way. So keep in mind: every era's beginning is arbitrary and artificial, and so is every ending. Scholars debate endlessly about how to frame the narrative of that period. The poet Wisława Szymborska noted that every beginning is a sequel, and the book of events is always open at the middle. That's true. But history is betrayed by its etymology. It's a story, and every story is itself an artifact—the product of artifice. So artificiality is unavoidable, and divisions are inevitable—and helpful.

The history of the Church is, moreover, *your* story. The artifacts you find in this book are *your* family heirlooms, locked in an attic till now, each a revelation of something in your character, something in your heritage, something in the faith you share with millions alive today, millions who have gone before, and millions, presumably, still to come. As Catholics we profess belief "in the communion of saints." In the original Greek, the phrase means the "communion of holy things"—yes, the blessed souls in glory, but also the things of the earth that are made holy by their contact with Christ, in the touch of baptized Christians. This is the stuff of our story. This is the stuff of our salvation as it plays out through the centuries.

The Church *of* *the* Apostles *and* Martyrs

In the beginning, the Church—and individual believers—needed to focus on very basic matters. How to survive persecution? How to distinguish Christianity from Greco-Roman religion and from Judaism? How to respond to critics? By the end of the first century, the Church already possessed the characteristics, and seeds of the doctrines, that define Catholicism today. Christian identity was strong and recognizable even to nonbelievers and persecutors. Christians distinguished themselves by their moral lives, their single-minded devotion, and their charity.

The star at the Grotto of the Nativity in Bethlehem. Photo by mtcurado / iStockphoto.com.

1

The Silver Star *in* Bethlehem

This silver, fourteen-pointed star marks the spot reputed to be the birthplace of Jesus. Its inscription reads, "Here Jesus Christ was born of the Virgin Mary." Fifteen candles light the small crypt around it. Every day thousands of pilgrims wait in long lines before crouching low to kiss this spot, whose access is guarded by Catholic and Orthodox monks.

The Grotto of the Nativity lies beneath the altar in Bethlehem's Basilica of the Nativity. Christians affixed the star to the marble in 1717. In the century and a half that followed, it was removed and replaced, and these actions precipitated the Crimean War in 1853.

But the spot was well established long before the eighteenth century. The Gospels of Matthew and Luke assert that Jesus was born in Bethlehem (Mt 2:1–16; Lk 2:4, 15). The Gospel of John then assumes that fact (Jn 7:42). The birth took place near a feeding trough for animals (Lk 2:7). That's all that the scriptural record tells us.

The artifacts of history confirm what we see in scripture and then hint at more.

The earliest Christians took special care to remember the actual sites of the major events of the Savior's life: his Passion but also his extraordinary birth. They learned of the sites, when they could, from eyewitnesses (Lk 1:2), possibly even from the Virgin Mary, who "kept these things and pondered them in her heart" (Lk 2:19, 2:51). They, in their turn, also kept these things in their hearts and pondered them.

The *Infancy Gospel of James*, a devotional work set down in the early second century, notes that Jesus was born in a cave. And Christians in Bethlehem claimed to know the very place. St. Justin Martyr, who was born in Palestine around AD 100, testifies that his contemporaries honored "a certain cave" as the site where Jesus was born. The Egyptian scholar Origen of Alexandria, writing in the third century, confirmed this by his studies and by his own visit to Palestine.

Though the practice of Christianity was illegal—and punished, now and then, by death—pilgrims made their way to the site. In the time of the Emperor Hadrian, the early second century, the Roman authorities built a pagan shrine at the cave, probably to discourage Christian visits. The shrine, honoring Adonis, stood until the early fourth century. With the legalization of Christianity, the pagan grove of trees was leveled and a Catholic basilica raised in its place, funded by the Emperor Constantine.

Later in the fourth century, St. Jerome, the greatest biblical scholar of his time, took up residence in a neighboring cave, and there he conducted his research, made his translations of the Bible, and sent letters abroad promoting pilgrimage to the holy sites where he lived.

Constantine's church lasted until 529, when it burned down, to be rebuilt later by the Emperor Justinian. In the early seventh century, a Persian army invaded the Holy Land and destroyed many churches. However, they left the Church of the Nativity unharmed. According to one tradition, the Persians spared the basilica for the sake of its mosaics depicting the Magi, who were depicted in Persian attire.

The basilica has, since then, suffered abuse by many forces invading, occupying, or just marching through. Yet the grotto has been protected, preserved, honored, and rebuilt by Christians in every age, at great cost and often at great risk. The rock of the Nativity is adorned with silver and still kissed by thousands of prostrate pilgrims each year. Why? Because the site itself—the object—is, like the gospels, evidence for a certain event, a certain work of God, not in mythic time, but in history. "*Here* Jesus Christ was born of the Virgin Mary."

Catholic faith is historical faith. Biblical religion situates itself in real times, real places, crowded with real people—historical figures. As the historian Cardinal Jean Danielou observed, "The Bible is a record of the evidence for certain events, certain historical works of God: as, the covenant with Abraham, the birth and resurrection of Jesus Christ, and Pentecost."

Certain places and things are objects of fascination for Christians in every age, and so they are objects of our study, our honor and care.

For More

Jean Danielou, S.J. *The Lord of History*. New York: Meridian Books, 1968.

Scott Hahn. *Joy to the World: How Christ's Coming Changed Everything*. New York: Image Books, 2014.

Paving stone from a first-century road in Jerusalem. Photo by Fr. Gaurav Shroff.

2

A Jerusalem
Paving Stone

This is a first-century flagstone from a street in Jerusalem. After two thousand years, it still bears the crude outline of a game of chance, cut perhaps by bored children or soldiers.

The stone may also have borne the footfalls of the apostles. And it may not have. But today it is given a place of honor, just for the possibility.

The important fact is that the apostles *did* walk out into the streets of Jerusalem. They didn't stay behind locked doors, within the enclosure of the Upper Room, where they had spent more than a week of prayer in the company of Mary, the mother of Jesus.

They didn't take up a life of reclusive contemplation, like the Jewish sect of the Therapeutai, who dwelt in Egypt. Nor did they retire to the desert like the ascetics of Qumran, who left the Dead Sea Scrolls to posterity.

Filled with the Holy Spirit on the Jewish feast of Shavuot (Pentecost), the apostles entered the streets—and so entered the great stream of history.

They preached in the public places of Jerusalem, where pilgrims "from every nation under heaven were gathered for the festival: Parthians and Medes and Elamites and residents of Mesopotamia, Judea and Cappadocia, Pontus and Asia, Phrygia and Pamphylia, Egypt and the parts of Libya belonging to Cyrene, and . . . Rome" (Acts 2:9–10). The apostles announced the kingdom and issued a call for repentance, and many people responded and asked to be baptized.

This apostles' first preaching was to Jews who had arrived to fulfill the command of the Law of Moses (Ex 23:16).

But the Jews who heard the apostolic preaching on Pentecost were destined to return to homes, jobs, families, and neighborhoods in distant lands, and they bore the Good News with them.

The apostles, too, would set out in turn to preach the Gospel "to all the world" (Mk 16:15). They could not have chosen a better time to embark on their mission. The Romans had begun to build an international system of roads, unprecedented in history. Under Caesar Augustus, the empire had also suppressed piracy on the oceans and so made travel safer. And a Greek sailor named Hippalus had just recently discovered the trade winds, enabling ships to travel on the open seas from the Red Sea to the Indian peninsula. It was almost as if the moment had been prepared in advance.

It has long been customary for Christians to observe the Feast of Pentecost as the birthday of the Church. From its origin, then, Christianity was in the middle of the street, in the marketplace, in the amphitheaters, at the docks, on the ships, in the common areas of the villages and farmlands. Though monastic movements would later arise and draw individual believers into hermitages and enclosed communities, Christianity has always been, in the main, immersed in the world, changing it from within—changing the hearts of people who walked the flagstones, worked the market stalls, and played games of chance in idle moments.

Nor would Christianity be contained within a single city, country, or ethnic group. The apostles received their commission to go out to all nations, all the gentiles, but "beginning from Jerusalem" (Lk 24:47). The mission started with that first rush of footsteps on the flagstones of Jerusalem's streets.

For More

Mike Aquilina. *Ministers and Martyrs: The Ultimate Catholic Guide to the Apostolic Age.* Manchester, NH: Sophia Institute Press, 2015.

Jaroslav Pelikan. *Brazos Theological Commentary Bible: Acts.* Grand Rapids, MI: Brazos, 2005.

The metal grate before St. Paul's tomb. Photo by REUTERS / Alamy Stock Photo.

3

A Roman Grate

This simple metal grate keeps pilgrims at a short, respectful distance from the remains of the ancient tomb they come to honor: the tomb that is the centerpiece of the Roman Basilica of St. Paul Outside the Walls.

Behind the grate is the stone casket discovered during archeological excavations from 2002 to 2006. The casket was buried beneath the main altar of the basilica, under a marble slab engraved with the Latin words for "Paul, Apostle and Martyr."

After carbon-dating tests on the bone fragments found inside, scientists confirmed that they likely date from the first century AD. What else was found inside the casket? Tatters of costly purple linen—the clothing of emperors—along with bits of incense and gold sequins. These are later additions, however, probably added when the apostle's body was reburied, amid great splendor, in AD 390.

Paul was a man of singular genius, born Saul in Tarsus, a major port and the capital of the Roman province of Cilicia (now southern Turkey). He was a Jew and a Roman citizen. His zeal for his religious heritage must have been evident from a young age, because he traveled a long way to study in Jerusalem with the greatest teacher of his day, Gamaliel.

Saul identified with the Pharisees, a lay movement that promoted strict adherence to the Law of Moses and separation from the Gentiles. Saul believed the "Way" practiced by the followers of Jesus—who were mostly Jews—was a violation of the Law. Their worship of Jesus he judged to be blasphemous; their rejection of ancient custom he found to be treasonous. He emerged as a leader among the Church's first persecutors, negotiating an unusual collaboration between the often rivalrous Pharisees and Sadducees (the latter being the priestly class).

His brilliance and effectiveness must have been obvious to everyone. The chief priests entrusted him with special missions (Acts 9:1, 9:14). Kings and governors recognized his erudition (Acts 26:24–32).

In the midst of a journey to arrest followers of Jesus in Damascus, Syria, Paul had a powerful encounter with the Risen Lord. Temporarily blinded by the experience, he emerged as a fervent disciple.

With his great learning and charisma, Paul soon established himself as a leader of the Jesus Movement, whose members were by then known colloquially as Christians.

Paul saw his conversion not as a renunciation but as a correction of course. He still identified strongly with the people and religion of Israel. But now he was convinced that Jesus was their long-awaited deliverer—the Anointed, the Messiah, the Christ—who would also bring salvation to the rest of the world.

He called himself "Apostle to the Gentiles" (Rom 11:13). He began to use his Greek name, Paul, instead of Saul. And indeed he went out to the shores of many nations. Yet he always began his preaching at the local synagogue and with the local Jewish community. This is the pattern of his apostolate in Damascus, Salamis, Pisidian Antioch, Iconium, Thessalonica, Athens, Corinth, and Ephesus.

He continued to identify himself, in the present tense, as a Jew (Acts 21:39, 22:3), an Israelite and member of the tribe of Benjamin (Phil 3:5), and even as a Pharisee (Acts 23:6).

He saw Jesus as the Savior common to Israel and the Gentiles, all of whom were in need of conversion (Acts 9:15, 4:27).

He exercised his apostolate energetically, by letter and by personal appearance. He traveled prodigiously, braving the hardships and dangers of both the highways and the seas. More than a dozen New Testament letters are attributed to him.

Paul's stated desire was to go to Rome; and the travelogue of his ministry shows that he was borne there by inner compulsion and providential purpose. Paul's most significant letter, his first in the New Testament canon, is addressed to the Church in Rome.

St. Peter, named by Jesus to be the leader of the universal Church, also made his way to the empire's capital. Both men would die as martyrs in the first Roman persecution, when Nero made Christians his scapegoats after the city's great fire in 64. According to local tradition, Peter and Paul were executed on the same day that summer, Peter by crucifixion and Paul by beheading—the method that afforded him more dignity and less pain, because he was a Roman citizen.

Their bones would serve, in time, as the foundations of great churches. Their martyrdom would serve as a special consecration of their adopted city.

For More

William Farmer. *Peter and Paul and the Church of Rome: The Ecumenical Potential of a Forgotten Perspective.* Mahwah, NJ: Paulist Press, 1990.

Margherita Guarducci. *The Primacy of the Church of Rome: Documents, Reflections, Proofs.* San Francisco: Ignatius Press, 2003.

Indian Catholics say that the Thomas Post held back the sea. Photo by Tom Brouns via tazmpictures.com.

4

Wooden Post *by* *the* Sea *in* India

There's not much to it. It's a rough wooden post stuck in the ground near the seashore in the city of Chennai, on India's southeastern coast. Until recently the post didn't even have a plaque or marker explaining its significance.

But the locals knew. According to legend, on that site St. Thomas the Apostle had thrust a wooden post into the ground and said the sea would never come up so far.

Well, the coastline has changed significantly since the first century, and some of the places visited by St. Thomas are now underwater. But the sea has never come up as high as the Thomas Post.

On the day after Christmas in 2004, just minutes after midnight, a great earthquake and tsunami struck the Indian Ocean. Seismologists say that it released energy equivalent to 23,000 Hiroshima-type nuclear bombs. Thousands of people lost their lives, and many coastal cities were laid waste.

Many Christians of the region, knowing that the floodwaters were coming soon, took refuge behind the Thomas Post, and they survived. The sea, according to local accounts, stopped short of the marker. Within days, the Indian bishops sent out a press release relating the incident. And soon afterward the locals, in gratitude, constructed a fence and a shrine around the post, with a bronze plaque recording the miracle of the tsunami.

There is no reliably datable first-century evidence of the presence of the Apostle Thomas in India. But the tradition thereafter is strong. Every single ancient writer who deals with the later careers of the apostles places Thomas either in India or Parthia (which ruled a vast territory in India). The witnesses include Origen of Alexandria, Eusebius of Caesarea, Rufinus of Aquileia, Socrates the historian, St. Ephrem of Syria, St. Gregory Nazianzen, St. Ambrose of Milan, St. Gaudentius, St. Jerome, St. Paulinus of Nola, St. Gregory of Tours, and others.

There is also a persistent Indian oral tradition—among both Hindus and Christians—which includes ancient epics about Thomas. At Hindu weddings in Kerala, it is customary to sing a long song about the deeds of the Apostle to India.

So popular was Thomas among the early Christians that, within fifty years of his death, his name was affixed to an apocryphal "gospel" as well as rather fanciful "acts" of his apostolate in India.

The Catholic community in southern India endured, proudly calling themselves "Thomas Christians," to distinguish themselves from later converts. An Indian Catholic recently boasted in the pages of the *New York Times* that his community "was Christian when the Vatican was still a pipe dream."

Without the usual historical markers, the Thomas tradition sometimes rouses the skepticism of some Western historians. But not all of them. And some of the standard histories of India, written by non-Christians, judge the story credible. In the first century, commercial shipping was experiencing a golden age, and ships were leaving regularly for India from Alexandria in Egypt.

And there was a prosperous, though small, community of Jews in India. If Thomas's apostolate followed the pattern of Paul's, then he could have begun his preaching in the synagogues and then expanded outward to the Gentiles.

According to the epics and *Acts of Thomas*, that's what he did. His success was so great that he drew the anger of the local ruler and the envy of the local priests of Kali. He was run through with a spear near Chennai, where the San Thome Basilica stands today.

An Indian bishop in the twentieth century warned that anyone who voices a doubt about Thomas's presence in India should be ready to receive a sudden punch in the nose.

That's hardly necessary. St. Thomas himself once harbored greater doubts (Jn 20:25). His spiritual children are numerous today, and they believe and have found refuge in a rich tradition.

For More

George Menachery, ed. *The Thomapedia*. Thiruvananthapuram, India: St. Joseph's Press, 2000.

A. M. Mundadan. *History of Christianity in India*. Bangalore, India: CHAI, 2001.

The mosaic near the altar at Tabgha, Israel. Photo by parys / iStockphoto.com.

5

Loaves *and* Fish

This mosaic, dating from the fifth century, adorns the floor of the Church of the Multiplication in Tabgha, Israel. It depicts a basket of loaves and two fish, recalling Jesus' miraculous feeding of thousands with just a few items (Mt 14:17, 15:34).

The image is situated next to a large rock, which has been left in place in the floor since the first church was built there in the fourth century. The early Christians likely marked that rock as the place where Jesus stood or sat when he took the loaves, blessed and broke them, and gave them to his disciples for distribution.

The mosaic rests beneath the church's altar, because Christians have always seen the multiplication of loaves and fish as a foreshadowing of the Eucharist. As the archeologist Graydon Snyder, an evangelical Protestant, put it, "The fish was, with the bread, the primary symbol for the Eucharist, the meal that developed, maintained, and celebrated the new community of faith."

Indeed, the Eucharist dominates the attention of the early Christian authors. The earliest surviving Christian document is likely the *Didache*, whose ritual portions may date back to AD 48. (That would predate the oldest portions of the New Testament.) The *Didache* includes full texts as well as rubrics for eucharistic prayer and advice for making a good Communion. It makes clear that Communion may be received only by baptized believers.

Other documents of the first and early second century share a common concern for proper eucharistic worship. The *Letter of Barnabas* considers the Christian sacrifice in light of the liturgy of the Jerusalem Temple, especially the rituals of the Day of Atonement. The *Letter to the*

Corinthians, by St. Clement of Rome, looks again to ancient Israel for liturgical order, with priests and laity faithfully fulfilling their respective roles. St. Ignatius of Antioch, writing around 107, also returns repeatedly to eucharistic themes. He calls the eucharistic bread the flesh of Christ, and he says the chalice contains the "blood of God." The very mark of a wayward Christian, Ignatius said, is to deny "the Eucharist to be the flesh of our Savior Jesus Christ, which suffered for our sins."

Even the Church's Roman persecutors recognized the centrality of the Eucharist. Pliny the Younger, a governor, when he made his report to the Emperor Trajan, mentioned Sunday Mass as the chief activity of the Christians. When pagans wanted to mock the faith, they accused believers of cannibalism for eating the flesh of Christ.

No other Christian practice or doctrine is so well attested from the Church's early years as the Eucharist. No other doctrine is portrayed so often (though the depictions are often symbolic, as at Tabgha).

Those early Christian writers were taking their cues from the writers of the New Testament. The story of the institution of the Eucharist is told in the first three Gospels and in Paul's First Letter to the Corinthians. At the Last Supper, Jesus broke bread, called it his body, and distributed it to his disciples, commanding them to "do this in remembrance of me" (Lk 22:19).

Immediately after his resurrection, Jesus broke bread with two disciples and was made "known to them in the breaking of the bread" (Lk 24:35). Even after Pentecost, the Church met for "the breaking of the bread and the prayers" (Acts 2:42). St. Paul's most extensive and theologically important letters are concerned largely with table fellowship (Romans, First Corinthians, Galatians), which in that first generation meant the Eucharist and the associated "*agape* meal" described in chapter 11 of First Corinthians. By the middle of the next century, the Church had decisively separated the Eucharist from other meals, probably because of the very abuses described by St. Paul.

The Mass described in the earliest Church documents is structurally the same as the Mass celebrated in typical Catholic parishes today. When the *Catechism of the Catholic Church* appeared in 1992, its editors chose not to draft a new description of the Mass but simply incorporated, verbatim, a passage from St. Justin Martyr, written in the middle of the second century, calling it "The Mass of All Ages."

For More

Mike Aquilina. *The Mass of the Early Christians*. Huntington, IN: Our Sunday Visitor, 2002.

Enrico Mazza. *The Celebration of the Eucharist: The Origin of the Rite and the Development of Its Interpretation*. Collegeville, MN: Pueblo, 1999.

An early Christian pendant plaque. Metropolitan Museum of Art 1984.32.

6

Lapis Lazuli Plaque

This pendant plaque, made of lapis lazuli, measures just two inches by two inches, but it is saturated with Christian symbols.

Consider the anchor, which is a traditional symbol of hope. "We have this as a sure and steadfast anchor of the soul, a hope that enters into the inner shrine behind the curtain" (Heb 6:19).

In this form the anchor also suggests the Trinity. The circular loop represents the eternal Father; the cruciform middle, the Son, Jesus Christ; and the dove-shaped hooks, the Holy Spirit.

Overlaying the anchor is the *labarum*, the combination of the Greek letters chi (X) and rho (P). XP is an abbreviation for the Greek word for Christ.

Flanking the anchor are the first and last letters of the Greek alphabet: alpha (A) and omega (Ω). These, too, represent the Lord God, who three times in the book of Revelation identifies himself thus: "I am the Alpha and the Omega" (Rv 1:8, 21:6, 22:13).

Finally, there is the fish, which we have already encountered in the Tabgha mosaic. The fish is a sign of the eucharistic Lord. The early Christians took the Greek word for fish, *ichthus*, to be an abbreviation, or acrostic, of the word formed from the initial letters of the words Jesus (*Iesous*) Christ (*Christos*), God's (*Theou*) Son (*Uios*), Savior (*Soter*). The fish, then, stands as a creed professing the Lord's humanity, divinity, and redemptive mission.

Then why are there two fish? Because the second one is the believer, who is identified with Christ, caught on the hook of the anchor.

Even the pendant's square shape could have symbolic value, representing the earth's four corners (Rv 7:1). The pendant tells the story, then, of the Incarnation: God entering world history through the humanity of Jesus Christ.

It is quite likely that most people—Christian or pagan—who lived in the Greco-Roman world could not read. (Literacy rates may have been somewhat higher for Jews.) Images were an important means of communication. They stood for complex truths. They served as reminders. They made life more beautiful. They were identity markers.

The first generations of Christians developed a complex language of visual and literary symbols. They invested meaning in geometric shapes, figures from plant and animal nature, colors, depictions of clothing, stylized letters, and almost anything else in the visible world. By his Incarnation Christ had blessed creation in an extraordinary way. It was suffused, now, with grandeur and significance.

The symbols show up everywhere: in graffiti at pilgrim sites; in artwork on the walls of the catacombs; on household items, such as lamps and bottles; and on jewelry like this pendant.

In a world hostile to Christianity, the symbols served also as a secret code, meaning one thing to believers and another to pagans.

In a world where few could read, many people used a seal or signet ring to affix their personal identity mark in lieu of a signature. Writing at the end of the second century, Clement of Alexandria urged his hearers to choose common symbols from the wider culture—but symbols that also admitted a deeper Christian meaning.

> Let our seals be either a dove, or a fish, or a ship with its sails full of wind, or a musical lyre, which Polycrates used, or a ship's anchor, which Seleucus got engraved as a device. And if there should appear a fisherman, remember the apostle, and the children drawn out of the water. For we are not to draw the faces of idols, and we are forbidden to cling to them; nor should we use a sword or a bow, since we are peacemakers; nor drinking cups, since we are temperate.

A ship could be just a ship to a pagan, but to a Christian it was the Church. A lyre reminded believers of the psalms of David. To sign one's name, then, could be an occasion of prayer.

These signs remained fairly constant across cultures. Christians in Syria, Greece, Italy, or Britain would all have understood the symbols on the pendant pictured here. And these same symbols have endured the centuries. Even today, they are engraved in altars and resplendent in stained glass.

For More

Mike Aquilina and Lea M. Ravotti. *Signs and Mysteries: Revealing Ancient Christian Symbols*. Huntington, IN: Our Sunday Visitor, 2008.

Jeffrey Spier et al. *Picturing the Bible: The Earliest Christian Art*. New Haven, CT: Yale University Press, 2009.

A carnelian intaglio with a lion-headed serpent. Metropolitan Museum of Art 81.6.303.

7

An Ancient Amulet

A lion-headed serpent uncoils, ominously, on this semi-precious amulet from the second century. Through the inscription, in the Coptic language, the chimera declares, "I AM, I AM CHNOUBIS."

The image of Chnoubis appears on many items from this period—mostly amulets and charms. His name also shows up in spells written out on papyrus.

Whoever wore this intaglio (or chanted the spells) believed that Chnoubis was the "archon" who ruled the earth and imposed suffering on humanity. The intaglio gave its owner power over Chnoubis—ultimately the power to get past the archon and return to the higher god.

Whoever wore this image also believed that Chnoubis was identical with the God of the Old Testament. (Thus the repetition of "I AM," the name revealed to Moses at the burning bush.)

Oddly enough, the wearer of this amulet probably self-identified as a Christian—though a *Gnostic* Christian.

"Gnostic" is an adjective we now apply to a large category of ancient Christian heresies—forms of religion that claimed the name Christian but deviated from the doctrines found in the New Testament and the apostolic tradition. Gnostic heresies emphasized esoteric knowledge (in Greek, *gnosis*) and private revelation. Though Gnostics acknowledged some of the New Testament writings, they claimed that the scriptures' meaning was veiled for ordinary believers. Only the elite were privileged with true understanding.

St. Paul may have been fighting against such ideas when he wrote: "Knowledge puffs up, but love builds up" (1 Cor 8:1). The Pastoral Epistles also speak of certain Christians who "occupy themselves with myths and endless genealogies which promote speculations rather than the divine training that is in faith" (1 Tm 1:4). This seems to describe the Gnostic tendency. Gnostics held that Chnoubis, for example, was an emanation from the one true God, a wayward offspring less powerful than his forebear—and devoid of goodness. The genealogy of the archons was key to the Gnostic explanation of the origin of evil.

Most Gnostics had a horror of the Old Testament and all things Jewish. They had, moreover, a loathing for the material world, which they believed the God of the Jews had created as a prison for Gnostic spirits.

Thus Gnostics tended to believe that Jesus' flesh was an illusion. They believed that he only *seemed* to be human (2 Jn 1:7–11 and 1 Jn 4:2–3). The Savior, for them, was a pure spirit, the *only* pure emanation of the god of light. Jesus redeemed humanity by coming to earth to teach spiritual people how to return to their origins—the god beyond the heavens. Salvation sometimes involved the memorization of passwords and the answers to riddles. Amulets were thought to help.

Since the Creator was also the Lawgiver, many Gnostics rejected the Law as well, including the parts about sexual morality. The New Testament Letter of Jude seems to speak of these when it mentions "ungodly persons who pervert the grace of our God into licentiousness" (Jude 4:1).

If the apostles were already troubled by "false teachers" and "destructive heresies" (2 Pt 2:1), how much more would the Church be vexed in the centuries to come, as strange doctrines had time to metastasize?

In the first millennium alone, teachers arose to deny Jesus' true divinity—and, in turn, his true humanity. Others sought to limit God's mercy. Still others denied that the Holy Spirit is a person. Some creative minds proposed a mash-up of Christianity with other world religions. Few of these experiments lasted for many years beyond the lifetime of their founders.

This amulet looks strange and unchristian today because Gnostic Christianity failed. Yes, the Church opposed it, but official opposition counted for almost nothing. The Church was itself persecuted and illegal and had no power to suppress anything. Gnosticism had every advantage but failed anyway. It failed because it was unsatisfying. What it proposed as knowledge was unbelievable.

For More

Birger A. Pearson. *Ancient Gnosticism: Traditions and Literature.* Minneapolis, MN: Fortress Press, 2007.

Carl B. Smith. *No Longer Jews: The Search for Gnostic Origins.* Peabody, MA: Hendrickson, 2004.

Large stones that were once in the walls of Jerusalem's Temple. Photo by dominiquelandau / iStockphoto.com.

8

Stones *of the* Jerusalem Temple

These massive blocks, recently unearthed, once composed the walls of the Jerusalem Temple—for Jews, the most sacred spot on earth. The gospels tell of the amazement of Jesus' disciples as they first caught sight of those mighty stones (Lk 21:5). And Jesus wept as he foresaw the destruction of the holy city (Lk 19:41). Today those hewn stones are a helter-skelter pile of colossal rubble, with individual blocks rising as high as a man's hip.

In the year AD 70, after four years of the bloody Jewish Rebellion, the Roman military leveled the city. The day came, as Jesus had predicted, "when there shall not be left here one stone upon another that will not be thrown down" (Lk 21:6).

The Romans wanted to prevent such a war from erupting again, and their efforts began with an erasure of all that was sacred to the Jews. On the Temple Mount they built a temple to the Roman god Jupiter. They expelled all Jews from Jerusalem and the nearby territory, enslaving many of them for labor in the capital.

There were few if any Christians among those captive and exiled Jews. The ancient histories say that followers of the Way received a vivid prophecy shortly before Jerusalem's destruction, and they withdrew to Pella, one of the ten cities built by the Romans in the Jordan Valley. Already, at Jerusalem's conquest, there seems to have been a parting of the ways. In the Acts of the Apostles, the first Christians clearly saw themselves as co-religionists with the Jews. Paul identifies himself as an Israelite, a Benjamite, a Jew, and a Pharisee. And outsiders saw the Jewish-Christian argument as a dispute between rival sects (Acts 23:29)—a running argument about a sacred text that both parties held in common.

At what moment did Christianity become something other than a variety of Judaism, like the Pharisees, Sadducees, Essenes, and Zealots? Each of these variations was granted some measure of legitimacy by the others. When did all begin to recognize Christianity as something else? When did Christianity begin to see itself that way?

The question of the "parting of the ways" is a vast field of study, hotly contested by scholars. At some point, both parties must have recognized that their differences were not incidental but essential and defining. Those who argue for an early separation point to the persecution of the Way by the authorities in Jerusalem. The Sadducees and Essenes had serious differences, but they didn't resort to killing one another. The "early" advocates note also that the apostles, at the Council of Jerusalem, chose to set aside the Torah's ceremonial law. Thus, each party *seems* to have rejected the other almost from the first moment of their coexistence.

Yet their coexistence continued, and there is ample evidence of Jews and Christians celebrating feasts together, in one another's homes and even in synagogues, until well into the fifth century. Some of the Church Fathers (John Chrysostom, for example, and Cyril of Alexandria) preached often on the subject. And they wouldn't have brought it up so frequently if it was happening only rarely. Meanwhile, two of the greatest scripture scholars in the early Church, Origen of Alexandria and St. Jerome, both learned to read Hebrew under the tutelage of rabbis.

The destruction of the Temple created a crisis for everyone who identified with the religion of Israel. Judaism, in the first half of the first century, was an essentially sacrificial religion, and sacrifice could be offered *only* in the Jerusalem Temple. All prayer was oriented in the direction of the Temple Mount. From the rubble of the destruction a new Judaism arose, contemporaneous with early Christianity. It is rabbinic Judaism, a non-priestly, non-sacrificial movement that grew from the methods and piety of the Pharisees, a lay movement.

Jews and Christians emerged, like siblings, from the same historical circumstances. And they have often fought like siblings. Domestic disputes tend to be the most passionate, volatile, and dangerous. There is no short-age of Christian anti-Jewish polemic from the first millennium (or the second). And there is plenty of Jesus-bashing to be found in the Talmud.

And yet Jews and Christians have gone forward in history together, each necessary, it seems, for the other's self-understanding. The stones may be scattered in Jerusalem—and so we can no longer meet on the porticos of the Temple—but our traditions and destinies are intertwined.

For More

Adam H. Becker and Annette Yoshiko Reed, eds. *The Ways That Never Parted: Jews and Christians in Late Antiquity and the Early Middle Ages.* Minneapolis, MN: Fortress Press, 2007.

Jacob Neusner. *Judaism When Christianity Began: A Survey of Belief and Practice.* Louisville, KY: Westminster John Knox Press, 2002.

Cardinal Wuerl kneels before the chains of St. Peter. Photo by Piotr Spalek.

9

The Chains *of* St. Peter *in* Rome

Two lengths of fetters are here fused in a single chain, displayed in a church all its own near the Roman Colosseum. The bonds, according to tradition, once held fast the limbs of St. Peter the Apostle and have been cherished by Christians since the first century.

The story of their veneration first appears in the ancient *Acts of Saint Alexander*, an early pope who died as a martyr in AD 115. As he awaited his own execution, he received a visit from Quirinus, the nobleman who oversaw the prisons in Rome. The man's daughter Balbina was desperately ill, and he had heard that Pope Alexander had the power to heal her. She was completely cured when the pope touched her with his chains. Balbina wanted to kiss the chains in gratitude—but Alexander instructed her to find the chains of St. Peter and honor them instead.

Balbina became a Christian—and, according to some accounts, a consecrated virgin—and she arranged for the construction of a shrine for St. Peter's fetters. It would be rebuilt and moved and expanded through the centuries.

In scripture we find St. Peter imprisoned twice in Jerusalem. Once he was jailed with the rest of the apostles and set free by an angel (Acts 5:17–25). The second time, the authorities took no chances. They assigned him two guards and bound him in his cell with double chains. But, again, "an angel of the Lord appeared, and a light shone in the cell; and he struck Peter on the side and woke him. . . . And the chains fell off his hands" (Acts 12:7).

Once freed, Peter brought the Gospel first to Syrian Antioch and then to Rome. In the imperial capital, during the reign of Nero, he was jailed briefly in the Mamertine Prison before suffering death by crucifixion.

Iron chains became, paradoxically, an early symbol of Christian freedom. They are, according to St. Polycarp, writing in the second century, "the fitting ornaments of saints, and . . . indeed the diadems of the true elect of God and our Lord." Though the emperors possessed the power to chain the popes—from Peter to Alexander and beyond—the Church endured and triumphed. Christians, from at least the fourth century, celebrated a feast of St. Peter's chains on August 1, the beginning of the month named for Rome's first emperor, Augustus.

As Rome's Christians honored Peter's chains from the Mamertine, so the Church in Jerusalem kept his chains from the Herodian prison. In the fifth century, the Christian empress Eudocia, the wife of Theodosius II, sent a length of Peter's Jerusalem chains to St. Leo the Great. According to tradition, Leo held it beside Peter's chains from the Mamertine Prison, and the two miraculously, inseparably fused together.

There are abundant testimonies to the presence of these chains in Rome. St. Gregory the Great, who reigned as pope from 590 to 604, was intensely devoted to the relic and often sent small filings as gifts to dignitaries—to Constantina Augusta, the Byzantine empress; to a bishop named Columbus; to King Childebert of the Franks; to King Rechared of the Visigoths; and to Theodore, the court physician at Constantinople. He would place the filing in a key-shaped reliquary—the key representing Peter's authority. He sent each particle with a prayer "that what bound [Peter's] neck for martyrdom, may loose yours from all sins."

The chains are today exposed for veneration in a gold and glass reliquary in the Basilica of San Pietro in Vincoli, on Rome's Oppian Hill, a church built in the fifth century during the reign of Leo the Great.

Peter's chains remain a sign of the relationship, often uneasy, between throne and altar, bishops and emperors. In 2010 Pope Benedict XVI granted the title of the basilica to the cardinal-archbishop of Washington, DC.

For More

Hugo Brandenburg. *Ancient Churches of Rome from the Fourth to the Seventh Century.* Turnhout, Belgium: Brepols, 2005.

Richard Krautheimer. *Rome: Profile of a City, 312–1308.* Princeton, NJ: Princeton University Press, 2000.

Fresco fragment with the Madonna and Child at Rome's Catacomb of Priscilla. Photo from Scala / Art Resource.

10

A Catacomb Painting

There are millions of images of the Virgin Mary scattered throughout the world, the material remains of two thousand years of devotion. Of all those images—from simple holy cards to colossal statues—this fresco painting is probably the oldest.

Reliably dated to the first half of the third century, it adorns a wall in the Catacombs of Priscilla, beneath a quiet neighborhood in Rome. The image is much faded from age, but the composition is clear. A woman holds a baby on her lap. He seems to be nursing but has pulled away to look at a visitor—perhaps the viewer or perhaps the male figure positioned to his left.

The male is dressed in the garb of a philosopher, and he points to a star. Art historians usually identify him as the Old Testament prophet Balaam, who foretold:

> I see him, but not now;
> I behold him, but not nigh:
> a star shall come forth out of Jacob,
> and a scepter shall rise out of Israel. (Nm 24:17)

Christians have always identified the star predicted by Balaam with the star of Bethlehem. So the scene in the fresco is set sometime after the birth of the Messiah, when the Magi followed the star to the home of the Holy Family.

Pilgrims to the tombs of the martyrs in the Catacombs—like the Magi who followed the star—would have found "the child with Mary his mother" (Mt 2:11).

In the canticle of the Magnificat, Mary herself predicted that "all generations will call me blessed" (Lk 1:48). And history has proven her right. Marian devotion has been a constant in Christian life.

It is evident in the art, graffiti, letters, sermons, hymns, and prayers of the earliest Christians. She is essential to the telling of the Gospel. Because Jesus was "born of a woman" (Gal 4:4), he was known to be truly human. Because he was born of a virgin (Mt 1:23), with God alone as his Father, he was known to be truly divine.

So the Word was preached in the earliest house churches. A first-century document, *The Ascension of Isaiah*, tells of the miracle of her virginal birth. The second-century *Protoevangelium of James*, which identifies Jesus' birthplace as a cave, purports to give Mary's backstory.

She is the only one of the disciples whose name appears in the ancient creeds. Her name appears also in ancient liturgical documents. The earliest known version of the Marian prayer known as the *Sub Tuum Praesidium* appears first in Coptic, in an Egyptian document also from the third century: "We fly to your patronage, O holy Mother of God: despise not our petitions in our necessities, but deliver us from all danger, O ever glorious and blessed Virgin Mary!"

Her image is common in the archeological record. In the Catacombs of Priscilla there is another fresco depicting the angel's annunciation to Mary. Similar scenes appear in other Roman catacombs and in the Christian cemeteries of the Fayum region in Egypt.

Apparitions of the Blessed Virgin were reported throughout the early centuries of the Church.

Later devotion to Mary has its deepest roots in those centuries. St. Irenaeus depicted her as the New Eve, her obedience untying the knot of Eve's disobedience. Likewise, many Catholics today invoke Mary as "Untier of Knots" and call upon her to intercede for a solution to their most difficult problems.

The Council of Ephesus was summoned in AD 431 because a prominent churchman, Nestorius, the Patriarch of Constantinople, refused to address Mary as "Mother of God." He would call her "Mother of Jesus" and "Mother of Christ" but not "Mother of God." She could not be mother to

God, Nestorius said, because she did not precede God, as a mother must precede her child. He conceded that Mary gave birth to Jesus' human nature, but certainly not his divine nature.

Defending the longstanding tradition, St. Cyril of Alexandria said that Nestorius's claim was heretical because it divided Jesus in two. A mother gives birth not to a nature but to a person—and in this particular case the person, Jesus, was both human and divine.

The Council of Ephesus invented nothing new but simply confirmed what the Church had always held. Cyril was known to history not as an innovator but as the "Seal of the Fathers"—the one who preserved, protected, and guaranteed the Marian doctrine of his predecessors.

For More

Mike Aquilina and Frederick W. Gruber. *Keeping Mary Close: Devotion to Our Lady through the Ages.* Cincinnati: Servant Books, 2015.

Luigi Gambero. *Mary and the Fathers of the Church.* San Francisco: Ignatius Press, 1999.

Fourth-century "Sarcophagus of the Shepherds," now in the Vatican Museums. Photo from Scala / Art Resource.

11

A Sarcophagus

It's crowded here, on the sculpted relief of this sarcophagus. Several shepherds dominate as they carry sheep on their shoulders. Smaller figures—either children or allegorical angels—are milking ewes and harvesting grapes from an arbor. Everywhere, baskets brim with abundant produce.

The imagery draws from the Bible, the liturgy, and the ordinary life of Christians. The shepherds, of course, represent Christ the Good Shepherd—but also the bishops, who were considered shepherds within the Church. The grapes are eucharistic, suggestive of the wine offered at Mass. The baskets symbolize plentiful grace.

While deeply symbolic, the crowd of figures is also simply realistic. The evidence seems to indicate that Church growth was rapid in the first three centuries—rapid enough to alarm the non-Christian authorities and provoke them to extreme measures of persecution.

The sociologist Rodney Stark concludes that the Church grew at a rate of 40 percent per decade through the first centuries of the Christian era—in spite of legal deterrents to conversion and social stigma. Even in times of natural disasters and epidemics, the Church continued to grow. Stark attributed some of this to Christians' openness to fertility. But mostly he credits the content of the Christian message. At the end of his book *The Rise of Christianity*, he writes, "Central doctrines of Christianity prompted and sustained attractive, liberating, and effective social relations and organization."

Stark argues that almost all Church growth occurred in the Roman Empire's cities. Urban populations are more likely, after all, to harbor enough "social deviants" to gather a community. And Christians were certainly deviating from the norms of Greco-Roman society. Yet they managed to establish significant subcultures in all the major population centers: Alexandria in Egypt, Antioch in Syria, Rome in Europe, and Carthage in North Africa. Christian social services, arts, and intellectual life were flourishing in these places, in spite of significant obstacles and deterrents.

Other experts have challenged Stark's analysis, arguing that the Church grew at the same rate in *rural* areas throughout the same time period.

By the end of the second century, Tertullian, in North Africa, could gloat: "We are of yesterday and already we fill the world and all your places: the cities, the islands, the towns, the municipalities, the councils, the very army camps, the tribunals, the assemblies, the palace, the senate, the forum. We have left you only your temples." Tertullian was probably not exaggerating. His pamphlet was addressed to pagans, who were able to confirm or deny his accuracy by a quick trip downtown.

Christians indeed were everywhere, and this ubiquity was threatening. For the Christian message ran contrary to many cultural norms in the Greco-Roman world. Christians observed a certain equality of the sexes. The Church respected the vocational freedom of women and forbade its members to practice contraception, abortion, infanticide, or divorce, all of which were common in the wider culture. Christians professed moral doctrines that seemed counterintuitive to pagans: universal brotherhood, the preferential treatment of the poor, and ethics on the battlefield and in law enforcement. Every conversion, then, seemed to be a further fraying of the Roman social fabric, and conversions apparently were frequent.

Thus, many Christian authors of the second century take care to reassure their pagan contemporaries. Though Christians are increasingly numerous, they insisted, they are also peaceable. These authors, known now as the "apologists," strove to explain and defend the faith to outsiders and to calm unreasonable fears. The anonymous *Letter to Diognetus* explains that Christians inhabit "Greek as well as barbarian cities" and follow "the customs of the natives in respect to clothing, food, and the rest of their ordinary conduct." They "obey the prescribed laws, and at the same time surpass the laws by their lives." Christians, the author laments, are misunderstood yet persecuted, "unknown and condemned."

The growth would continue unabated through the centuries that followed. So would the misunderstanding and persecution.

For More

Thomas A. Robinson. *Who Were the First Christians? Dismantling the Urban Thesis.* New York: Oxford University Press, 2016.

Rodney Stark. *The Rise of Christianity: How the Obscure Jesus Movement Became the Dominant Religious Force in the Western World in a Few Centuries.* San Francisco: HarperCollins, 1997.

The libellus *was a get-out-of-jail-free card in the third century. Photo courtesy Luther College Archives, Decorah, Iowa.*

12

Certificate *of* Sacrifice

This is a certificate, a ticket—in Latin, *libellus*—and it enabled the holder to continue living, but at a certain price.

The holder of this particular certificate was a man named Aurelius Sarapammon, a donkey driver from Theadelphia, near Alexandria in Egypt. Sarapammon acknowledges that he has "sacrificed, poured the libations, and tasted the offerings," as commanded by the Roman emperor Decius in the year AD 250. Two provincial officials co-sign his certificate as witnesses. Aurelius thus enjoyed full freedom in the Roman world.

The *libellus* was the empire's way of separating the increasingly numerous Christians from the rest of a city's population. Biblical religion was unique in its demand that worship be reserved for only one God. The cults of Egypt, Greece, Babylon, and elsewhere gave preference to their local divinities but recognized the existence and power of others as well. It was inconsequential for an Egyptian to bow and sacrifice to a Roman god—unless that Egyptian was also a Christian.

For a Christian, to offer sacrifice—even just a pinch of incense—was an act of apostasy, a rejection of Jesus Christ, the gravest sin of all.

In times of persecution, the temptation to blend in was always great. And persecution was part of the Christian experience from the beginning. In the Acts of the Apostles, Paul confesses that he "persecuted this Way to the death" (Acts 22:4). The New Testament elsewhere seems to assume that those "slain for the word of God" (Rv 6:9) were already many by the end of the first century.

The Roman persecution began in earnest in 64, when the Emperor Nero blamed Christians for setting the great fire of Rome. According to Roman contemporaries, the Christians were scapegoats, made to suffer for a crime committed by Nero himself. Nevertheless, as Tertullian said in the following century, "the cruelty of Nero sowed the seed of Christian martyrdom at Rome." Nero felt the need to fabricate a crime. But his decision established legal precedent, so that later emperors could act more freely. Trajan instructed the governor of Bithynia, Pliny, to execute Christians if they refused to renounce their faith but not to hunt them down.

Other local authorities had this ability as well. St. Justin Martyr said that, while he was still a pagan, he was impressed by the fearlessness of Christians, who would incriminate themselves, knowing that "the consequence would be death."

As the second century turned to the third, the Severan emperors issued the first universal decree forbidding conversion to Christianity. There were other intermittent efforts by emperors, and between them there was an enduring climate of anti-Christian prejudice. Nero was not the last to blame the Christians for whatever problems afflicted his people. Tertullian observed, "Christians are to blame for every public disaster, every misfortune that happens to the people. If the Tiber floods, if the Nile fails to flood, if the sky is rainless, if there is an earthquake, a famine, a plague, immediately the cry arises, 'The Christians to the lion!' What—so many Christians to one lion?"

Decius, in the year 250, was the first to issue an edict affecting every Christian in the empire. He ordered all citizens to perform some act of worship before Roman idols and have it confirmed by official witnesses. After doing so, they would receive a certificate. If they refused, they could be killed.

Many were. The bishop of Alexandria, St. Dionysius the Great, testified that many Christians didn't wait to be asked. "Before anyone could lay hold of them, they ran quickly up to the bench of judgment and declared themselves to be Christians."

On the other hand, he also saw a sight less edifying. "But some advanced to the altars more readily, declaring boldly that they had never been Christians," he said, as quoted in Eusebius's famous *Church History*. St. Cyprian of Carthage lamented that *so many* from his congregation went forward to offer sacrifice that they overwhelmed the magistrates, who asked them to come back the following day.

In times of persecution, many Christians died—and others left the faith by committing apostasy. Yet the Church continued to grow! Tertullian taunted the Church's tormentors: "The more you mow us down, the more we spring up in greater numbers. The blood of Christians is seed."

For More

Robert L. Wilken. *The Christians as the Romans Saw Them*. New Haven, CT: Yale University Press, 1984.

Cardinal Donald Wuerl. *To the Martyrs: A Reflection on the Ultimate Christian Witness*. Steubenville, OH: Emmaus Road Press, 2015.

The walls of the Roman catacombs are lined with slots for burial. Photo by franklx / iStockphoto.com.

13

Catacomb Niches

Each niche (in Latin, *loculus*) pictured here was carved out of soft tufa stone to hold the mortal remains of at least one Christian. Some held the bones of many. The corpse was laid out during funeral rites and covered with quicklime to speed the decomposition process. The niche was then closed up with plaster. When the body was reduced to bones, the niche could accommodate another, and then another. All the family had to do was remove the plaster covering.

The Roman catacombs are a vast network of tunnels whose walls are lined with these—as well as larger "cubicle" slots and even dedicated tombs for the wealthy. More than sixty miles of underground corridors have been discovered so far, and archeologists are still finding more. Estimates of their "population" range into the millions.

The catacombs are our richest source of evidence of early Christian life. The human remains, sometimes still clothed when found, tell us what people were eating and wearing, how long they lived, and how hard they worked. The graffiti scratched into plaster tell us what they believed and what kind of work they did. The ornaments and artworks tell us what they valued.

The catacombs, first begun in the late second century, were a clear message that the Christians had "arrived" on the Roman scene. Their faith was illegal, and they were scorned. But they were numerous and could marshal enough manpower and money to undertake a large public work.

And contrary to popular misconceptions, the catacombs were a public work. Yes, they were underground; and, yes, they were constructed outside the city walls (as mandated by law for a cemetery). But they involved the labor of many hands, and that means traffic. They involved the noise of many tools—picks repeatedly hitting stone. And they required the removal of tons of dirt and stone. None of this could be done in secret. The project probably began during a lull in official persecution. It was nonetheless daring.

Oddly enough, it was also trend-setting. Romans (and most others) had long preferred cremation over ground burial. It's cheaper and tidier. But around the same time the Christians began digging their catacombs, it became fashionable for wealthy Romans also to bury their dead.

Ground burial was another heritage from ancient Israel. For Christians, the practice represented a profession of faith in the resurrection of the body. It was an expression, too, of faith in the Incarnation and the wondrous exchange of salvation. Through Baptism, Christians enjoyed communion with the humanity and divinity of Jesus Christ. Thus their human bodies, after death, were sacred relics. Their burial places were holy ground. The Church looked upon the work of grave diggers as a sacred task. In some ancient sources it is listed among the offices of the Church hierarchy after bishop, priest, and deacon.

Burial was valued by all Christians but affordable by few. From the contributions of the wealthy—which must have been lavish—the Church was able to provide burial for the poor. Most of the catacombs include richly decorated rooms reserved for the family of a rich patron. Some of the catacombs, such as those of Priscilla, were named for their benefactors.

This was not just a local phenomenon. Rome's native volcanic stone was congenial to the construction of labyrinthine tunnels; similar arrangements were possible elsewhere in Italy as well. But Christian necropolises—literally, cities of the dead—appear above ground in other, far-flung lands: Egypt, Greece, Asia Minor, the Holy Land.

The "Church of the catacombs" may have been operating underground, but it was hiding in plain sight.

For More

Vincenzo F. Nicolai, Fabricio Bisconti, and Danilo Mazzoleni. *The Christian Catacombs of Rome: History, Decoration, Inscriptions*. Regensburg, Germany: Verlag, Schnell, and Steiner, 2009.

James Stevenson. *The Catacombs: Life and Death in Early Christianity.* Nashville: Thomas Nelson, 1985.

ΤΙΓΕΓΡΑΜΜΕΝΟΝ
ΕΣΤΙΝΟΖΗΛΟΣΤ[Η]
ΟΙΚΟΥΣΟΥΚΑΤΑΦΑ
ΓΕΤΑΙΜΕ·
ΑΠΕΚΡΙΘΗΣΑΝΟΥ
ΟΙΙΟΥΔΑΙΟΙΚΑΙ
ΠΟΝΑΥΤΩΤΙΣΗΜΙ
ΟΝΔΙΚΝΥΕΙΣΗΜΙ
ΟΤΙΤΑΥΤΑΠΟΙΕΙΣ·
ΑΠΕΚΡΙΘΗΟΙΣΚΑΙ
ΕΙΠΕΝΑΥΤΟΙΣΛΥ
ΣΑΤΕΤΟΝΝΛΟΝΤ
ΤΟΝΚΑΙΕΝΤΡΙΣΙΝ
ΗΜΕΡΑΙΣΕΓΕΡΩΑΥ
ΤΟΝ·ΕΙΠΟΝΟΥΝ
ΙΟΥΔΑΙΟΙΤΕΣΣΕΡΑ
ΚΟΝΤΑΚΑΙΕΞΕΤ
ΟΙΚΟΔΟΜΗΘΗΟ
ΝΛΟΣΟΥΤΟΣΚΑΙ
ΤΡΙΣΙΝΗΜΕΡΑΙΣ
ΡΕΙΣΑΥΤΟΝΕΚΕΙΝ
ΛΕΛΕΓΕΝΠΕΡΙΤ
ΝΛΟΥΤΟΥΣΩΜΑ
ΤΟΣΟΤΕΟΥΝΗΓΕΡ
ΘΗΕΚΝΕΚΡΩΝΕ
ΜΝΗΣΘΗΣΑΝΟΙ
ΜΑΘΗΤΑΙΑΥΤΟΥ·
ΤΙΤΟΥΤΟΕΛΕΓΕΝ·
ΚΑΙΕΠΙΣΤΕΥΣΑΝ
ΤΗΓΡΑΦΗΚΑΙΤΩ
ΛΟΓΩΟΝΕΙΠΕΝ
ΟΙΣ·ΩΣΔΕΗΝΕΝ
ΤΟΙΣΙΕΡΟΣΟΛΥΜ
ΕΝΤΩΠΑΣΧΑΕΝ
ΤΗΕΟΡΤΗΠΟΛΛΟΙ
ΠΙΣΤΕΥΣΑΝΕΙΣΤ
ΟΝΟΜΑΑΥΤΟΥ·
ΘΩΡΟΥΝΤΕΣΑΥΤ
ΤΑΣΗΜΙΑΛΕΠΟΙ·
ΑΥΤΟΣΔΕΟΙΣΟΥΚΕ
ΣΤΕΥΕΝΑΥΤΟΝΑ
ΤΟΙΣΔΙΑΤΟΓΙΓΝΩ
ΣΚΙΝΠΑΝΤΑΣΚΑ
ΟΤΙΧΡΙΑΝΟΥΚΙΧ
ΙΝΑΤΙΣΜΑΡΤΥΡΗ
ΣΗΠΕΡΙΤΟΥΑΝΟΥ
ΠΟΥΑΥΤΟΣΑΓΕΓΙ
ΝΩΣΚΕΝΤΙΗΝ·Ν

ΤΙΗΝΕΝΤΩΑΝΘΡΩ
ΠΩ·
ΗΝΔΕΑΝΘΡΩΠΟ
ΕΚΤΩΝΦΑΡΙΣΑΙ
ΝΙΚΟΔΗΜΟΣΟΝ
ΜΑΤΙΑΡΧΩΝΤΩΝ
ΙΟΥΔΑΙΩΝΟΥΤΟ·
ΗΛΘΕΝΝΥΚΤΟΣ
ΠΡΟΣΑΥΤΟΝΚΑΙ
ΠΕΝΑΥΤΩΡΑΒΒΙ
ΟΙΔΑΜΕΝΟΤΙΑΠ
ΘΥΕΛΗΛΥΘΑΣΔΙ
ΔΑΣΚΑΛΟΣΚΑΙΟΥ
ΛΙΣΔΥΝΑΤΑΙΤΑΥΤΑ
ΤΑΣΗΜΙΑΠΟΙΕΙΝ
ΑΣΥΠΟΙΕΙΣΕΑΝΜΗ
ΗΟΘΣΜΕΤΑΥΤΟΥ· ΚΑΙΕΙΠΕΝΑΥΤΩ
ΑΠΕΚΡΙΘΗΟΙΣΑΜΗ
ΑΜΗΝΛΕΓΩΣΟΙ
ΑΝΜΗΤΙΣΓΕΝΝΗ
ΘΗΑΝΩΘΕΝΟΥΔΥ
ΝΑΤΑΙΙΔΕΙΝΤΗΝΒΑ
ΣΙΛΕΙΑΝΤΟΥΘΥ·
ΛΕΓΕΙΠΡΟΣΑΥΤΟΝ
ΝΙΚΟΔΗΜΟΣΠΩ·
ΔΥΝΑΤΑΙΑΝΘΡΩ
ΠΟΣΓΕΡΩΝΩΝΓΕΝ
ΝΗΘΗΝΑΙΜΗΔΥ
ΝΑΤΑΙΕΙΣΤΗΝΚΟΙ
ΛΙΑΝΤΗΣΜΗΤΡΟΣ
ΑΥΤΟΥΔΕΥΤΕΡΟΝ·
ΣΕΛΘΕΙΝΚΑΙΓΕΝΝΙ
ΘΗΝΑΙΑΠΕΚΡΙΘΗ
ΙΣ·ΑΜΗΝΑΜΗΝ
ΛΕΓΩΣΟΙΕΑΝΜΗΤΙ
ΕΣΥΔΑΤΟΣΚΑΙΠΝ
ΓΕΝΝΗΘΗΟΥΔΥΝΑ
ΤΑΙΕΙΔΕΙΝΤΗΝΒΑ
ΣΙΛΙΑΝΤΩΝΟΥΡΑ
ΝΩΝ·ΤΟΓΕΓΕΝΝΗ
ΜΕΝΟΝΕΚΤΗΣΣΑ
ΚΟΣΣΑΡΞΕΣΤΙΝΚΑΙ
ΤΟΓΕΓΕΝΝΗΜΕΝ
ΕΚΤΟΥΠΝΣΠΝΑ·
ΜΗΘΑΥΜΑΣΗΣΟΤΙ
ΕΙΠΟΝΣΟΙΔΙΥΜΑ
ΓΕΝΝΗΘΗΝΑΙΑΝ
ΘΕΝΤΟΠΝΧΟΠ

ΛΕΙΠΝΙΚΑΙΤΗΝΦ
ΝΗΝΑΥΤΟΥΑΚΟ
ΕΙΣΑΛΛΟΥΚΟΙΔΑ
ΠΟΘΕΝΕΡΧΕΤ
ΚΑΙΠΟΥΥΠΑΓΕ
ΤΩΣΕΣΤΙΝΠΑΣΟ
ΓΕΓΕΝΝΗΜΕΝΟ
ΕΚΤΟΥΠΝΑΤΟΣΚ
ΤΟΥΠΝΣΑΠΕΚΡΙ
ΘΗΝΙΚΟΔΗΜΟ
ΚΑΙΕΙΠΕΝΑΥΤΩ
ΠΩΣΔΥΝΑΤΑΙΤΑΥ
ΤΑΓΕΝΕΣΘΑΙΑΠ
ΚΡΙΘΗΟΙΣΚΑΙΕΙΠ
ΑΥΤΩΣΥΕΙΟΔΙΔΑ
ΣΚΑΛΟΣΤΟΥΙΗΛ
ΚΑΙΤΑΥΤΑΟΥΓΙΝΩ
ΣΚΙΣ·ΑΜΗΝΑΜΗΝ
ΛΕΓΩΣΟΙΟΤΙΟΟΙ
ΔΑΜΕΝΛΑΛΟΥΜ
ΚΑΙΟΕΩΡΑΚΑΜΕΝ
ΜΑΡΤΥΡΟΥΜΕΝΚΑΙ
ΤΗΝΜΑΡΤΥΡΙΑΝΗ
ΜΩΝΟΥΛΑΜΒΑΝ
ΤΑΙΕΙΤΑΕΠΙΓΑΕΙΠ
ΥΜΙΝΚΑΙΟΥΠΙΣΤ
ΕΤΑΙΠΩΣΕΑΝΕΙΠ
ΥΜΙΝΤΑΕΠΟΥΡΑΝ
ΑΠΙΣΤΕΥΣΕΤΑΙΚΑ
ΟΥΔΕΙΣΑΝΑΒΕΒΗΚ
ΕΙΣΤΟΝΟΥΡΑΝΟΝ·
ΜΗΟΕΚΤΟΥΟΥΡΑΝ
ΚΑΤΑΒΑΣΟΥΣΤΟΥ
ΑΝΘΡΩΠΟΥ·
ΚΑΙΚΑΘΩΣΜΩΥ
ΥΨΩΣΕΝΤΟΝΟΦ
ΕΝΤΗΕΡΗΜΩΟΥ
ΤΩΣΟΥΨΩΘΗΝΑ
ΔΙΤΟΝΥΝΤΟΥΑΝ
ΙΝΑΠΑΣΟΠΙΣΤΕΥ
ΩΝΕΙΣΑΥΤΟΝΕΧ
ΖΩΗΝΑΙΩΝΙΟ·
ΟΥΤΩΣΓΑΡΗΓΑ
ΣΕΝΟΘΣΤΟΝΚΟ
ΩΣΤΕΤΟΝΥΝΤΟΝ
ΜΟΝΟΓΕΝΗΠΝΑ
ΠΑΣΟΠΙΣΤΕΥΩΝ
ΕΙΣΑΥΤΟΝΜΗΑΠ

A page from the fourth-century Codex Sinaiticus. Photo: Universal Images Group / Art Resource, NY.

14

Codex Sinaiticus

This book is a Bible, specifically the Codex Sinaiticus, produced in the years AD 330–350. It contains the earliest complete copy of all the texts of the New Testament. It also contains the Old Testament in Greek translation, including the deuterocanonical books (Tobit, Judith, Wisdom, Sirach, and 1 and 2 Maccabees). The page shown here tells the story of Nicodemus, from the Gospel According to St. John.

The Codex Sinaiticus is important to scripture scholars and historians. It is a key witness to the Bible's text and canon. It is abundantly annotated and corrected by later readers, so it also tells us how certain passages were received and interpreted.

But it is also important for the history of technology.

The book is a technology we take for granted, even today as it can disappear easily into batches of electrons stored in a "cloud." We assume that its format is inevitable, almost natural, but it's not.

The book—as we know it—is made by binding multiple folded sheets of paper between thick covers. This form is called the codex. And it was one way of recording, delivering, and preserving a literary text. But it wasn't the only form, and it wasn't the most popular form.

In the first century AD, the codex was a recent innovation, and it wasn't catching on. Some people liked it, but most preferred to stick with the old-fashioned, tried-and-true scroll. Jews preferred scrolls, and so did Greeks and Romans. When the New Testament speaks of "books," it almost certainly means scrolls.

Soon after the apostolic age, however, Christians seem to have turned decisively to the codex as their preferred form for books. Almost all the earliest Christian literary remains have survived in the codex form.

Though it did not originate with the Christians, the codex became a distinctively Christian technology. Consider just a few of the great caches of documents discovered from antiquity. The Dead Sea Scrolls are (obviously) scrolls; the Greco-Roman library found under the volcanic ash in Herculaneum is also made up entirely of scrolls; but in the Nag Hammadi collection, compiled by Christians, everything is in codex form.

The codex served Christian purposes very well. It was relatively inexpensive to make and convenient to store. It was portable, easily carried about by missionaries.

But perhaps the greatest benefit was that it accommodated use in the liturgy. You could lay it down on a table or lectern, and it would stay flat. A preacher could move from passage to passage with little trouble. St. Justin Martyr records that the "memoirs of the Apostles" were customarily read at Mass in the city of Rome in 150. The codex made it possible to bind all four gospels (handwritten) between a single set of covers, and it seems that these were the first "canonical" collections of originally Christian scriptures.

The codex proved most useful for biblical research and critical studies. The great scholar Origen amassed a library at Caesarea in Palestine, and he himself produced no small number of books to fill out its shelves. Among his greatest achievements was the *Hexapla*, an edition of the Bible that placed six different versions in parallel columns, enabling easy word-by-word comparison. It was the codex that made such research useful and accessible to scholars. The form was tested and proven in the laboratory of Christian libraries and churches.

Origen's work was continued by his disciple, St. Pamphilus, and then later by the great historian Eusebius of Caesarea. When the Roman Empire first legalized Christianity, the emperor commissioned Eusebius to produce a number of Bibles in codex. Why? Because it should be in the way "most needful for the instruction of the Church . . . written on prepared parchment in a legible manner, and in a convenient, portable form," Eusebius recounted.

The book as we know it—in the form called the codex—was born with Christianity. It was championed by Christianity. It was useful to

Christianity; it brought the Word to the world. And it has Christianity to thank for its triumph and long endurance (at least until now).

For More

Anthony Grafton and Megan Williams. *Christianity and the Transformation of the Book: Origen, Eusebius, and the Library of Caesarea.* Cambridge, MA: Harvard University Press, 2008.

Larry W. Hurtado. *The Earliest Christian Artifacts: Manuscripts and Christian Origins.* Grand Rapids, MI: Eerdmans, 2006.

*The Tomb of Diocletian and the Catholic cathedral in Split, Croatia. Photo by majaiva /
iStockphoto.com.*

15

Diocletian's Tomb

The Emperor Diocletian built this massive structure—in what is today the city of Split, Croatia—to be his own mausoleum, a tomb worthy of a god. It was the year AD 305. He was beginning his retirement and thinking about his legacy. So he ordered the construction of an unforgettable building, with walls of white marble topped by a bright, shining dome.

Taking the throne in 283, Diocletian found himself constantly putting down civil wars. He concluded that something was wrong with the basic structure of the Roman Empire.

The problem was that there was no set way to choose an emperor. Usually whoever had the largest part of the army behind him became emperor. But often different emperors were proclaimed in different parts of the empire, and civil war was the inevitable result.

So in 293 Diocletian decided to scrap the whole system. Instead of one emperor for the enormous empire, there would be four—two Augusti and two Caesars. Each Augustus would rule for twenty years and then retire. During those twenty years, he would choose his Caesar, someone he trusted, and when the Augustus retired the Caesar would become a new Augustus. The elder of the two Augusti would be the head of the whole empire. This way, there would be no doubt about who was to become the next emperor.

Diocletian was quite tolerant of Christians. His court was filled with them. It was rumored that his wife and daughter were believers. For most of his reign, the Church was left at peace, and it continued to grow.

But that growth worried the priests of the old Roman religion. If Christianity continued to flourish, they saw that they would soon be out of jobs. Diocletian was old and scheduled to retire soon. Here was the priests' last chance to get rid of the Church. They found eager support from other fanatics at court, including Galerius, Diocletian's named successor.

Diocletian wasn't about to start a war against a large portion of his own people. But he made every decision by consulting omens, as interpreted by pagan priests. One day Tagis, his chief priest, was offering sacrifice before the whole court. When the priest killed the sacrificial animal, the Christians made the Sign of the Cross, as they always did.

But this time something unheard-of happened. Tagis announced that the omens hadn't appeared. He ordered the priests to make another offering, but still no omens appeared. Tagis pointed his finger at the Christians.

"The gods refuse to appear," he shouted, "because these profane men are keeping them away with that sign, the sign that the gods hate!"

That was enough to convince Diocletian. And so the persecution began. A hand-picked squadron swooped down on the beautiful church in Nicomedia—built during the decades of peace since the last persecution—and broke down the doors. They made a bonfire of the scriptures, then destroyed the whole building.

All the Christians in the court were given a choice: sacrifice to the emperor or die. Soon the persecution fanned out to the remotest provinces. Even children were executed. More edicts came out in Diocletian's name. Clergy were imprisoned. Finally, all Christians were ordered to sacrifice. With ruthless efficiency, persecutors surrounded towns, rounded up all Christians, and called each by name to sacrifice. The ones who refused were carried off to horrible tortures.

Meanwhile, Diocletian lay sick in bed, his dream of a peaceful empire torn to shreds. From Gaul came news that Constantius Chlorus, one of the Caesars, was refusing to persecute the Christians. The four emperors were no longer acting as one. And Diocletian had to watch helplessly as the persecution raged into something worse than civil war. Meanwhile, the time had come when he had said he would step aside. Galerius practically pushed him out the door in 305, and the old man retired to the land today known as Croatia. Soon, six emperors were claiming the title of Augustus.

Diocletian came out of retirement and made a futile attempt to paste the empire back together, but he saw there was no hope. He found a comfortable spot to lie down and took poison.

His mausoleum? Not long after his death, it was repurposed as the Christian cathedral and dedicated to St. Domnius, one of the local martyrs who died in Diocletian's persecution.

For More

Marta Sordi. *The Christians and the Roman Empire.* Norman, OK: University of Oklahoma Press, 1994.

D. Vincent Twomey and Mark Humphries, eds. *The Great Persecution.* Dublin: Four Courts Press, 2009.

The Church *and* *the* Empire

The "Peace of the Church" arrived with the coronation of Emperor Constantine and the promulgation of his Edict of Milan. Now the Church was free to develop distinctively Christian institutions—the hospital, the almshouse, the orphanage, and many others. But imperial favor also introduced challenges. Some emperors wished to control the Church, and different bishops responded in markedly different ways. Religious freedom brought conflicts into the open. Disputes over doctrine suddenly became important matters of state. Councils and creeds arrived to settle matters of biblical interpretation.

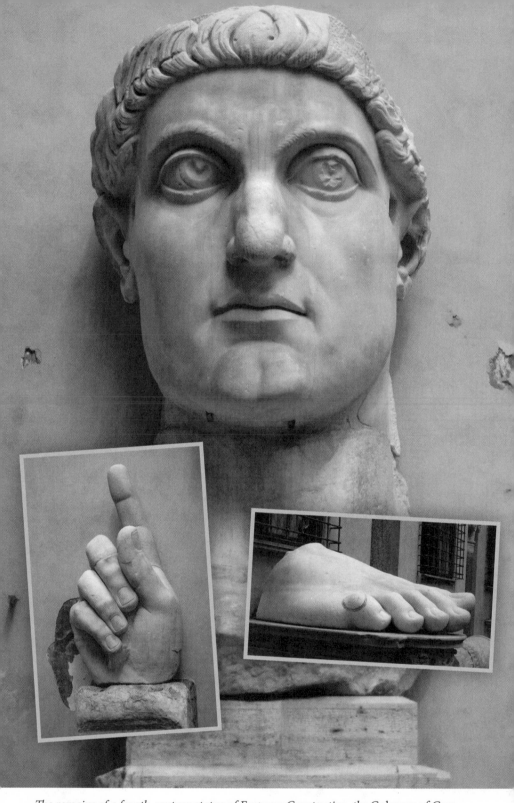

The remains of a fourth-century statue of Emperor Constantine, the Colossus of Constantine. *Photos by James Papandrea.*

16

The *Colossus of* Constantine

These are some of the marble remains of the colossal figure of Constantine that once stood near the Roman Forum. The statue—of the emperor enthroned—stood forty feet tall when it was raised. That probably took place in the years AD 312–315, immediately after Constantine's accession to the throne.

The head alone is eight feet tall. Today it rests with some of the statue's other extremities in the courtyard of the Capitoline Museum in Rome. The rest of the statue was made of lighter and less durable materials. Otherwise the overall weight would have been too much of a temptation to gravity.

Few figures loom so large in history as Constantine. Ruling for more than a quarter century, he established the conditions for a Christian civilization. The developments of the next 1,700 years would be unthinkable apart from the foundational acts of his long reign.

For two and a half centuries, Christians had endured intermittent persecution, which occasionally grew intense. Sometimes there were long stretches between the imperial crackdowns. But even in times of peace, Christians lived with persecution as a recent memory and possible future. They knew that there was substantial legal precedent for the suppression of the Church and the making of martyrs. They knew that anti-Christian violence, outside the law, probably would not be punished. In the years leading up to Constantine's reign, the Church endured the empire's most thoroughgoing persecution to that point in history.

In February 313—after seizing control of the empire's western lands—Constantine, with his eastern counterpart Licinius, issued the Edict of Milan, decreeing toleration of Christianity throughout the empire.

Constantine and Licinius could have presented their decision in many ways, but they chose to speak in terms of widespread tolerance. "We have also conceded to other religions the right of open and free observance of their worship for the sake of the peace of our times, that each one may have the free opportunity to worship as he pleases. This regulation is made that we may not seem to detract from any dignity of any religion," they said. These were revolutionary ideas, and their influence, at least in western Christian lands, would be profound.

Both Constantine and Licinius had family members who were practicing Catholics, and both seem to have had some level of personal interest in the faith. They also were shrewd politicians, and they could see which way the wind was blowing. In every sector of society—military, education, commerce, government—Christians were present and making great contributions. In pragmatic terms: persecution had become counter-productive.

One of Constantine's court intellectuals, a Christian named Lactantius, wrote eloquently in defense of religious freedom. He may have been an important influence in shaping the young emperor's understanding of conscience: "Torture and piety are quite different things," he wrote. "Truth cannot be joined to force or justice to cruelty."

Constantine's later edicts—to the Palestinians and to the Eastern Provincials—show even more mature doctrine, put sometimes in poetic terms: "Let no one disturb another. Let each man hold fast to that which his soul wishes. Let him make full use of this."

Constantine was a believer, and he favored Catholic interests. It was he who summoned the Church's first ecumenical council, at Nicaea, near the imperial capital, in 325. But he knew that the success of Roman rule depended on collaboration among subjects whose religious commitments were widely diverse. Contrary to the myths promoted by secularist historians, Constantine did not coerce conversions. Nor did he invent and impose any elements of the Catholic faith. The faith he embraced, the

Church he favored, was well established in all its doctrinal, disciplinary, and practical particulars long before Constantine was born.

His reign was revolutionary but not in the ways some people make it out to be. He invented the notion of religious liberty. He established, by decree, the principles of a civilization that would endure and come to dominate the world.

For More

Peter Leithart. *Defending Constantine: The Twilight of an Empire and the Dawn of Christendom.* Downers Grove, IL: IVP Academic, 2010.

David Potter. *Constantine the Emperor.* New York: Oxford University Press, 2013.

The dirt at this Roman church is from Jerusalem. Photo by James Papandrea.

17

Empress Helena's Dirt

Beneath the glass panel in the floor is dirt—just dirt. It's soil that was transported to Rome from Jerusalem by command of the Empress Helena.

As she returned from pilgrimage around the year AD 328, Helena brought a boatload of the stuff with her. Though she could not remain in the Holy Land, the Holy Land would remain with her. She had the soil spread on the floor level of the church known today as the Basilica of the Holy Cross in Jerusalem. The church's name reflects the fact that it's built on Jerusalem's soil though it stands in Rome and the cities are almost 1,500 miles apart.

Helena is a fascinating but elusive figure. Her birthplace is uncertain. She's claimed by both Bithynia (in modern Turkey) and Britain (whose legends say she was the daughter of Old King Cole, the merry old soul).

In her youth she became the wife (or concubine) of Constantius, a Roman general serving under the Emperor Aurelian. Together they had a son, future emperor Constantine, born around 272. As Constantius advanced in his career, he separated from Helena in order to marry the daughter of the Emperor Maximian—a politically expedient move. His star rose, but he seems to have maintained a remarkable degree of principled independence. When he eventually rose to the imperial purple, he refused to take part in the persecution ordered by Diocletian. Some speculate that he did this out of affection for Helena, who may already have had Christian sympathies (though the historian Eusebius, her contemporary, said she came to faith through her son).

Helena remained close to Constantine, who revered her. When he ascended the throne, in 306, he summoned his mother to join him in honor. He gave her the title empress and struck coins with her image.

Eventually she moved into a grand palace in Rome, at the site where the basilica would be built.

Around 325, when she was probably in her mid-seventies, she set out on pilgrimage at the request of her son. Though the Church had only recently been legalized, it was already suffering divisions because of heresies. Constantine may have wanted his mother to act as a goodwill ambassador.

The ancient historians say she made her pilgrimage an expedition to visit the sites—and discover the relics—of Jesus' life. St. Ambrose, writing a half century later, claimed that it was Helena herself who unearthed the true cross. (Constantine's letters make reference to the recent discovery of the cross but do not credit his mother.) According to various ancient sources, Helena spent her time in the Holy Land commissioning repairs of existing churches and the construction of new churches, and she returned to Rome with wood from the cross, the nails from the crucifixion, and the *titulus* that hung above the cross with the text "Jesus of Nazareth, King of the Jews" (Jn 19:19–20)—items that are on display today in the Basilica of the Holy Cross in Jerusalem.

Helena established the model that would be followed by Christian empresses afterward. She was renowned for her generosity, her piety, and her concern for the Church. She died at age eighty in 330, just seven years before the death of her son.

She is sometimes given credit with founding the field of archeology. She was perhaps the first to be sent on expedition with the resources to make genuine discoveries. Local Christians had preserved traditions about the sites of the events in the gospels, but never before had they had the freedom or the means to make excavations. Helena, as empress, had both.

A mysterious figure in many ways, she found ways to move the earth. Pilgrims today, to Rome and to the Holy Land, follow in her footsteps, pray in the churches she built, and worship at the ground she walked on.

For More

Carsten Peter Thiede and Matthew d'Ancona. *The Quest for the True Cross*. New York: Palgrave, 2002.

Evelyn Waugh. *Helena*. Chicago: Loyola Press, 2005. Note, this is a novel.

An Arian Baptism of Jesus in Ravenna, Italy. Photo by udokant / iStockphoto.com.

18

A Ravenna Mosaic

What is the object here? Jesus' body is objectified to make a doctrinal point. This mosaic adorns the ceiling of a baptistery built by Arian heretics in the city of Ravenna, on Italy's Adriatic coast.

The image is unusual for many reasons but most noticeably because Jesus is portrayed entirely naked, with everything exposed, though somewhat distorted by water. The artist wished to emphasize Jesus' humanity, as the Arians rejected his deity and coeternity with the Father. In artwork, Catholics afforded Jesus a measure of modesty. The Arians wanted to make a point.

Jesus is portrayed, furthermore, as a beardless youth, suggesting his subordination to the Father. And of course, he is depicted at his Baptism in the River Jordan, confirming (the Arians would say) his divine adoption from the Father.

Arianism was, like many heresies, a seemingly rational proposition. It seemed to make sense, and that's why it succeeded to such a remarkable degree. What, after all, were Christians to make of the Trinity—of threeness that is oneness? What were Christians to make of the intersection of eternity and time in the life of Jesus? The Gospel proposed mysteries it did not explicate.

In the second and third centuries Christians attempted a variety of approaches to the mysteries. Sometimes even great minds—like Justin Martyr and Origen—spoke of them with language that would be judged erroneous or imprecise by later generations. During times of persecution, however, such controversies tended to remain brush fires that blazed up and burned out quickly.

Arius was a priest of Alexandria, Egypt, though he had studied in the rival city of Syrian Antioch. In his teaching he emphasized God's transcendence and utter solitude. He insisted that the Word of God was not truly God—not coeternal or coequal—but rather received divinity as a gift. The Word, then, was a creature, though the greatest of creatures by far. The Word became "Son" upon adoption by the Father. And God assumed the title "Father" only upon adopting the Word.

Arius was an effective teacher. He often summed up his principles in tidy slogans: "There was [a time] when he was not," he said of the divine Word. And "As long as the Son did not exist, God was not Father." He wrote hymns with catchy tunes that spread his doctrines abroad with astonishing speed.

In the years AD 318–322 he came into conflict with his bishop, Alexander of Alexandria. Alexander was bright, but he was no match for Arius, who was a genius of public relations. Intellectuals gravitated toward Arius. The secular authorities liked what he had to say. And a growing number of bishops were inclined to give him time in their pulpits.

Arius forced the crisis one Sunday by interrupting a homily that Alexander was preaching. The priest publicly denounced his bishop for teaching that God was eternally Father and Jesus his coeternal Son.

Soon afterward an Egyptian synod excommunicated Arius and his followers and expelled them. On his way out of the country, Arius wrote a tract to plead his case before the widest possible audience. Then the dispute was no longer a local brush fire. It became an international conflagration. St. Jerome later recalled the rapidity with which the heresy spread: "The world awoke to find itself Arian."

Free at last after centuries of persecution, the Church seemed now to be fragmenting from forces within. The contention often erupted into violence.

Constantine grew alarmed and in 325 summoned the bishops to Nicaea, a suburb of Constantinople, to meet in council and settle the matter. After heated discussion, the bishops declared that Arius's doctrine was irreconcilable with the apostolic faith. They issued a creed as the Church's doctrinal standard, and so the Nicene Creed remains today. In the Creed the Church proclaims that the Son is "consubstantial with the Father."

Arius was vanquished, though his followers sought to keep his doctrine alive by finding safer expressions that could *almost* pass for the faith of Nicaea. But the creeds and councils held the day, at least within the borders of the empire. Arians were safer among the barbarian peoples, however, and it was Ostrogoths who commissioned the mosaic pictured here, around the year 490.

For More

Lewis Ayres. *Nicaea and Its Legacy: An Approach to Fourth-Century Trinitarian Theology.* New York: Oxford University Press, 2006.

Christoph Schonborn. *God Sent His Son: A Contemporary Christology.* San Francisco: Ignatius Press, 2010.

A scene from Homer's Iliad, *cast on the handle of a mirror. Photo from bpkBildagentur / Art Resource, NY.*

19

A Scene *from* Homer's *Iliad*

The cast is from Greek mythology. The medium is the bronze handle of a mirror. And the scene is from Homer's *Iliad*. Achilles has killed Hector and is abusing the man's corpse. Hector's father, King Priam, arrives, escorted by the god Hermes, to retrieve the body.

This small bronze was cast in the sixth century before Christ. But the story was still vividly familiar to educated men and women nine hundred years later. Even after the Edict of Milan, and even for Christians, the ancient epics remained part of the curriculum and were often committed to memory.

A young man named Julian found the stories attractive—and all the more because they had *nothing* to do with Christianity. Julian was the nephew of Constantine, and he had been raised Christian, like all the imperial family. When he was a young child, however, his faith was shaken as his older cousins, the heirs to the throne, killed off all the male relatives they perceived as rivals. Among the victims of the massacre were Julian's father, his older brother, an uncle, and six cousins. They spared Julian because he was very young and posed no credible threat.

Though Julian continued to live a privileged life, he kept the memory of that purge, and he nursed the grudge. He learned, however, to keep his thoughts to himself. Constantius, his murderous uncle, was also his patron, and alienation from the emperor meant certain death. So the boy went about his studies quietly and diligently.

At Athens he took up philosophy and rhetoric, and he secretly began his investigations of the traditional mysteries of Greek and Roman religion. He found a group that secretly practiced the old rituals, and he joined them. Though he kept up his outward practice of Christianity, his mind and heart now belonged to old gods.

Appointed to leadership in the military, Julian rose rapidly with stunning campaigns in the barbarian lands. He gained a reputation for toughness. Unlike other generals, he shared the hardships of his troops. He ate what they ate, slept where they slept. And he rewarded them handsomely. All this made for tenacious loyalty. Not surprisingly, they eventually declared him emperor.

So in AD 360 Julian began to march toward Constantinople to confront his cousin Constantius. But the meeting never happened. Constantius died of natural causes while Julian was on his way.

Thus began the reign that gave Julian his place in history. He is remembered as "The Apostate"—the man who renounced Christianity in a public and forcefully institutional way. The Christian Church had enjoyed the favor of emperors for a half century. But Julian made clear that his reign would be different.

He made vast sums available to restore temples that had fallen into disrepair and disuse. He promoted pagans to prominent positions in the capital and boosted the wages of pagan priests. He presented a scheme for an organized paganism—and it looked a lot like the Christian Church. It had three levels of hierarchy, and the emperor was more or less its pope. When he spoke of this in Antioch, the majority-Christian population openly laughed.

This infuriated him, of course, and led to harsher restrictions on Christians. He began by banning believers from teaching grammar, rhetoric, and philosophy. Christians could not teach the ancient epics, because the epics were about the gods. Julian made requirements for schoolteachers so stringently pagan that no Christian could fulfill them. Banished from the public square, Christianity could be minimized as a cultural force.

And yet Julian retained the appearance of religious freedom. Believers remained free to do and think whatever they wanted on Sundays . . . as long as they didn't let it seep into the wider society. Julian wanted to remove Christians from public discourse—neutralize their public influence—and drive them into a cultural ghetto. Briefly, he succeeded.

From Antioch Julian led his troops toward Persia—and to their devastating defeat at the hands of the Persian emperor Shapur II. On the battlefield at the Persian frontier, Julian fell hard, and with his death the eastern empire began to crumble.

For More

Michael Curtis Ford. *Gods and Legions: A Novel of the Roman Empire.* New York: St. Martin's Press, 2002. Note, this is a novel.

Adrian Murdoch. *The Last Pagan: Julian the Apostate and the Death of the Ancient World.* Rochester, VT: Inner Traditions, 2008.

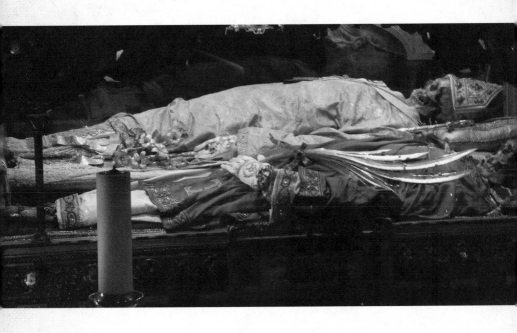

The relics of St. Ambrose lie in state in Milan. Photo by Fr. Gaurav Shroff.

20

St. Ambrose's Bones

The skeletal remains of St. Ambrose lie in state, in bishop's vestments, in the crypt of the church he built. Beside him lie the bones of the second-century martyrs Gervasius and Protasius, discovered through archeological explorations conducted by Ambrose himself.

As bishop of Milan from AD 374 to 397, Ambrose encouraged devotion to the martyrs and actively sought their relics. It was a tense moment in the conflict between Arians and Catholics, and a new age of martyrdom seemed a real possibility for Ambrose and his church.

He was adept at reading the political signs of the times. Before becoming bishop, Ambrose had served as governor of the region of Liguria and Emilia, with headquarters at Milan. It was a position of tremendous power. Milan was by then the administrative and military center of the western empire. Rome remained the symbolic capital, but it was geographically too vulnerable. The emperors, the court, and the armies had gradually moved to Milan in the second half of the fourth century. In these key developments, Ambrose played an important role.

The bishop of the city during Ambrose's governorship was Auxentius, an Arian who enjoyed the favor of the ruling class. When Auxentius died, there was much anxiety over who would succeed him in office. People poured into the streets of the city, and the governor, of course, worried that the demonstrations were devolving into riots.

Ambrose went out to calm the mobs—and the mobs acclaimed *him* as bishop. He refused. He wasn't even a baptized Christian! But word came from Rome that the emperor expected Ambrose to accept the office. So the governor was fast-tracked through his preparation and, in short order, received the sacraments of Initiation—plus Holy Orders and consecration as a bishop.

Since Ambrose came from the ruling class, surely the emperors hoped he would be a reliable ally, no matter what they demanded. Ambrose, however, proved to be his own man. He stared down three emperors in succession. He informed Gratian that he had no authority to summon bishops to attend a council. He told Valentinian that the emperor had no authority in matters of faith. Theodosius he refused to admit to Communion until the man had done public penance. But his greatest act of defiance, perhaps, was his peaceful occupation of a church that Valentinian's mother and guardian, Justina, had ordered the army to commandeer for Arian worship. While the military closed in, Ambrose and his parishioners sang hymns. The soldiers could not go forward in good conscience.

While the Arians—all the way back to Constantine—tended to look to the emperor as the earthly head of the Church, Ambrose made clear that this would not be the Catholic way.

His primary response to heresy, however, was educational, not political. He formed his congregation in every manner at his disposal. He composed hymns in the eastern style, making sure to end them with a Trinitarian verse that was clearly Nicene in its expression. (Such "doxologies" have remained a standard feature of hymns down the ages.) He delivered a series of lectures to his clergy for their ongoing formation. He preached persuasively. And he wrote prolifically for every conceivable audience.

Somehow, though, he managed to die of natural causes after long years as bishop of Milan. The basilica he had only just finished building was named for him; there he rests with the martyrs.

For More

Angelo Paredi. *Saint Ambrose: His Life and Times.* Notre Dame, IN: University of Notre Dame Press, 1964.

Boniface Ramsey, O.P. *Ambrose.* London: Routledge, 1997.

*The base of the Obelisk of Theodosius in Istanbul, Turkey. Photo by danishkhan /
iStockphoto.com.*

21

The Winner's Wreath

The winner is the one who receives the wreath from the hand of Theodosius. That's the message of the bas relief sculpture at the base of the great obelisk in the city once known as Constantinople.

The great needle, almost a hundred feet tall, came from Egypt at the command of the emperor in the year AD 390. It had stood in place in Egypt for two millennia before Theodosius decided it would be a fitting monument to his power. He had the front and back filled with figural sculpture. He had the sides inscribed with praise of himself, composed as testimony of the obelisk: "Once I opposed resistance, but I was commanded to obey. . . . Everything yields to Theodosius and to his descendants in perpetuity. This is true of me, too. I was dominated and overcome."

The red granite obelisk stood as the emperor's pride in the Hippodrome of the capital city, where the people thronged for chariot races.

During the reign of Theodosius I, the greatest winner—at least in worldly terms—was no charioteer. It was Nicene orthodoxy.

Since the death of Constantine, the emperors had been divided among themselves between the Catholic and Arian factions. Some bishops tried to curry favor for their respective parties. They jockeyed for position—like charioteers, perhaps. The instability made the people anxious and prone to violence when they didn't get the brand of bishop they preferred.

Theodosius, the last emperor to rule over both the eastern and western halves of the empire, saw that religious disunity was weakening his kingdom. He made his decision for the Nicene faith. His piety and ardor were genuine. He accepted Baptism not in old age, as Constantine did, but in the vigor of youth. Then he chose to make it *more* than a personal choice. He made the decision for the entire empire. He enacted laws against Arianism and Donatism, the two besetting heresies of his time. And he did away with the last vestiges of state subsidy for traditional pagan rites. He even issued an edict forbidding the *discussion* of any religious matter!

Many bishops were happy to see this. But it didn't exactly bring peace. Orthodox Christians took the imperial favor to mean they could (finally) do away with the straggling remnants of the old Roman religion. Mobs destroyed ancient temples in several major cities.

Theodosius is the man who did the deed for which Constantine is often blamed: the suppression of every religious variety except Nicene Christianity. Constantine did *favor* the Catholic faith. But Theodosius *enforced* it.

And he had a reputation as a brutal and impulsive enforcer. In 390, the same year the obelisk was raised in Constantinople, the people of Thessalonica rioted to complain about the placement of a military garrison. The mob managed to kill the commanding officer. So Theodosius had the population of the town summoned to the circus, and there the military killed everyone—seven thousand people in all.

The bishop of Milan, St. Ambrose, was furious and publicly refused to admit the emperor to Communion until he did public penance for several months—terms that Theodosius accepted.

When Theodosius died in 395, the empire was divided between his sons Arcadius (age eighteen) and Honorius (age ten). They were unprepared to rule, and they ruled like men unprepared for the task.

Faith won by force is not faith. It's an open question whether Theodosius did Catholicism any favors by granting it the wreath.

For More

Karl Baus et al. *The Imperial Church from Constantine to the Early Middle Ages.* New York: Seabury, 1980.

Michael Grant. *The Roman Emperors: A Biographical Guide to the Rulers of Imperial Rome.* New York: Barnes and Noble, 1985.

An unguentarium from the ancient world. Photo by Susan Brown.

22

Glass Unguentarium

An unguentarium like this one—small and made of glass—was probably used to hold medicine or cosmetics in powder or ointment form. In fact, the Latin word *unguentarium* could also mean a drugstore.

When this vessel was made in the fourth century, Christian doctors were bringing about a revolution in health care. Immediately after the legalization of Christianity, the hospital emerged for the first time and became ubiquitous. It was, according to the modern historian Gary Ferngren, a distinctively Christian institution, unlike anything that had gone before.

What passed for the medical profession until then was a riot of different types of practitioner: herbalists, magicians, folk healers, as well as doctors in the empirical tradition of Hippocrates and Galen. Most were traveling salesmen, offering their services in one village before moving on to the next. In the course of their careers, they could range across continents. The profession was unregulated and anarchic, and training happened through apprenticeship.

From the documents and inscriptions of the first three centuries, it seems that physicians were drawn to Christianity—and Christians were drawn to the practice of medicine. No other profession is as well represented as doctors are. They make up the single largest cohort by far. St. Justin Martyr confirms their prevalence in the second century, as does Origen in the third.

In the middle of the third century, Christian physicians distinguished themselves for their brave and generous service during the so-called Plague of Cyprian, the smallpox epidemic that lasted for decades and claimed the lives of thousands of city-dwellers in a single day. Christian doctors did not abandon their stations; the Church was the only institution willing and able to organize relief efforts. Christians, moreover, extended their care not only to their co-religionists but to everyone—even their persecutors.

In another epidemic, which began during the great persecution of Diocletian, Christian physicians performed no less heroically. Even nonbelievers praised the work and virtue of Christian physicians.

What were established as habits during the centuries of persecution became institutions during years of imperial favor. The first hospitals arose in the years immediately after the Edict of Milan. By the end of the century, every city was expected to have several hospitals.

Hospitals extended Christian "hospitality" to anyone in need. Their complexes often included not only wards for the sick but also homeless shelters, hospices for the dying, hostels for travelers, and even trade schools to provide beggars with a better future. In Pontian Caesarea, the complex built by St. Basil the Great was so extensive that the locals called it the "New City." One observer said it rivaled the Seven Wonders of the Ancient World.

Pagan antiquity had had all the material ingredients for the creation of such an institution. The Greeks and Romans had doctors. They had *valetudinaria*, which were essentially repair shops for broken slaves and wounded soldiers. There was ample demand for medical care. Yet neither Greeks nor Romans ever produced a hospital. Modern historians of medicine agree on this point.

What was missing was a Christian sense of virtue that exalted *charity*—sacrificial, self-giving love. Charity was far more demanding than the classical virtue of philanthropy. So was the Christian ideal of hospitality, which required a welcoming attitude toward everyone.

Once the hospital was in place, other developments soon followed. The first primitive ambulance, for instance. These are developments that would have been unlikely without Christianity.

For More

Gary B. Ferngren. *Medicine and Health Care in Early Christianity*. Baltimore: Johns Hopkins University Press, 2009.

Timothy S. Miller. *The Birth of the Hospital in the Byzantine Empire*. Baltimore: Johns Hopkins University Press, 1997.

Stylized Ethiopian cross. Photo by Rosemary Aquilina.

23

Ethiopian Cross

The cross is the focal point of this brass pendant, but it is decorated with symbolic geometric shapes. It is simple for an Ethiopian cross. It has only minimal knotwork, visible on only one side of the pendant.

Xs mark the points of Jesus' five wounds—at the head, foot, hands, and heart. The cross's middle portion is enclosed by a rectangle, perhaps representing the Ark of the Covenant, which Ethiopian Christians claim to have possessed since antiquity.

Ethiopia is first associated with biblical religion in the Old Testament, when the Queen of Sheba went to Jerusalem to learn wisdom from King Solomon (1 Kgs 10:1–13 and 2 Chr 9:1–12). According to tradition, she returned pregnant by Solomon, and the son they conceived was heir to the throne of Aksum. There have been Jews in Ethiopia ever since.

The New Testament tells of at least one Ethiopian making pilgrimage to Jerusalem for the Jewish holy days: the eunuch who served as treasurer to the queen of Ethiopia (Acts 8:27–39). When he first appears, he is reading the prophet Isaiah from a scroll. Soon he is instructed and baptized by Philip the deacon. As the story ends, we are told, "he went on his way rejoicing."

His way surely went back to sub-Saharan Africa. It is likely that there was some Christian presence in Ethiopia since the first century. But no evidence has survived. Ethiopian Christianity first clearly enters the historical record in the fourth century, when two shipwrecked Syrian youths, Frumentius and Aedisius, came to serve at the court of the king in Aksum. They won the trust of the king; when the king died, the queen asked them to stay and rule until the young prince came of age. At the prince's accession, Frumentius went to Alexandria, where St. Athanasius consecrated him a bishop and sent him back to Aksum. Ethiopian Christianity flour-ished afterward. Always associated with the See of Alexandria in Egypt, it nonetheless developed its own distinctive traditions of liturgy, art, and monasticism, and it retained many Jewish customs.

Already in the fourth century, Ethiopian coins attest to the conversion of the country's royal family. Inscriptions also confirm the accounts of Ethiopian Christian origins preserved in the works of Athanasius in Egypt and Rufinus in Italy. Soon, local Christians were translating the scriptures, the liturgy, and a wealth of theological and devotional literature into the Ge'ez language.

Ornate crosses were (and are) the universal sign of Ethiopian Chris-tianity. The clergy hold hand crosses, and they carry processional crosses in the liturgy. Family homes bear rooftop crosses. Individuals have crosses tattooed on their bodies and faces.

The Ethiopian cross is usually elaborately decorated, like this one, although it rarely shows the body of Jesus. Common design elements include stylized ram's horns, doves, foliage, and intricate knotwork. The loops upon loops sometimes resemble the decoration of crosses in Ire-land—and Celtic and Ethiopian monasticism may indeed share common precursors in the deserts of Egypt.

Ethiopian Christian culture has been unique and distinctive since its origins. The designs seem unusual to Western eyes. But what is common is the cross, which is squarely at the center.

For More

Wolf Leslau, ed. *Falasha Anthology: Translated from Ethiopic Sources.* New Haven, CT: Yale University Press, 1979.

Milos Simovic. *Daughter of Zion: Orthodox Christian Art from Ethiopia.* Jerusalem: The Israel Museum, 2000.

Pilgrim flask of St. Menas. Photo by Susan Brown.

24

St. Menas's Flask

We call them knickknacks or tchotchkes—the souvenirs we pick up on vacations and accumulate on our shelves. Pilgrims, too, pick them up. They always have.

This tiny terra cotta flask is one of many that have been unearthed from sites all through Europe and the Middle East. It once held holy water from the popular Egyptian shrine of St. Menas.

On the front of the flask appears the martyr-saint in his traditional pose, standing between two camels.

Ancient sources tell us that Menas was born around AD 285 to a wealthy Christian family in Egypt. In his teen years he joined the Roman army and was given an officer's commission because of his family's status. After three years of service he left the army in order to live as a hermit in the desert. During the Great Persecution under Emperor Diocletian, Menas was inspired to present himself publicly as a Christian. For this he was sentenced to death.

According to tradition, the martyr's shrine was established near Lake Mariout when the camels carrying his remains simply stopped, knelt down, and refused to go any further.

Like the catacombs in Rome and the Way of the Cross in Jerusalem, the shrine of St. Menas flourished as a pilgrim destination. Its natural spring reportedly had curative powers, and Christians traveled there to bathe in its healing waters. They also filled flasks to carry home for friends and family members.

In time, a veritable city arose around the burial place of St. Menas. Once the Roman Empire was officially Christian, Emperor Arcadius built a basilica there. The shrine flourished till Muslim rule began in the seventh century, when it fell into disuse. Its ruins were excavated in the early twentieth century, turning up thousands of flasks and other religious mementos. The flasks, like this one, often bear an inscription, usually in Coptic, meaning "Blessing of St. Menas" or even "Remembrance/Souvenir of St. Menas."

Flasks of St. Menas traveled to the ends of the earth—or the known world, at least—and today testify to the tremendous popularity of Christian pilgrimage. In a world united in peace by Christian faith, "spiritual tourism" once flourished.

St. Jerome, a fourth-century resident of the Holy Land, asked rhetorically, "For what race of men is there which does not send pilgrims to the holy places?" In a famous letter on pilgrimage, he held up his late friend St. Paula as a model pilgrim: "So great was the passion and the enthusiasm she exhibited upon visiting each of the holy places, that she could never have torn herself away from one had she not been eager to visit the rest."

Pilgrims made their way to the Holy Land to walk in Jesus' footsteps. They made it to Rome to venerate the tombs of Sts. Peter and Paul. They even traveled to India to visit the sites associated with St. Thomas the Apostle. They returned home changed by the experience. St. Jerome said, "The man who has seen Judea with his own eyes . . . will gaze more clearly upon Holy Scripture."

They also brought back their remembrances—what the Church would later call "sacramentals"—to renew their piety for the rest of their lives.

Pilgrims would even journey to distant monasteries to visit "living saints," holy men and women in other lands. St. Anthony of Egypt fled to the desert for solitude, but great crowds of inquirers followed after him. Some stayed. Others returned home to tell of what they saw—and inspire yet another generation of pilgrims.

Such travel would become more difficult as Christianity declined in Egypt, Syria, the Holy Land, and elsewhere. But the knickknacks have made sure the ancient devotion will never be forgotten.

For More

Jas Elsner and Ian Rutherford, eds. *Seeing the Gods: Pilgrimage in Graeco-Roman and Early Christian Antiquity*. New York: Oxford University Press, 2007.

Georgia Frank. *The Memory of the Eyes: Pilgrims to Living Saints in Christian Late Antiquity*. Berkeley: University of California Press, 2000.

The pool where St. Augustine was baptized in Milan, Italy. Photo by Robert Fernandez.

25

A Milan Baptistery

It's likely that thousands of new Christians were born to new life from this baptistery—though it is best known by far for one: St. Augustine.

Today the fourth-century chapel is a ruin beneath Milan's cathedral. At the heart of the baptistery is an eight-sided shallow in-ground pool.

St. Ambrose composed the inscription on its walls: "This font has eight corners. It is proper to build this baptismal hall around the sacred number eight, for here the people are reborn." The octagon is indeed the typical shape of early Christian baptismal fonts. In the Old Testament sacrament of initiation, Jewish children had been circumcised on the eighth day, so the octagonal font represented the "eighth day" of a new creation in Jesus Christ.

In the early Church, the ordinary day for baptisms was Sunday (properly Easter), the first day of the week. Christians observed Sunday also as the "eighth day"—the day that followed the Sabbath and completed the creation story, as told in the book of Genesis. Jesus' Resurrection on a Sunday brought to fulfillment God's work in history.

St. Augustine's Baptism took place on Easter Vigil in AD 387. It had been a long time coming. The son of a devout Christian mother, he grew up in a village in North Africa. Augustine went astray as a teenager and young adult, indulging his sensuality and pride even as he excelled in his studies. He slept around and conceived a child out of wedlock. He even dabbled in the practices of an eastern cult, Manicheism.

His career soared in his chosen field, rhetoric, as he attracted powerful patrons. His mother, Monica, continued to plead with him and pray for his return to the faith. Augustine paid no heed—and even fled from her, taking jobs across the sea in Rome and then at the imperial court in Milan. She continued praying and followed him all the way to Milan.

At court in the city, Augustine came into contact with Christian philosophers, who helped him to see the sense of the faith. He also heard the preaching of Milan's brilliant bishop, who had by then been in office for a decade. As a rhetorician, Augustine admired Ambrose's skill. As an intellectual, he appreciated Ambrose's depth. The old man began to move the younger man's heart.

On Easter Vigil in 387, Ambrose baptized Augustine and his son, Adeodatus, who was by then in his late teens. (The fad in the fourth century was to delay Baptism until old age, for fear of committing a post-baptismal mortal sin.) Their Baptism—by immersion in the octagonal pool pictured here—is arguably one of the most important events in history for Augustine appears prominently on any short list of the most influential thinkers of all time. His literary works synthesized the best of the classical heritage with emerging Christian thought. His social doctrine, expressed magnificently in his *City of God*, served as the foundation of medieval civilization. He wrote standard texts in Trinitarian theology, biblical interpretation, catechetics, apologetics, monastic community life, and many other fields (more than a hundred works in all). Literary historians say he invented the genre of the memoir with his *Confessions*.

Augustine is as important to history as any king or general, inventor or theorist. From his pen came the inspiration, justification, and impetus for many later events and movements.

He exercised his influence, moreover, far from the cultural centers of his time. Shortly after his Baptism, he returned to Africa and founded a community for prayer and study. Eventually he was ordained a priest and then a bishop. As a pastor he established a model for generations to follow. For his people he was a preacher, teacher, judge, and father. All roles are evident in the voluminous sermons and correspondence he left behind.

He had a strong but critical appreciation of the classical Roman culture he had inherited—its literary and legal traditions and institutions. He lived to see the beginning of their dissolution. As he lay in bed dying, his city was besieged by Vandals, a Germanic tribe that would sack Rome in 455.

Because Augustine had been born to new life, the Roman world would also find new life as a new civilization, continuous with the old but more clearly Christian.

For More

Peter Brown. *Augustine of Hippo: A Biography*, 2nd ed. Berkeley: University of California Press, 2000.

Allan D. Fitzgerald, O.S.A., ed. *Augustine through the Ages: An Encyclopedia*. Grand Rapids, MI: William B. Eerdmans, 1999.

The cave where St. Eustochium did scholarly work. Photo by Linda Mertz.

26
Eustochium's Cave

Beneath the main floor of St. Catherine's Church in Bethlehem—close to the Grotto of the Nativity—there is a corridor that opens onto several caves. The cave pictured here was once the workplace and later the burial place of Eustochium, a woman renowned for her intelligence and industry, and her mother, Paula.

Members of a Roman senatorial family, Eustochium and Paula dedicated their lives to prayer, study, and charitable work. Paula, upon her husband's death, consecrated herself to widowhood and began to gather a community of consecrated women into her home. Paula had a vast fortune at her disposal, and she had the kind of boldness that wealth can foster. So she approached Jerome and asked him to serve as spiritual director and tutor to her community.

This took remarkable chutzpah. Jerome was one of the most respected scholars of his day, and to say he was a curmudgeon would be an understatement. In the course of his lifetime, he left a caustic paper trail, dismissing or insulting many great saints and scholars, including Augustine, Ambrose, John Chrysostom, and Rufinus.

Paula was not intimidated. And Jerome, perhaps astonished by her temerity, took up her offer. He was immediately impressed by the level of scholarship in Paula's community—not just study but genuine academic rigor. He invited the women to submit questions to him but soon found himself overwhelmed by the research required to answer them. He complained that Paula was a "slave driver." He also complained that the women soon surpassed him in their mastery of Hebrew. When they chanted the psalms, they did so without an accent, while he still sang like a tourist with a phrase book.

Jerome had a day job as secretary to Pope Damasus I, who commissioned him to produce a new translation of the Latin Bible. He found able assistance in the community of women gathered in the house of Paula.

After the death of Damasus, Jerome decided to return to monastic life in the East. He was accompanied by some from the women's community and soon followed by Paula and Eustochium themselves, who had pledged to spend their remaining days in the Holy Land.

They passed through Egypt, stopping along the way to study the various ways of organizing religious communities. Arriving in Bethlehem, they founded four monasteries there, three for women and one for men, and devoted the rest of their lives to producing biblical and theological scholarship. Many of Jerome's works were produced at Eustochium's request. Without her assistance, it is unlikely he could have produced such volume and quality of work. Eustochium was an able administrator as well, corresponding confidently with bishops and popes.

Paula died in AD 404 and Eustochium in 420. It was Jerome's sorrow to outlive his closest colleague in biblical research. He died a few months afterward.

It is difficult to imagine women finding such opportunities before the rise of Christianity. Roman law treated women as perpetual children. They were forbidden to testify in a court of law. One of the earliest critics of Christianity, Celsus in the second century, derided the Church for speaking directly to women.

In the Roman world, a woman derived her identity and value from her relationship to a male: her father, her husband, or her sons. But then Christianity came along making the revolutionary claim of equality between the sexes (Gal 3:28); that principle had immediate practical consequences. Women emerged as leaders in the Christian community from the earliest generations. The New Testament presents the examples of Mary the mother of Jesus (Acts 1:14), Priscilla (Acts 18:2), Tabitha (Acts 9:36), and many others. Following those biblical examples were Perpetua and Felicity in the first years of the third century. Imprisoned with other Christians, they assumed a role of inspired leadership—though their parish priest was jailed with them. Other women emerged as founders, hermits, teachers, and spiritual guides: Macrina, Monica, Egeria, Scholastica, Olympia, and (of course) Paula and Eustochium.

By the fifth century, it became possible for pagan women, such as the Egyptian philosopher Hypatia, to achieve a prestigious place in the academic world. But they probably have Christian women to thank for preparing the way.

For More

Mike Aquilina. *The Witness of Early Christian Women: Mothers of the Church*. Huntington, IN: Our Sunday Visitor, 2014.

Carolinne White, trans. and ed. *Lives of Roman Christian Women*. New York: Penguin, 2010.

A Byzantine marriage ring, from the collection of the British Museum.

27

A Wedding Ring

The wedding ring is solid gold and rather large. It must have adorned the hand of a wealthy man. Perhaps he was very much in love. The signet depicts a man and a woman looking contented. Above them—uniting them—is the cross.

The British Museum of Art estimates that this band was made in the fifth century. Many similar rings survive from the early Byzantine Era. They often show the couple united around a single word or symbol: the *chi-rho* christogram; the word *homonoia* (meaning harmony), *hagia* (holy), *charis* (grace); or the Greek letters alpha and omega (see Rev 1:8).

The message is consistent: marriage is something sacred, divine, sacramental.

With the rise of Christianity came a reconfiguration of society. Indeed, it was the revaluation of family roles that most alarmed the persecutors of the faith. Christian teachers condemned practices that were considered normal in Greco-Roman family life: easy divorce, contraception, abortion, and child marriage, to name just a few examples. In contrast to Roman law, Christian doctrine presented women as men's equals, not their property or their perpetual wards. Thus, on rings like this one, the spouses are depicted as equals.

In the wedding rings of the early Christians we see the union prescribed by St. Paul: "Husbands, love your wives, as Christ loved the church and gave himself up for her" (Eph 5:25).

It was not always a smooth transition from pagan to Christian wedlock. Vows were rarely exchanged in a church ceremony. Even for Christians the setting was usually at home or in a public place—and the form remained what it had been for centuries. The common people still held on to some of the old pagan fertility rites, such as throwing seeds of grain. Grooms still carried their brides over the threshold of the home they would share. Wedding guests foretold the young couple's sexual happiness with bawdy songs.

Against such customs, the Church Fathers railed. Hear St. John Chrysostom, in the fourth century: "Is the wedding then a theater? No! It is a sacrament, a mystery, and a model of the Church of Christ. . . . They dance at pagan ceremonies; but at ours, silence and decorum should prevail, respect and modesty. Here a great mystery is accomplished."

In calling marriage a "mystery," Chrysostom harks back again to St. Paul: "For this reason a man shall leave his father and mother and be joined to his wife, and the two shall become one flesh." "This mystery," St. Paul says, "is a profound one, and I am saying that it refers to Christ and the Church" (Eph 5:31–32).

Christian marriage was intended to be something essentially different from pagan marriage, and that fact should be evident in the couple's grace and charity. The family is now a privileged image of the Church—and even an image of the Trinity. Chrysostom said it is the third family member, the child, who strengthens the bond of husband and wife.

As marriage was a sacrament, so the wedding ring was seen as a sacred item capable of warding off the demons assigned to trouble Christian homes. Some wedding rings—with simple, deep, and prominent features— were also designed to serve as personal seals, signs of a new personal identity, bound indivisibly to another and to Christ.

For More

Ioli Kalavrezou. *Byzantine Women and Their World.* Cambridge, MA: Harvard, 2003.
Patrick Riley. *Civilizing Sex.* Edinburgh: T and T Clark, 2002.

This mosaic in Ravenna, Italy, shows Empresses Theodora and her court. Photo by gaveover2012 / iStockphoto.com.

28

Theodora's Halo

Among the mosaics at the Basilica of San Vitale in Ravenna, Italy, are panels depicting Justinian and Theodora, the Roman emperor and empress who commissioned the construction of the church. Their heads are surrounded by haloes, which distinguish them from their courtiers. In Theodora's panel, presented here, the empress bears the chalice of wine that is necessary for the celebration of the liturgy.

Justinian was a devout man with a strong sense of Christian mission. He wanted to restore the empire's glory and unity. He also wanted to give the empire an identity more completely Christian. He pursued these goals rather single-mindedly and according to a plan.

His most lasting legacy would be the compilation and codification of all previous Roman laws. It was a stunning achievement, and it gave coherent legal expression to many Christian principles—including the rights and protections of women and the humane treatment of slaves. It stands as the "Roman law" upon which the constitutions of many modern nations have been built.

His costlier project, however, was the reunion of the empire, East and West. For a century, barbarians had been eating away at the edges of Roman territory. But, with the aid of his brilliant general Belisarius, Justinian re-conquered much of the West, including Rome itself, and the whole Mediterranean was once again a Roman sea.

Justinian sought also to unify Christianity by suppressing the heresies in their lingering outposts. He was urged on by his wife, Theodora, who had her own idiosyncratic opinions in matters of religion. Justinian's agents went abroad to suppress any dissent from the faith of the councils, as interpreted by Justinian—and sometimes differently by Theodora.

Justinian thought that his pogroms would force the population of the empire into religious unity. They only served to alienate people in provinces remote from the imperial capital. His military campaigns had similar results. Though the old territories were re-conquered, lands were left battered and deserted from the ferocity of war. People, moreover, were impoverished from the taxes that funded Justinian's wars.

But they also funded his churches, which were glorious indeed, like San Vitale in Ravenna and, most glorious of all, Hagia Sophia in Constantinople. Hagia Sophia, Greek for "Holy Wisdom," stood for 900 years as the center of Christianity in the eastern empire. It still stands today, though the last liturgy was offered there in 1453.

Justinian nearly bankrupted Constantinople to build it. His architect, Anthemius, was brilliant but eccentric. Anthemius designed his church around a huge, shallow dome. Nothing like it had ever been done before—a big dome usually has to be tall in order to hold itself up. Anthemius solved the problem by setting the dome on half domes, so that the whole structure could rest on four widely spaced piers. Around the circumference of the dome were so many windows that the dome seemed to float over the church.

When Justinian finally entered the finished church, he cried out that he had surpassed even Solomon in building such a glorious temple. A few years later, the impossible dome fell down and had to be rebuilt with more safeguards.

When Justinian died in AD 565, his reunited empire also began to fall apart. Within three years, Lombard tribes rather easily invaded a weakened Italy; soon afterward the eastern lands, one by one, would fall to a fiercer enemy, the Arabs led by Muhammad.

Justinian had entrusted the telling of his story to the court historian, Procopius, whose florid prose exalted the buildings and military campaigns of his boss. But all the while Procopius kept a "secret history" locked away; in it he vented his resentment and rage against Justinian, whom he claimed was a demon, and Theodora, whom he portrayed as a prostitute.

Today the haloes remain on the imperial mosaics in Ravenna, and the domes upon domes still stand in Istanbul. But the image of Theodora and Justinian—in history—is not so pretty.

For More

John Julius Norwich. *Byzantium: The Early Centuries*. London: Penguin, 1990.

School days in antiquity: a wax tablet for taking notes. Photo: © RMN-Grand Palais / Art Resource, NY.

29

A Boy's Notebook

This notebook contained the math exercises—and prayers—of an Egyptian boy named Theodore. Between two beech wood covers are ten tablets of waxed wood. At his lessons Theodore used a pointed stylus to scratch notes into the wax. When he no longer needed those notes, he could apply a new coating of wax. If he chose to keep his notes, he could replace the old boards with fresh ones.

Theodore was fortunate to receive an education. It was not universally valued, and there was no public subsidy for schools.

Education was a luxury in late antiquity. The wealthy owned slaves for the purpose of schooling their children. The merchant or middle class might send their children out to a tutor. For the poor, it was usually not an option.

Christians, in the years of Roman rule, were ambivalent about schooling. The curriculum was fairly standard, emphasizing a literary heritage saturated with stories of the gods and heroes of Greece and Rome. Thus, teachers like Tertullian in the second century warned believers away from the teaching profession. A tutor must, after all, spend his entire day in close proximity to "manifest idolatry," as Tertullian put it, pronouncing the names of the gods and instructing children in the correct pronunciation of those names.

It's interesting that even later Fathers of the Church, such as Basil the Great, who lived a generation after Christianity's legalization, could not quite imagine an educational system that was Christian in its content and methods. Yet Basil spoke more favorably about the Greco-Roman tradition as a preparation for Christian studies later on. For this he invoked biblical precedent. Moses, after all, "trained his mind in the learning of the

Egyptians, and Daniel is said to have studied the lore of the Chaldeans."
And Homer, in any event, was all about "praise of virtue."

So a Christian might handle the epic texts—as long as they viewed
such study as preparation for nobler things.

Basil's contemporary, the emperor Julian, disagreed vehemently. Julian,
who had formerly been a Christian, was now a born-again idolater who
wanted to ban Christians from any jobs in education. He enacted a law to
that effect, saying, "It seems absurd to me that men should teach what they
do not believe. . . . Instead, let them retire to their churches to expound
Matthew and Luke." But Julian died soon afterward, and Christian teachers
returned to their classrooms—and went back to teaching their Homer
and Hesiod.

In the Roman world, primary studies occupied children from ages
seven to eleven, secondary from twelve to fifteen. Those who were so
inclined might pursue further studies until age twenty or so. But nothing
was compulsory, and students might drop in for as long as their parents
wished—and drop out when their parents tired of paying. Most of those
who received primary schooling probably didn't proceed to secondary;
few went on to the more advanced coursework.

As the world became more Christian, little changed. Origen taught the
natural sciences, geometry, and astronomy alongside the sacred sciences
of theology and scripture in the third century. Clement of Alexandria, a
generation earlier, quoted widely from Greek literature. If those giants
had no fear of secular learning, why should their intellectual and spiritual
descendants?

By the time of the sixth century—when Theodore took up his notebook in the Fayum—the Church had begun to experiment with a new
idea: schools run by parishes, dioceses, or monasteries. Roman tutors
had been freelancers, like Roman doctors, but this new wave of Christian
teachers was rooted in the community, and their schools were more stable
institutions. They taught their students math, among other subjects, and
they taught them to pray.

Around the same time, Christians in Ethiopia, Armenia, Georgia, and
elsewhere were developing alphabets in order to transmit the Church's

literature, especially the scriptures. In order to be used, an alphabet had to be taught and learned.

This was the beginning of something big.

For More

F. R. Cowell. *Life in Ancient Rome*. Toronto, ON: Perigee, 1980.

H. I. Marrou. *A History of Education in Antiquity*. New York: Mentor Books, 1964.

The Dark Ages

Things flew apart as the center did not hold. The unthinkable happened: Rome fell. The West experienced a decline in communications and commerce. Travel became difficult. And the people of Europe found new ways of governance. Christian bishops emerged as important secular leaders. Monasteries began to preserve what they could of the old culture. And missionaries reached out to people long dismissed as barbarians and enemies. The Church found innovative ways to Christianize warlike peoples and redirect their energies. However, soon in the East, nascent Islam began to chip away the edges of the old empire, until many of the original Christian lands were completely lost.

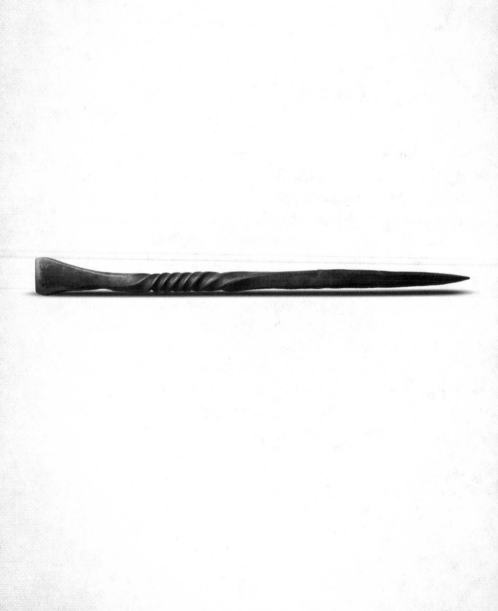

A metal stylus was used to write notes on a wax tablet. Photo by Rosemary Aquilina.

30

A Scribe's Stylus

A stylus was among the chief tools of the scribal trade. Scribes would use a metal stylus, like this one, for writing on a wax tablet. Writing on paper, papyrus, or parchment required a gentler touch, and so the preferred tool was a quill pen, made from a feather plucked from a goose, swan, or turkey.

Paradoxically, scribes used the more permanent stylus to mark up the more ephemeral medium. They used the disposable, degradable quill to set down words they wished to last for the ages. So while we possess many *words* written in the sixth century with quill pens, archaeologists are more likely to find a metal stylus if they're digging at the site of a monastery.

It is a modern stereotype to equate monks with scribes, and for that we can thank Cassiodorus. It was he who first proposed that monastic communities should be dedicated to the task of crafting books and building libraries.

Cassiodorus lived a long and almost impossibly rich life near the pinnacle of earthly power during a very tumultuous period. He was raised in a ruling family; his father was governor of Sicily. While young, Cassiodorus attracted the notice of Theodoric the Great, the barbarian king who was then ruling over the western empire. Educated and eloquent, Cassiodorus provided valuable assistance to the king. He gave his letters and decrees the dignity and refinement expected of a statesman's work. And by his conversation and counsel, he provided the king with a rudimentary education. Cassiodorus sought to elevate the culture of the Gothic rulers by synthesizing it with Rome's ancient heritage. His older colleague at court was the great philosopher Boethius.

Justinian succeeded in his pyrrhic war of recovering the Western lands, and Cassiodorus went to live in Constantinople for a time. When he returned to Italy, he found a land ravaged by war, its people overtaxed and badly ruled. A witness to the destruction of the old culture, he decided that a new, truly Christian culture must rise on the foundations of the old.

He retired to his family estate in southern Italy, far from the ravages of recent events, and there launched a program of preservation. He kept gardens and fishponds—but most importantly, he founded a monastery, which he named after his fishponds. He called it the Vivarium.

He gathered all the books he could find out of the wreckage that was Italy and built a great library there. Though it seems he never took monastic vows himself, he wrote a set of rules for his monks, tasking them with reproduction, by hand, of the important books in the library, both religious books and secular.

He could wax poetic about math, astronomy, grammar, and handwriting. He clearly valued history and rhetoric. But in his vision of Christian culture, all these were secondary, necessary preconditions for the understanding of scripture and doctrine. He told his copyists, "Every time you write one of the Lord's words, Satan is wounded." Because of the Vivarium's example, other monasteries began to take up the idea, and soon copying books was one of the expected duties of a monk.

But the Vivarium itself did not endure. The community seems barely to have outlived its founder, who died at almost a hundred years of age (writing to the end) in AD 585.

Fortunately, at the same time Cassiodorus was doing his work, another man, St. Benedict of Nursia, was founding communities of men and setting down his own rule. His sister, Scholastica, founded communities of nuns. Benedict was a man of practical temperament and wise. With his Rule he showed monks clearly what they should be doing from one hour to the next. It boiled down to prayer and labor. He wasn't particular about what work they should be doing, but they needed to be productively occupied. In time, many of them came to fill their days in scribal work, striving to meet the standards of Cassiodorus as they observed the Rule of Benedict.

For More

Gregory the Great. *The Life of Saint Benedict*. With commentary by Adalbert de Vogüé. Petersham, MA: St. Bede's Publications, 1993.

James J. O'Donnell. *Cassiodorus*. Berkeley: University of California Press, 1979.

St. Patrick's bell shrine. Photo by Fr. Bernard Healy.

31

St. Patrick's Bell

The bell beneath the plating is plain, rough, and fashioned from hammered iron—two sheets riveted together. It's coated with bronze, though, and the bronze is decorated with silver and gold. This particular bell merits the precious metals because it once belonged to Patrick, the fifth-century apostle of Ireland.

Panels on the sides depict stylized serpents, because Patrick is reputed to have driven all snakes from the island he came to serve. The back of the bell records the names of the king who commissioned the decoration (around 1100), the man who did the metalwork, and the family charged with care for the bell. The relic remained with that family until the end of the nineteenth century.

Patrick was born in Britain to a family of churchmen. His father was a deacon; his grandfather was a priest. But according to Patrick's own testimony, the family was not particularly fervent in faith. In Britain at the time, there were worldly advantages to the reception of Holy Orders.

When Patrick was sixteen he was kidnapped by pirates and taken to Ireland, where he was enslaved as a shepherd for six years. In the misery of that time he underwent a deep conversion and resolved to accept his hardships as penance. One night, however, he had a dream in which he received instructions for his escape. He rose and followed them, ultimately boarding a boat loaded with hunting dogs and destined for Gaul (modern France). Eventually he made his way back to his parents' home in Britain. But he would not remain there for long. He discerned a call to be a priest and a missionary—returning to the very people who had held him captive.

For his training he returned to Gaul, where the Church at Auxerre was thriving under a mission-minded bishop named Germanus. Still, he was eager to get to Ireland. The British bishops, moreover, decided that Ireland was ready to receive its first missionary bishop. But some who knew Patrick recommended against him, dredging up the sins he had committed before his conversion. So a bishop named Palladius was chosen instead—and he, in turn, invited Patrick to follow after him. Before Patrick could leave, however, word arrived of the death of Palladius. So Patrick was, after all, consecrated bishop and sent to Ireland.

His apostolate there was phenomenally successful. He strove to convert the tribal chieftains, hoping that the rest of the people would soon follow. His hunch was right. He recruited his clergy from the ruling families. He established monasteries with a strict rule of life, and they attracted many from the tribal aristocracy. Though the priests of the traditional religion, the Druids, opposed him, Patrick persisted, and he mostly prevailed. Though he didn't Christianize the entire land, he made the triumph of Christianity practically inevitable.

What we know reliably about Patrick comes from his own writings: his autobiographical *Confession* and his *Letter to the Soldiers of Coroticus*. We also possess a hymn he may have authored, the "Breastplate" or *Lorica*, as well as several sayings and rulings attributed to him. And we have a hymn written about him by a contemporary, St. Secundinus.

These are the earliest documents of Irish Christianity. But much more was to follow—more texts and more activity. Within a generation, the island became a thriving monastic center. Ireland, which had only recently been mission territory, would soon send missionaries to renew the churches all over Western Europe. The Irish Church had a profound influence on the development of Christian art and scholarship and especially on the practice of sacramental Confession. The poet-monk St. Columba continued Patrick's work of founding monasteries.

It was Columba who opened Patrick's grave and removed the three items that were buried with him: a Gospel book, a chalice, and his iron bell. Those were the basic tools of a priest and monk. The book and the chalice were for the Mass. The bell was to summon others to prayer.

Many Irish saints shared Patrick's two-hearted love for monastic life and missionary action: Finian, Brendan, Brigid of Kildare, and

Columbanus, who founded monasteries in distant Gaul and Italy. One recent author goes so far as to say that the efforts of these Irish monks "saved civilization." It's not much of an exaggeration.

For More

Oliver Davies, trans. and ed. *Celtic Spirituality*. Mahwah, NJ: Paulist, 1999.

Máire B. de Paor. *Patrick: The Pilgrim Apostle of Ireland*. Dublin: Veritas, 1998.

An amphora for holding wine or oil, on display at Castel Sant'Angelo in Rome. Photo by Marc Hagen.

32

A Vessel *for* Wine *in* the Dark Ages

These large earthenware containers, called amphoras, were the preferred method of transporting large quantities of liquid. Archaeologists have recovered shipwrecks whose entire cargo consisted of sealed amphoras, some brimful with olive oil or fish sauce (similar to Worcestershire). But most held wine.

If Christians didn't skimp on wine, perhaps they had Gregory the Great to thank.

He was pastor to the world at a critical moment, reigning as pope from AD 590 to 604. The old Roman order was crumbling. Once-great cities, like Rome, had suffered a steep decline in population, with a corresponding disappearance of infrastructure. There was hardly any military or law enforcement. Banditry flourished. Travel was risky, and long-distance communication increasingly difficult.

The Church suffered from all these circumstances. Once upon a time, a bishop like Ambrose could count on his priests to have a modicum of social graces and culture, but those days were long gone. Discipline and formation of the clergy were more difficult now that the ages were darkening.

The Church—and indeed the world—needed a leader like Gregory.

He was born into a noble family and received an excellent education. Like his father before him, he rose very quickly to the top civic office in Rome. Gregory was made prefect—essentially mayor—at age thirty-three.

He didn't remain in office long. He converted his family's estate into a monastery, and he retired there to a life of contemplation.

But he didn't remain long in the monastery, either. He was summoned to serve as the ambassador of Pope Pelagius II to the court of the emperor in Constantinople. So off he went. While at court he composed his great commentary on the book of Job. After seven years he was recalled to Rome, and he returned to his old monastery.

Soon, Rome suffered a series of disasters. The Tiber River flooded, leaving many people homeless—and leading to an infestation of rats. Then followed a deadly plague, probably spread by the rats. Sickness claimed thousands of lives, including the pope's. The people clamored for Gregory to be pope, and he tried to refuse the office, but he soon saw it was futile. He took strong command and led the people in penitential processions, to beg heaven for mercy and relief from the pestilence and sickness. According to an ancient tradition, Gregory and his people were marching past Hadrian's tomb, which sits between the river and Vatican hill. Gregory said he saw the archangel Michael atop the monument, sheathing his sword, and immediately he knew that Rome's trial was over.

Gregory's papacy was a storm of activity. He carried on a voluminous correspondence. He set an agenda for reform—reform of the liturgy, the papacy, and the episcopacy. The finances of the Church also came under Gregory's eye. When the Church spent money, he made sure that everyone knew how it was being spent.

He wrote a book, his *Pastoral Rule*, to serve as a textbook in spiritual direction, training the clergy to see virtue as a middle course between opposing vices—helping them to avoid laxity on the one hand and fanaticism on the other. "Let the one hear, 'It is right not to eat meat or drink wine or do anything that makes your brother stumble' (Rom 14:21). Let the other hear, 'Use a little wine for the sake of your stomach and your frequent ailments' (1 Tm 5:23). Thus both the former may learn not to desire inordinately the food of the flesh, and the latter not dare to condemn something God has created, but which they do not desire."

Gregory was a master of clarity. For every task of the clergy he stated principles that were easy to understand and to apply in individual cases.

As he sent missionaries away to far-off lands, he taught them to respect local cultures and assimilate all that was good. He prepared bishops for the role they would play in the disintegrating social order. As the Roman ways and institutions vanished—as it became increasingly difficult for amphoras of wine to go from one land to another—the Church's hierarchy would gradually assume new roles as leaders and sometimes governors and judges.

Though Gregory labored tirelessly and productively, he suffered poor health, and he conducted much of his work from his sickbed. Undoubtedly, he allowed a little wine for his stomach's sake.

For More

Gregory the Great. *Forty Gospel Homilies*. Kalamazoo, MI: Cistercian Publications, 1990.

Carole Straw. *Gregory the Great: Perfection in Imperfection*. Los Angeles: University of California Press, 1988.

An early Islamic coin. Photo by Rosemary Aquilina.

33

A Coin *of the* Umayyad Caliphate

This is one of the simple coins of the Umayyad Caliphate, the second of four major dynasties that exercised governance—religious and secular—over the lands conquered by Islam. The Umayyads began their reign in AD 661, just twenty-nine years after the death of Islam's founder, Muhammad. They were supplanted by the Abbasid dynasty in 750.

The coins of the Umayyads are, like most Islamic art and craft, aniconic. They bear no images. Muhammad's sacred book, the Qur'an, forbade the worship of idols, and early interpreters took this a step further, prohibiting the production of any representation of persons or animals. Islamic art has made do since then with geometric designs and calligraphy.

Umayyad coins are engraved with Qur'anic verses in Arabic script: "There is no god but God alone" and "Muhammad is the prophet of God." These particular coins were minted between the years 698 and 705, and with such coins all adult non-Muslim males—mostly Christians and Jews—were to pay the heavy jizya tax prescribed by Muhammad.

In the year 610, Muhammad, an Arab merchant, announced that he had received a vision from God, or Allah, as the Arabs called him. Allah had given him a great message to bring to all the world, a message written in the Qur'an—which means, "the reading." At first, Muhammad had little success, but soon his movement grew, and he also became a military leader. In 630 he captured Mecca, and the new religion began to spread as quickly as Christianity had spread before. But there was a difference: Christianity had spread by persuasion. Islam was spreading by force.

Christ had allowed his enemies to kill him. Muhammad, armed with a sword, wasn't about to take that chance.

Under Muhammad's successors, the Caliphs, the conquests spread with amazing speed. Within ten years of Muhammad's death, Muslims had conquered almost the entire eastern and southern parts of the Roman Empire. Jerusalem, Alexandria, and all of Egypt and Syria had fallen, and Arabs were threatening Constantinople itself. Soon the rest of North Africa was theirs and then Spain. There the expansion finally stopped, halted in its tracks by the resistance of the Franks under Charles Martel.

Why did the empire fall apart so quickly? Partly it was the enthusiasm of the Muslim soldiers and the talent of their leaders. But at least some of it was because many people were sick of Roman rule. The emperors' rigid enforcement of their religious sympathies had left gaping wounds in just those places where Muslims conquered most easily.

The Church Fathers consistently treated Islam not as an "other" religion but as a Christian heresy. It was strikingly similar to other Christian aberrations that had been popular in the East. The Arians had denied the divinity of Christ; they would agree with the Qur'an that Jesus is not to be worshiped as God. The Nestorians denied Mary the title Mother of God. And the Montanists believed that God continued to send new revelations through new prophets.

All these people had suffered persecution under Justinian and his successors. And they had been taxed heavily to support Justinian's wars in the West. Is it any wonder that some welcomed the Islamic Arabs as liberators? And is it any wonder that some chose to submit to Islam?

The conquered didn't turn Islamic all at once. In some places, they were given a stark choice: convert, submit to the tax, or die. But the Umayyads were more tolerant, recognizing the value of Christians and Jews as a steady tax base.

They tolerated followers of biblical religions but only as inferiors. Christians could continue to worship, but they couldn't build new churches or rebuild old ones. They had to pay extra taxes, so there was a strong financial incentive to convert. In some places, Christians were forbidden to ride horses and restricted to donkeys.

Taking a long-term view, the Muslim conquerors were mostly content to let Christianity wither away rather than try to eliminate it all at once. After a while, Christianity—once the dominant religion in northern Africa, southern Europe, and western Asia—became just a tiny minority in the very lands where Christian history began.

For More

Bernard Lewis. *The Middle East: A Brief History of the Last 2,000 Years.* New York: Simon and Schuster, 1995.

Bat Ye'or. *The Decline of Eastern Christianity under Islam: From Jihad to Dhimmitude.* Madison, NJ: Fairleigh Dickinson University Press, 1996.

Many formal features of icons have remained constant for centuries. Photo by the authors.

34

An Icon

This icon was hand-painted at a monastery in Greece during the twentieth century, but it strictly follows forms established in the first millennium. It is the *Panagia Glykophilousa*. *Panagia* means "All-Holy," recognizing Mary's preservation from sin. *Glykophilousa* means "sweetly kissing." Her expression is sorrowful, as if she foresees her son's eventual Passion and Death. The baby Jesus comforts her by his touch and kiss.

Icons of the *Glykophilousa* type survive from the first millennium. It's a marvel that they do.

The Greek word *eikon* means simply "image." The New Testament uses the word to describe Jesus himself: "He is the image of the invisible God, the first-born of all creation" (Col 1:15). As Jesus is the image of God the Father, his representation in art has always been an important element in the Church's devotion. Tertullian, in the second century, spoke of pictorial engravings on vessels used in the liturgy. Eusebius, in the fourth century, spoke of sculpture in churches. Some of the frescos in the catacombs date from the third century. And other sacred images have survived from ancient times—on medals, jewelry, silver plate, and other materials. These items bear images not only of Jesus but also of other biblical figures and of martyrs and saints.

In the East the techniques of devotional art became standardized according to strict canons. Icons range in style, though they share some common characteristics: a two-dimensional quality, symbolic use of color and shape, and slightly distorted proportion in bodily and facial features: elongated fingers, for example, impossibly large eyes, or long necks. They speak a rich symbolic language. Every color, gesture, garment, shadow, and prop is significant. The oversized eyes represent the vision of God. The brilliant gold background indicates the divine aura.

In the eighth century, some Byzantine Christians fell under the influence of ascendant Islam, particularly in their attitude toward religious art. In the late AD 720s, Emperor Leo III (the Isaurian) faced a crisis over his recent military losses. He wondered why Muslims were succeeding consistently in their conquest of Christian territories. He concluded that the Byzantine use of devotional images was idolatrous, causing them to lose favor with God.

Leo sprang into action. He commanded that a prominent image of Jesus should be removed from his palace gate in Constantinople. Bystanders were outraged by what they saw and killed the workers who were following the order. But Leo was not intimidated. He issued an edict forbidding all religious artwork and had his agents seize and destroy much Church property. Thus they became known as *iconoclasts*—literally, picture-smashers. Some believers died as martyrs rather than hand over their icons to thugs.

Leo's son and successor, Constantine V, continued his father's policies and protocols, and was similarly loathed. They dubbed him *Copronymos*, which means his "name is excrement," and so he is remembered in history. Constantine summoned a puppet synod of bishops who were reliably in his camp, and they obediently confirmed his policy.

But the monasteries opposed him, and the monks had the respect of ordinary Christians. Two monks in particular, John of Damascus and Theodore the Studite, argued effectively against the emperors' campaign. Said John of Damascus, "Since God has appeared in the flesh and lived among men, I can represent what is visible in God. I do not worship matter, but I worship the creator of matter who became matter for my sake . . . and who, through matter, accomplished my salvation. Never will I cease to honor the matter which brought about my salvation!"

Leo III's grandson, Leo IV, was unmoved. He kept his father's and grandfather's iconoclast project moving forward, but with little support. Not even his wife, Irene, agreed with him. He was about to have her put away when he suddenly died of a fever.

Irene, acting as regent for her young son Constantine VI, called for a true ecumenical council, known now as the Second Council of Nicaea (787). There the bishops restored icons to the churches, homes, and street corners—and decisively declared iconoclasm to be a heresy. A couple of later emperors tried to revive the old iconoclastic campaign but failed.

For More

John Lowden. *Early Christian and Byzantine Art*. London: Phaidon, 1997.

Jeffrey Spier et al. *Picturing the Bible: The Earliest Christian Art*. New Haven, CT: Yale University Press, 2009.

A pin to celebrate a native son of Britain, St. Boniface. Photo by Rosemary Aquilina.

35

St. Boniface's Ax

Boniface took an ax to a mighty oak in the mid-eighth century—and the blows resounded 1,200 years later in his hometown of Crediton, England.

If the ax blows weren't actually heard, they were at least memorialized in this brass pin.

For Boniface remains the favorite son of Crediton. He is a key figure in the conversion of Europe—and in the story of the continent's defense against a seemingly unstoppable Islam. The historian Norman Cantor numbers Boniface among the "creators" of Europe as we know it.

He was born Winfrith, and he took up monastic life at a young age. His monastery, however, was close to a port; perhaps there he heard travelers tell how the Germanic tribes were still mostly pagan. These tribes lived in the ancestral lands of Boniface's countrymen. He felt impelled to go to them.

His first foray was to Frisia (in modern Holland), but there he accomplished little before returning home. A year later he made another voyage, this time to Rome, to receive a commission from the pope to evangelize the Germans. Along the way he also met Charles Martel, the Frankish king, who would eventually turn back the armies of the Muslim Caliphate. Charles saw the value in Boniface's mission. If Europe were unified in religion, it would present a surer defense against Islam.

So Boniface and his missionaries went forward with the blessing of the pope and the promise of protection from Charles.

In Germany they faced a motley mix of pagans, Arian heretics, and backslidden and badly catechized Christians. Most of the local pagan beliefs were informal and non-exclusive in their demands. Thus, some people thought of Christianity as another round of rituals they could add to their accumulated pagan practices. A substantial number of homilies from the period urge congregations to stop worshiping at pagan shrines and offering sacrifice to idols.

Boniface clear-cut his way through this confusion. In order to prove the powerlessness of the pagan gods, he took an ax to a tall oak that was sacred to the Thor, the god of thunder. He had made only a superficial cut when the tree fell forward and crashed to the ground.

The tree fell, though the sky didn't. And the thunder god remained silent. Boniface had made his point—and made an impression on both the pagan and somewhat Christian onlookers.

He and his missionaries baptized thousands, founded monasteries in the land, and began to establish bonds of common belief between the Germanic people and the rest of the continent. He labored to educate and discipline the clergy, and he enjoyed some degree of success.

It was a beginning but not a work he would live to complete. After three decades in the German lands, he decided to return to Frisia, the place of his first (failed) efforts as a missionary. He enjoyed some success this time and baptized a large number. But a gang of robbers ambushed him and his companions as they made their way to confirm the recent converts. Boniface and his men voluntarily disarmed themselves, and then the bandits killed them.

Immediately he was honored as a saint by the Germans and by the folks back home in Crediton, with whom he had stayed in regular contact through his many years abroad. His correspondence remains a key source for understanding of the period—and the ages to follow.

For More

Ephraim Emerton, trans. *The Letters of Saint Boniface.* New York: Columbia University Press, 2000.

Richard Fletcher. *The Barbarian Conversion: From Paganism to Christianity.* New York: Henry Holt, 1998.

The Middle Ages

Charlemagne, the first Holy Roman Emperor, imposed unity on European lands and instilled a new vigor—a new sense of common culture. Monasteries promoted renewal in spiritual life and liturgy. Religious arts once again flourished, now lavishly funded by monarchs. Gothic cathedrals pointed heavenward. A new literature emerged, in Latin and in languages of the common people. Soldiers and ordinary people bore the cross to defend the freedom of Christians abroad. The Church, meanwhile, in many lands struggled to maintain its independence from the influence of monarchs and purify its bishops from the corrupting power of money.

A large stone tile marks the spot in Rome where Charlemagne was crowned. Photo by the authors.

36

The Porphyry Stone

This gigantic purple tile rests in the floor near the entrance of St. Peter's Basilica in Rome. It arguably marks the spot where the Dark Ages ended.

Historians differ, of course, about the opening and closing of any era. But it's convenient to say that darkness began to descend in the West with the fall of the western empire in AD 476. And it's just as convenient to say that darkness began to lift with the crowning of Charlemagne as Holy Roman Emperor, which took place in old St. Peter's on Christmas day in 800. Centuries later, when the new St. Peter's was built atop the foundations of the old, the builders insisted on preserving the memory of the exact location of the event.

Charles had ruled as sole king of the Franks since 771. Immediately he showed that he had more than the common ambition of a barbarian king. What Charles wanted was nothing less than the restoration of Roman civilization in the West.

Under the supervision of Alcuin, a scholar from England, Charles gathered all the best thinkers and set them to work civilizing his kingdom. They collected all the old manuscripts they could find and made copies; today many of the ancient Latin works we have exist only because Charles's learned monks copied them. Alcuin set high standards for the copies. In place of the almost illegible scripts that were popular in many monasteries, he introduced a style of writing known as "Carolingian minuscule," named after King Charles. It would become the basis for our modern printed letters.

He encouraged the reform of the clergy, insisting that they be literate and that bishops especially should live exemplary moral lives. Charles also demanded that his nobles learn to read and write. He had schools set up all over the kingdom, and for the first time since the end of the empire in the West, large numbers of non-religious were becoming literate. In fact, Charles hoped to make education available to anyone. Charles himself tried very hard; he learned to read fairly well, but his writing was always strained. He liked to have books read to him at dinner. His favorite was St. Augustine's *City of God*, which must have greatly influenced his ideas of government.

Meanwhile, his kingdom was expanding. Every time barbarian neighbors attacked his frontiers, Charles rushed to the defense, and he always ended up conquering the barbarians. He seemed to be invincible. He began to be known as Charles the Great—in the Frankish dialect, Charlemagne.

When he conquered the stubborn Saxons in 782, he slaughtered 4,500 prisoners before inviting the remaining barbarians to accept Baptism. It seems cruel, but we must remember that the Saxons themselves had excelled in cruelty, raiding Frankish towns, burning churches, and killing indiscriminately. Nevertheless, the Church disapproved of forced conversion; the pope objected, and Charlemagne's friend and advisor Alcuin issued a stinging rebuke: "A man can be drawn to the faith, but he can't be forced. You can be forced to be baptized, but it does the faith no good at all."

In 799, Pope Leo III was suddenly attacked in Rome. Armed men dragged him into a church and beat him so badly they thought they had killed him. He survived and sought refuge with Charlemagne. The king sent him back to Rome with a heavy guard, and the conspirators were captured and imprisoned.

Charlemagne himself visited Rome the next year, and the pope received him with great honor. What Charlemagne probably didn't know was that the pope had made a momentous decision. All these years the West had waited for an emperor. Here was one king who had done more to revive civilization than any other since the barbarian invasions. Pope Leo saw his opportunity.

On Christmas Day, Charlemagne attended Mass at St. Peter's. As he knelt before the altar to pray, he suddenly felt something heavy on his head. The pope had placed an imperial crown there, and suddenly all the nobles in attendance were shouting, "To Charles Augustus, crowned by God, great and pacific Emperor of the Romans, long life and victory!"

Charles died in 814 after a long and glorious reign. Soon after, however, his empire fell apart. He had failed in his dearest wish—to bring back Roman civilization. The world simply wasn't ready. But Charles had preserved and revived enough of the ancient learning that we can truly say he ended the Dark Ages.

For More

Roger Collins. *Charlemagne*. Toronto, ON: University of Toronto Press, 1998.

Johannes Fried. *Charlemagne*. Cambridge, MA: Harvard University Press, 2016.

...на главѣ̀ є҆гѡ̀, глаго́ла:

Вѣнча́етсѧ ра́бъ Бж҃їй (и҆ма́къ), во и҆́мѧ Ѻ҆тца̀ ✠ и҆ Сы́на ✠ и҆ ст҃а́гѡ Дх҃а ✠. А҆ми́нь.

Та́же вѣнча́етъ невѣ́стꙋ, глаго́ла:

Вѣнча́етсѧ раба̀ Бо́жїѧ (и҆ма́къ), во и҆́мѧ Ѻ҆тца̀ ✠ и҆ Сы́на ✠ и҆ ст҃а́гѡ Дх҃а ✠. А҆ми́нь.

І҆ере́й: Гдꙋ помоли́мсѧ. Ли́къ: Гдⷭ҇и поми́лꙋй.

МОЛИ́ТВА

Влады́ко Гдⷭ҇и Бж҃е на́шъ, всѣ́хъ щадѧ́й и҆ ѡ҆ всѣ́хъ промышлѧ́ай, та́йнаѧ вѣ́дый человѣ́ческаѧ, и҆ всѣ́хъ разꙋмѣ́нїе и҆мѣ́ай, ѡ҆чи́сти грѣхѝ на́ша, и҆ беззакѡ́нїѧ простѝ свои́хъ рабѡ́въ, призыва́ѧ и҆́хъ на покаѧ́нїе, пода́ѧ и҆мъ проще́нїе согрѣше́нїй, грѣхѡ́въ ѡ҆чище́нїе, ѡ҆ставле́нїе беззакѡ́нїй во́льныхъ же и҆ нево́льныхъ; свѣ́дый не́мощное чл҃овѣ́ческагѡ є҆стества̀, зижди́телю и҆ созда́телю. Раа́вꙋ блꙋдни́цꙋ про-

A page in Cyrillic script. Photo by Fr. Justin Charron.

37

Cyrillic Script

These are pages from the *Trebnyk*, the Byzantine equivalent of the Latin Church's *Book of Blessings*. But for our purposes, we could just as easily have included pages from a Ukrainian phone book or a Russian newspaper. What they share in common is the Cyrillic alphabet, which is used today by more than a quarter of a billion people.

The Cyrillic alphabet is named for the missionary who developed it in the ninth century—and he developed it for the express purpose of creating a Christian culture.

Cyril and Methodius were brothers from Thessalonica. Their father, a government official, died when they were young; and their guardian was a high-ranking administrator of the Byzantine Empire. He made sure they received an excellent education. Cyril especially was a prodigy of languages, with fluency in Arabic and Hebrew. The brothers also studied theology and were ordained as clerics.

As Cyril reached adulthood, the emperor began sending him on diplomatic missions that were also evangelistic. Cyril's early mission was to the Khazars. It was in AD 862, however, that he and Methodius received the assignment for which they're known in history. The duke of Moravia had asked the Byzantine emperor to send missionaries to Christianize his lands. It seems that the people had already accepted Christianity, but their practice was rough around the edges. As in other places that were superficially Christianized, the ordinary folk still clung to old superstitions and the Church had minimal order.

The duke, moreover, was anxious to improve relations with Constantinople and hoped that common faith would make for a stronger alliance.

Off the brothers went. As they evangelized those lands, they needed to set down the liturgy and the scriptures in the local languages, but there was no native literary tradition. So Cyril and Methodius invented a new alphabet to represent the sounds of the language.

Based on the Greek alphabet, Cyril's new script also included characters from an older alphabet (called Glagolitic), to convey sounds quite alien to the Greek tongue. His students developed the language further after their master's death. The Cyrillic alphabet, modified to suit modern eyes, is still used to write Russian, Ukrainian, Bulgarian, Serbian, and many other Slavic languages.

It was ingenious—but for that very reason it raised suspicions. After the brothers finished their work in Moravia, they made their way to Rome, where some churchmen blanched at the innovation. The only proper languages for liturgy, they said, were Hebrew, Greek, and Latin. The pope disagreed. He had the brothers welcomed in triumph, and he arranged for the Slavonic liturgy to be celebrated in Roman churches.

Neither Latin nor Greek, Slavonic established the condition for another, distinctive medium of Christian tradition. Slavic Christianity, though indebted to the cultures of Rome and Constantinople, became a *tertium quid* in European Christianity. Cyril and Methodius had launched something more than a language. Over a few short centuries, what had begun as catechesis would become a civilization—a Christian civilization.

In 1980 Pope John Paul II acknowledged this in a fitting way by naming Cyril and Methodius among the patron saints of Europe. He did this, he said, in "the firm hope of a gradual overcoming in Europe . . . of everything that divides the Churches, nations, and peoples." A mission that began long ago, with jots in a new alphabet, continues today through the continued work and witness of the men who invented the script of the Slavs.

For More

Leo XIII. Encyclical Letter. *Grande Munus*. 1880.
John Paul II. Encyclical Letter. *The Apostles of the Slavs (Slavorum Apostoli)*. 1985.

A silver censer for use in the Divine Liturgy. Photo: Metropolitan Museum of Art 1985.123.

38

A Censer Used *in the* Divine Liturgy

This censer (or thurible) was found with other liturgical vessels among the Attarouthi Treasure in Syria. It was fashioned by a master silversmith and engraved with religious symbols and phrases. Its donor spared no expense because it was destined for use in the Divine Liturgy.

Such accoutrements are as grand as the Byzantine ritual itself, whose prayers have accumulated over centuries and have been artfully arranged by geniuses such as St. Basil the Great and St. John Chrysostom. In the large churches—and especially in the capital cities—the Byzantine liturgy was usually accompanied by abundant incense, sounding bells or gongs, and haunting chant.

It was to the imperial capital, Constantinople, that Vladimir, prince of Kiev, sent his emissaries to inquire about the Christian religion. There are differing accounts of his conversion to Christianity, but all agree that he conducted due diligence before submitting himself—and his subjects—to Baptism.

His neighboring realms were in perpetual conflict—some were Christian and others Muslim—and he would, eventually, have to ally himself with one side or the other. He was also, perhaps, experiencing personal discontent with the local brand of paganism.

According to Kievan chroniclers, Vladimir wanted to judge among the religions of the Jews, Western Christians, Eastern Christians, and Muslims. Judaism he soon dismissed because its adherents had, in a thousand years, been unable to rebuild the Temple. Such weakness did not appeal to a warrior prince.

Then he sent out emissaries to observe the life and worship of Christians and Muslims. They reported back to him that Islam, as they had found it, was joyless and dour: Muslims ate no pork and drank no alcohol.

The Western churches of the Germans they judged to be dark and relatively devoid of beauty.

But everything was different when they attended a liturgy at the grand church of Hagia Sophia in Constantinople. They were enchanted. "We no longer knew whether we were in heaven or on earth," they said.

The Eastern Christian liturgy the emissaries witnessed was a festival of light, incense, icons, and chant. It was an earthly image of the biblical seer's vision of heaven: "And another angel came and stood at the altar with a golden censer; and he was given much incense to mingle with the prayers of all the saints upon the golden altar before the throne; and the smoke of the incense rose with the prayers of the saints from the hand of the angel before God" (Rv 8:3–4).

Eastern Christians had always adorned their liturgy with as much splendor as possible. Of course, in times of persecution, splendor could be difficult and dangerous to provide. But even the earliest Christians associated the oracle of the prophet Malachi with the Church's liturgy: "For from the rising of the sun to its setting my name is great among the nations, and in every place incense is offered to my name, and a pure offering; for my name is great among the nations, says the Lord of hosts" (Mal 1:11).

The earliest ritual books include blessings with incense, and records from the fourth century indicate that the great basilicas were resplendent with light during the celebration of the Mass. When Vladimir's emissaries saw such a liturgy, they were convinced—and they were converted.

In 988, Vladimir was baptized; immediately afterward he married the sister of the Byzantine emperor. Returning home to Kiev, he ordered all pagan shrines to be demolished and replaced by churches.

Vladimir identified himself and his people with Eastern Christianity and its distinctive culture. It was a decisive moment not only for the spirituality but also for the future politics, literature, and visual art of the now-Christian Slavic lands.

For More

Joseph Andrijisyn. *Millennium of Christianity in Ukraine: A Symposium*. Ottawa, ON: St. Paul University, 1987.

Paul Robert Magocsi. *A History of Ukraine*. Seattle: University of Washington Press, 1996.

Chivalry was the means by which warriors were converted to Christianity. Photo by Rex Harris, Oxford, UK.

39

Arms *and* Armor

Weapons, shields, and protective plate line the walls of the armory in the Alcázar of Segovia, a fortified castle in Spain. Such is the stuff of a warrior's life.

A fort has stood at the site of the Alcázar since Roman times. The current structure was built in 1120.

From the fall of Rome onward, the missionary activity of the Church was directed to the tribes and peoples who lived beyond the frontiers of the old empire. The world was divided between Romans and "barbarians," and these were the barbarians.

They were warrior cultures, the Germanic, Frankish, and Slavic hordes. Their livelihood and their sport involved violence and plunder. Men proved themselves as men in battle with other men.

What was the Church to do with such men as they accepted the faith?

Centuries before, at the beginning of the Dark Ages, Pope Gregory the Great had laid down rules for conversion of the barbarians. He wanted his missionaries to keep what was good from other cultures and give it a new Christian meaning. Any traditional pagan celebrations, he suggested, could be converted into Christian celebrations. Pagan temples could be made into churches. "It is doubtless impossible to cut out everything at once from their stubborn minds," Gregory said. "Just as the man who is attempting to climb to the highest place, rises by steps and degrees and not by leaps."

But, again, what to do about the habitual waging of war? What do to about jousting and tournaments that almost always ended in gore? Temples and feast days are relatively easy to change compared to the warrior's way of life.

The Church found ways to sanctify even knighthood but "rising by steps and degrees and not by leaps."

The Church established a baseline for knightly behavior. It was called the Peace of God. This principle forbade any violent act against clergymen, monks, and consecrated virgins and widows. It placed churches, monasteries, and graveyards out of bounds for any violent act.

The Church also enforced the Truce of God, which limited the times when a tournament might be held: never on Sunday, for example, or feast days. Knights who transgressed these boundaries could face excommunication. Popes and councils enacted bans on dueling, with the same consequences for transgressors.

Over time the Church stretched the Peace of God to cover other groups: pilgrims, sacristans, and the poor. Over time the Church extended its Truce to cover some weekdays as well: Thursday (to honor the Ascension), Friday (the Passion), and so on. Eventually, all of Advent and Lent were figured in. Rising by steps and not by leaps.

Over the course of centuries, these small changes produced a change in culture. They elevated the virtues that were already present in warrior culture—fortitude and forbearance—and supplemented them with the most sublime religious ideals. The goals of knighthood were elevated from plunder and conquest. The knight was commissioned to protect the defenseless and to serve—serve God, serve his earthly lord, and serve his country.

Now the warriors, who were members of the nobility, were expected to behave in a noble way. This culture found its summary expression, beginning in the twelfth century, in codes of chivalry. Knighthood began to mimic the forms of religious life. Men took vows of chivalry. They bore their arms and armor to church to receive a prescribed blessing.

Military orders arose whose members were celibate and dedicated to charitable works as well as defensive war. This does not mean that most warriors strove daily to practice the rules of chivalry. If that were the case, the Church's hierarchy would not have felt the necessity to renew the prohibition of dueling, repeatedly, at council after council.

But, by steps, certain actions that were once considered honorable came to be seen as shameful and indefensible: looting, marauding, plundering, raping, and killing indiscriminately. In the history of warfare, these are great advances.

For More

Richard Barber. *The Knight and Chivalry*. Woodbridge, UK: Boydell, 2000.

Jean Leclerq et al. *A History of Christian Spirituality, Volume II: The Spirituality of the Middle Ages*. New York: Seabury, 1982.

The crozier of Archbishop Hubert Walter, who was not noted for his holiness. Photo used with permission of Canterbury Cathedral Archives and Library.

40

A Bishop's Crozier

A crozier is the hooked staff used by a bishop as a ceremonial walking stick. Shaped like a shepherd's crook, it is a symbol of Church office. In biblical religion, the earthly leaders of God's people have always been designated "shepherds." Such were the judges and kings of Israel (2 Sm 5:2, 7:7). Jesus appears as the perfect fulfillment of this ancient type. He is the Good Shepherd (Jn 10:11). He knows his sheep, and they know him. He is the Shepherd who is also a Lamb (Rv 7:17), identifying himself with the most vulnerable in his flock. Jesus was to be the model for bishops, who would guide, bless, and teach the Church in his name.

The guidance of the Church became a challenging occupation in the Dark Ages. The bishops were, by and large, educated men experienced in administration of large properties. The local bishop, after all, might oversee parish churches, monasteries, cemeteries, hospitals, poorhouses, and schools—and all of these required maintenance and governance. So the bishops were often chosen from the aristocracy, the class that could afford advanced education.

The crozier pictured here belonged to Hubert Walter, archbishop of Canterbury, the primary see in England, from 1193 to 1205. Historical sources all take pains to emphasize that Walter was *not* a saint and *not* a scholar, but he was one of the most able administrators in the history of English government.

In England and elsewhere the office of bishop had gradually become another position of power. The same was true for the position of abbot in the larger monasteries. The king customarily awarded these offices at his pleasure. Some families of the nobility came to count the episcopacy among their possessions, a legacy inherited by the firstborn son. Inevitably it became, in some cases, little more than a title. Nobles delegated the duties of office to hirelings. Many bishops were absentee rulers of churches they seldom or never visited. The office, moreover, could be sold to families eager for power or status.

Investiture was the ceremony by which bishops and abbots received their office and authority. They were given their rings and croziers—but by whom? Usually, it was the king who ceremonially invested these men. The king's action was then confirmed by the bishop's act of consecration.

In the eleventh century, the popes began to condemn lay investiture as a violation of the Church's rights. The great reforming pope St. Gregory VII decreed that all clergy who had bought their offices should cease immediately to act as ministers of the Church. At the Councils of Bari and Rome in 1098–1099, the pope excommunicated anyone who participated in a lay investiture. St. Anselm of Canterbury, a brilliant and holy predecessor of Archbishop Hubert, tried to enforce the Church's law and was exiled twice for his trouble.

People accustomed to ruling do not usually give up power easily. Rulers routinely ignored the canons of synods and decrees of the popes. The Holy Roman Emperor, Henry IV, did. But Pope Gregory decided to move forward with enforcement against Henry, who was horrified to see his allies and partisans begin to distance themselves from him. Fearing for his crown, he traveled across the Alps and approached the pope as a penitent, dressed in rags and walking barefoot in the snow. After three days the pope received him, and Henry was able to return home with his crown secure. But the encounter had little effect on his subsequent behavior—or the behavior of other European kings. Henry would be excommunicated again in due time.

At the heart of the controversy were serious questions about the Church's influence in the secular sphere and the laity's role in the Church. Disputes would continue to erupt down the centuries, and even today certain secular governments demand a role in the choice of their country's bishops.

Simony—the buying and selling of sacred goods and offices—had been condemned by the Church since apostolic times (Acts 8). In the eleventh and twelfth centuries, the investiture controversy served at least as a reminder of that fact. The shepherd's crozier belongs to the Church, not to the highest bidder and not to the secular state.

For More

Uta-Renate Blumenthal. *The Investiture Controversy: Church and Monarchy from the Ninth to the Twelfth Century.* Philadelphia: University of Pennsylvania Press, 1988.

Brian Tierney. *The Crisis of Church and State: 1050–1300.* Toronto, ON: University of Toronto Press, 1988.

Bell works in the tower of an English church. Photo by Simon Garbutt.

41

Bell Works

The parish church of St. Medardus and St. Gildardus, in Little Bytham, Lincolnshire, England, was built up gradually over the twelfth and thirteenth centuries. These are its bell works, seen from the top of the tower. The church and its bells, here as elsewhere in England, played no small part in the drama of their time.

England, like much of Europe, was caught up in the controversy over lay investiture. Tensions ran high between the throne and altar. In 1170 Thomas Becket, the archbishop of Canterbury, was killed in his cathedral at the prompting of King Henry II. Within two years, the Church canonized Thomas, and Henry took on public penance, suffering to be scourged by prelates at the new tomb of the saint.

Whatever Henry's faults, they were small compared to those of his grandson John, who ruled as king from 1199 until 1216. King John governed whimsically, taxed impulsively, punished those who disagreed with him, and meddled senselessly in Church affairs. On his watch, England lost its overseas territories.

John displayed contempt for the Church's authority. He was known to cut short a bishop's homily when he thought it had gone on long enough. When the see of Canterbury came open, he took it upon himself to appoint a successor and then inform the pope. But the pope consecrated a different man for the task: Stephen Langton, a scholar who had been teaching in Paris.

John refused to recognize Langton and forbade him to enter the country. So Pope Innocent III placed the English Church under the most severe discipline: interdict. That meant that, until King John recognized Langton's legitimacy, there would be no Mass in England, no weddings blessed in the churches, no burials in consecrated ground, and no church bells rung. Priests were permitted to baptize babies and hear confessions but little more than that. This strange imposition of silence lasted from 1208 until 1214.

Discontent grew among the barons, who had long since tired of John's volatility in rule and taxation. The barons revolted, taking one town after another. Word came that the king of France was marshaling troops and a fleet for the invasion of England. The barons presented John with terms of peace, a treaty, and he accepted.

The treaty became known as the "Great Charter"; in Latin, *Magna Carta*. It was revolutionary in what it proposed: government limited by the rule of law. This was a radical departure from the status quo. The Roman code of Justinian, which was widely respected, held that "the emperor is not bound by laws." That principle had legitimized the whimsy of men like King John. Now it was superseded.

The Magna Carta begins and ends with guarantees of the freedom of the Church. This was reasonable since John's conflict with the pope was a precipitating cause of the barons' revolt. The first article mandates "that the English Church shall be free, and have its rights undiminished and its liberties unimpaired." The Church "shall be free" from interference by secular powers; free to follow the pope, even if he should come into disagreement with the king. The Magna Carta's final article reprises the theme: "We wish and firmly command that the English Church be free." Thus the Church's freedom is the Magna Carta's "Alpha and Omega," as the American legal scholar Dwight Duncan has put it.

The papally appointed archbishop, Stephen Langton, was an active participant in the process of drafting and implementing the charter.

The principles set down in the Magna Carta would profoundly influence subsequent legal thought in England—and then in its colonies—and then in the founding of the United States.

For good reason the church bells rang throughout the land when King John signed the charter.

For More

Thomas Andrew. *The Church and the Charter: Christianity and the Forgotten Roots of the Magna Carta.* London: Theos, 2015.

Dwight G. Duncan. "Magna Carta's Freedom for the English Church." *Faulkner Law Review* no. 6 (2014): 87–102.

One of the claimants for the title of Holy Grail. This one is at the Cathedral Church in Valencia. Photo: Album / Art Resource, NY.

42

The Holy Grail

This is the Holy Grail. At least the top part is reputed to be. According to legend, the stone cup has been in Spain since the third century—sent by the deacon St. Lawrence to his Spanish hometown for safekeeping. During centuries of Muslim rule, the relic was kept in a monastery in the Pyrenees. It was concealed again during the Spanish Civil War in the 1930s.

In antiquity and the Middle Ages, Christians customarily dressed their sacred relics with precious metals and jewels. The more holy the artifact, the greater the ornaments added to it. Much of what we see here is ornament. The cup itself is simple but well made, cut from a solid block of brown agate. The gold handles, the jewels, and the alabaster base were added in the Middle Ages.

The earliest mention of the stone cup is in an eleventh-century inventory of a monastery in Huesca. In the fourteenth century it was handed over to the king of Aragon, and from there it made its way to Valencia.

Relics were an object of intense devotion and holy desire, and the cup from Jesus' Last Supper, the cup with which he instituted the Eucharist, was considered the greatest relic of all. The kingdom or the cathedral that possessed it would enjoy tremendous prestige.

Eventually, authors identified the cup of the Last Supper with the Grail, a mythic vessel from Celtic lore. In the original folk tales, the *graal* dispensed whatever foods people wanted and in great abundance.

The most famous of the medieval Grail authors was Chrétien de Troyes; it is in his work that the Grail first appears with eucharistic associations. It looks like a well-made chalice. It is carried in procession like a monstrance. It is preceded by a relic of Jesus' Passion, a lance—that still drips fresh blood.

Unfortunately, Chrétien died with his book unfinished. That circumstance inspired a cottage industry of Grail stories. Authors vied with one another to fashion an ending for Chrétien's masterpiece.

Grail literature, mostly set in the court of the legendary King Arthur, came to dominate the literary scene—and it became more pervasively eucharistic with each passing generation. In the greatest of the Arthurian romances, *The Quest of the Holy Grail*, attributed to Walter Map, the Grail comes to represent the entirety of the mystery of the Eucharist. The quest for its possession becomes a spiritual allegory, in which Christian knights relive the human drama, from paradise to mortal sin, from hard-won repentance to final glory.

Grail stories were the first European fictions and were written specifically for the laity. They were grand entertainments—with steamy romance for the women and action-adventure for the men—but they were furtively catechetical, too. Readers, drawn into the tales of Lancelot, Guinevere, and Galahad, found themselves drawn also to the quest. And the quest led inexorably through penance to Holy Communion.

Grail legends and the much-decorated Valencia cup are different manifestations of the same deep eucharistic piety that defined medieval Catholicism. Such piety, said the British historian Miri Rubin, created a culture hospitable to the "body of Christ" wherever it was found: at the altar and in the tabernacle, yes, but also in the poor and the sick.

For More

Mike Aquilina and Christopher Bailey. *The Grail Code: Quest for the Real Presence.* Chicago: Loyola, 2006.

Richard Barber. *The Holy Grail: Imagination and Belief.* Cambridge, MA: Harvard University Press, 2004.

Rose window at Notre Dame Cathedral in Paris. Photo by Alyssa Lewis.

43

The Rose Window *at* Notre Dame

This is the south rose window at the Cathedral of Notre Dame in Paris, France. Built in 1260, it was the second of the church's three rose windows to be completed. Its panes are divided into groups of four, twelve, and twenty-four. The designers chose the geometric shapes, the colors, and the numbers for their symbolic richness and aesthetic power. It is more than forty-two feet in diameter.

With bays included, the windows are sixty-two feet high. The subjects depicted are from scripture and the lives of the saints. Saints and angels radiate out from the center, which is the image of Jesus Christ in glory. Below the rose, sixteen prophets stand tall, one in each bay.

The giant kaleidoscopic pattern has (mostly) survived wars, revolutions, fires, storms, and other disasters. It has suffered long periods of disrepair punctuated by brief bursts of restoration (which was occasionally worse than the damage it sought to repair).

The stained glass of Notre Dame—and of all the original Gothic churches—is, today, a monument of culture. Colored glass had been used to decorate churches since the fourth century, but stained glass as we know it arrived on the scene only with the twelfth and thirteenth centuries. It required the combination of profound artistic vision and rather advanced chemistry—and both chemistry and art were flourishing in the monasteries of the later Middle Ages.

Stained glass is time-consuming, labor-intensive, and phenomenally expensive to make. But for the kings and nobles who commissioned it, not to mention the workers who produced it, it was worth the effort and the price.

In the single century between 1170 and 1270, the French built eighty cathedrals and almost five hundred churches big enough to be cathedrals. Each was a collaborative effort involving heavy labor. There were no engines for the lugging of heavy stones and no power tools for the cutting into blocks and hoisting into place. These Gothic marvels arose out of thought, vision, and sweat—and money willingly spent for the glory of God and the honor of the Virgin Mary.

They differed significantly from churches of the past. The old basilicas had been built squat and square, lit more by lamps than by windows. But the Gothic cathedrals featured spires and flying buttresses that angled upward—drawing the eye heavenward and seeming to take the soul as well. The large windows were resplendent with the glory of the sun—magnified, filtered, projected—but their figures could only be seen from inside the church. Thus the stone and glass themselves stood as an allegory for the life of grace.

Suger, the twelfth-century French abbot, is considered one of the early patrons of Gothic architecture. His words, in fact, are engraved on the gilded main doors of the abbey church he built at Saint-Denis. "The dull mind," he said, "rises to truth through that which is material, and, in seeing this light, is resurrected."

For More

Robert Barron. *Heaven in Stone and Glass: Experiencing the Spirituality of the Great Cathedrals.* New York: Crossroad, 2002.

Otto von Simson. *The Gothic Cathedral: Origins of Gothic Architecture and the Medieval Concept of Order.* Princeton, NJ: Princeton University Press, 1974.

Chemistry class started with the medieval universities. Image copyright © The Metropolitan Museum of Art. Image Source: Art Resource, NY.

44

A Medieval Beaker

In such sturdy glass, the stuff of this medieval beaker, the empirical sciences began—there, and in the minds of pioneering thinkers such as Hildegard of Bingen and Albert the Great, both Germans and canonized saints.

Hildegard, abbess of a monastery of nuns, is best known for her mystical visions and her musical compositions. But she also wrote medical and scientific works based on her own observation and practice. Chief among them are the *Physica*, which catalogs the medicinal properties of herbs, minerals, and the organs of animals, and *Causes and Cures*, a diagnostic manual that details the origins of various ailments as well as their remedies. No less a scholar than Pope Benedict XVI has credited her with a renewal of interest in the natural sciences.

The time was right for such a development, and a place had been prepared. The eleventh century, which witnessed the birth of Hildegard, also saw the creation of the university—the formal institute of higher education, operating somewhat autonomously, largely independent of the monasteries, bishops, and civil government. The first of the great ones was the University of Paris, in France, founded in 1045. It was followed by the University of Bologna, in Italy, in 1088, and the University of Oxford, in England, in 1096, and then many others.

It soon became a necessary part of a major city. If you didn't have a *studium generale*, with faculties in theology, law, and medicine, you weren't a serious city. The universities had a distinctively Catholic ambience. They attracted students and teachers from distant lands. They granted degrees that were recognized throughout the Christian world.

Theology was taught as the "Queen of the Sciences," and works of popular history sometimes give the impression that the medieval universities occupied themselves with obscure matters irrelevant to ordinary life—such as how many angels can dance on the head of a pin. That's untrue and unjust. The medieval universities established the system used by higher education ever since, and their faculties laid the necessary foundations for disciplines in the experimental sciences, the liberal arts, and across the curriculum.

Albert the Great embodied the academic ideal of his time. A Dominican of his order's second generation, he was the most prolific author of the Middle Ages. His collected works fill thirty-eight thick volumes. He wrote commentaries on all the works of Aristotle. He wrote seminal works of theology, botany, chemistry, physiology, astronomy, and other sciences.

During his first teaching assignment, at the Dominican house in Cologne, he built a laboratory and began his collection of plants and insects. In 1250 he isolated the element of arsenic. He is the first scientist known to have discovered an element. He was interested in questions that would later be addressed by the field of biochemistry: How do men and women differ in their constituent chemistry? How does aging affect our elemental makeup?

He was renowned, too, for his teaching. Among his students was St. Thomas Aquinas, the most influential theologian and philosopher of his time.

Albert's knowledge was so singularly large and wide-ranging that it became the stuff of legends. In the field of alchemy, for example—which hovered near the edges of empirical science while dabbling in magic—it became customary to attribute treatises to "Albert the Great." The name increased the value of the book and enabled the actual author to avoid any legal or ecclesiastical troubles. But Albert's own principles seem to invalidate the very possibility of alchemy. In his treatise *On Minerals*, he wrote, "Art alone cannot produce a substantial form." The alchemists, meanwhile, went on with their attempts to turn mercury and lead into gold.

Albert became a bishop but continued his researches. He is the only figure of the High Middle Ages to be known to history as "the Great."

For More

Irven Resnick, ed. *A Companion to Albert the Great: Theology, Philosophy, and the Sciences.* Leyden, Netherlands: Brill, 2013.

Priscilla Throop, trans. *Hildegard von Bingen's "Physica": The Complete English Translation of Her Classic Work on Health and Healing.* Rochester, VT: Healing Arts Press, 1998.

Tunic purported to be St. Francis's. Photo by REUTERS / Daniele La Monaca / Files.

45

St. Francis's Tunic

This is one of several surviving tunics that, according to tradition, were worn by St. Francis of Assisi during his lifetime. In 2007 the Franciscan order submitted two of them to carbon-dating tests, and the results were inconclusive. The results suggested that some parts of one tunic (its belt, for example) could be dated to Francis's lifetime, while other parts could not.

Of course, that very result has a ring of Franciscan authenticity about it. It's possible, in other words, that friars continued using Francis's gently worn clothes after he had died and no longer needed them.

In the earliest version of the Rule he composed for his community, Francis declared that the "brothers who have already promised their obedience may have one tunic with a hood, and, if necessary, another without hood and a cord and pants." Also, "they may then mend them, lovingly patching them with sackcloth and other pieces."

The tunic shown here, on exhibit in Gubbio, Italy, in 2006, fits the description rather nicely. It's probably more patch than tunic.

The saint's name at Baptism was not Francis but John. His father, Pietro, was a merchant who built his fortune in trade with France. Pietro's affection for France shows in the nickname he gave his son. He called him the little Frenchman—Francesco—*Francis*. The family lived in the picturesque village of Assisi, in the geographic center of Italy.

In his young manhood Francis had many friends, and he liked to party. "He was an object of admiration to all," wrote his first biographer Thomas of Celano, "and he endeavored to surpass others in his flamboyant display of vain accomplishments: wit, curiosity, practical jokes and foolish talk, songs, and soft and flowing garments." He spent money freely, indulging "every kind of debauchery."

Like many young men, Francis had a romantic view of military valor. He volunteered for service and went to battle—but was soon captured and kept prisoner for a year. Some biographers see in those days the small beginnings of his religious conversion. Once free, however, he returned to his old life. But he was increasingly dissatisfied. He experienced a strong sense of vocation but no clarity about how to respond to God. He began to spend more time in solitude and wandering, sleeping outdoors and in the ruins of churches.

His father grew alarmed and tried to put a stop to his son's eccentricities. He asked his local bishop to talk sense into the young man. But Francis literally divested himself of all ties to the family and the town. He "took off and threw down all his clothes and returned them to his father," writes Thomas of Celano.

The bishop threw his own mantle over the young man, and Francis then went off into the countryside, experiencing one adventure after another and drawing kindred souls to share his unusual life. This was the beginning of what would be called the Franciscan movement—the band of "little brothers" (Friars Minor) living without earthly attachments. Before long, they would be joined by a community of sisters, the Poor Clares, founded by (and eventually named for) Francis's friend Clare of Assisi.

While begging on the streets of Rome, Francis fell in love with poverty, and ever afterward he called it his "Lady," to whom he was wed. He became known simply as Poverello, the Poor One. Poverty was the defining condition of his life and of the lives of his followers.

Poverty was the deep source of his characteristic freedom. Since he had no possessions, he had nothing to lose. He could be daring. He could drop everything and take a journey to Egypt on a mission to convert the Sultan and put an end to the Crusades. He could abandon himself to the will of God and expose himself to countless dangers—the contagion of leprosy, the violence of bandits, and the real possibility of martyrdom.

God gave him a special mission, commanding Francis to "rebuild my Church." Francis thought the Lord meant only the repair of a local chapel.

But the project was far greater than that. Francis and his followers would revive the sagging spirits of Christendom with their joyful witness. They did it in tunics "lovingly" patched.

For More

Jon M. Sweeney, ed. *The Complete Francis of Assisi: His Life, the Complete Writings, and "The Little Flowers."* Brewster, MA: Paraclete Press, 2015.

Thomas of Celano. *The Francis Trilogy.* Hyde Park, NY: New City Press, 2004.

سَمَكَةُ الَّتِي يُشْبِهُ التِّمْسَاحُ اذا اَلْكَلَامَنْ

Philosophy textbooks, such as this, were central to medieval education. Photo: © British Library Board / Robana / Art Resource, NY.

46

A Philosophy Textbook

This book, copied in the Middle East in the thirteenth century, is an anthology of texts gleaned from the works of Aristotle and the family of Bukhtishu. Most educated people today know the name Aristotle; in the Middle Ages, Bukhtishu was similarly renowned in Eastern lands. The name belonged to a dynasty of Persian Christian physician-philosophers who lived in the seventh through ninth centuries. They practiced Nestorian Christianity. First they wrote in Persian and later, after the land was Islamized, in Arabic.

Their works made their way to Europe, in translation, along with the works of Aristotle. This rich document illustrates the international character of intellectual discourse in the universities of the thirteenth century. Schoolmen in France, Italy, and Germany were rediscovering the works of an ancient Greek philosopher in Latin translations made from Arabic editions.

It was controversial, to say the least, for Christians to take up the study of these texts. They had arrived with such strange and seemingly dangerous associations: Aristotle's paganism; the ancient heresy of Nestorianism (which exaggerated the distinction between the human and divine in Jesus); and the perpetual threat to Europe's security, Islam.

Officially, the Church forbade the study of Aristotle. But most universities ignored the ban, and the man who soon became known as "*The Philosopher*" was taught freely at the University of Naples, in Italy. And to that campus, around the year 1240, arrived a teenager from southern Italy named Thomas Aquinas. At Naples Thomas encountered the philosophy of not only Aristotle but also the Spanish Muslim Ibn Rushd (also known as Averroes) and the eminent rabbi Maimonides.

Thomas also encountered Dominican friars. Their mendicant order had only recently been approved by the pope. Dominicans took vows of poverty, as monks did. Unlike monks, however, they lived not behind walls but in the cities—in the universities and parishes—as the Order of Preachers. The Dominicans were, like the philosophers Thomas was reading, still a novelty in the Church. He was attracted to their way of life, and he entered the order. His family opposed the move—and they enforced their prohibitions more strictly than the Church. They had Thomas kidnapped and imprisoned in their home. They hired a prostitute to try to seduce him (she failed). Finally they gave in.

As a Dominican, Thomas went to Paris to study with the century's most famous commentator on Aristotle, Albert the Great (also a Dominican). Thomas didn't wear his brilliance on his sleeve. He rarely spoke in class. He was so silent that his classmates called him "the Dumb Ox." Albert prophesied that the world would one day resound with the Ox's bellowing.

He was right, of course. Thomas was, by far, the most important theologian of the second millennium. His works were comprehensive. He wrote with clarity and charity. He sought to engage every argument at its strongest. So he often stated the case for heresies more persuasively than any of their adherents ever had. He was able to find the good in every argument and sift out the bad by making fine distinctions. He strove to reconcile opposing points of view whenever possible. He wrote two summary presentations of Christian doctrine, the *Summa contra Gentiles* (against the pagans) and the *Summa Theologica* (addressed to Christians). The latter, which was to remain unfinished, was to be a complete, systematic presentation of Christian doctrine. He put it aside one day after he had a vision in prayer. Compared to his vision, he said, all of his writing seemed to be nothing more than a heap of straw.

But there was still the whiff of novelty about his work, and the old guard remained suspicious. Thomas's work was condemned, in his lifetime, by the archbishop of Paris. The condemnation was renewed several years after his death.

Thomas died at age forty-nine, but by then he had produced an extraordinary amount of work. In time the Church would recognize its value (as the poet Dante did from the start). Indeed, at the end of the nineteenth century, his *Summa*s would receive almost official status as theological statements.

Thomas's genius was to assimilate, synthesize, and make a system of truths he had gleaned from authors as diverse as Aristotle, Averroes, Maimonides, and Dominic.

For More

Etienne Gilson. *The Spirit of Medieval Philosophy*. Notre Dame, IN: Notre Dame University Press, 1991.

Josef Pieper. *Guide to Thomas Aquinas*. San Francisco: Ignatius Press, 1986.

A mortuary cross buried with a plague victim. Photo: SSPL / Science Museum / Art Resource, NY.

47

Mortuary Cross

This artless cross, hastily fashioned from lead, was one of many discovered among heaps of human bones. Pits were dug deep to accommodate many corpses and to keep their contagion far from the surface ground.

The dead were victims of the Black Death, the bubonic plague that raged through Europe in the middle of the fourteenth century. The disease killed between a third and half of the people in the lands it reached. Estimated fatalities range from 50 million to 200 million.

Sometimes thousands died in a single day. As they were lowered into a common grave, their loved ones placed a leaden or wooden cross with their remains. It was possibly the only religious rite available.

The plague, after all, claimed an outsized share of the clergy. Priests were often a town or village's first responders to anoint the sick or hear a last confession. Thus they were usually among the first exposed to a contagious disease. Going from home to home, they would also be exposed to the fleas that usually bore the plague bacteria.

The great Italian storyteller Giovanni Boccaccio was an eyewitness, and he left us a vivid description, in his *Decameron*, of the plague's course in a typical victim.

> In men and women alike there appeared, at the beginning of the malady, certain swellings. . . . From these two parts the aforesaid death-bearing plague-boils proceeded, in brief space, to appear and come indifferently in every part of the body. After a while, the fashion of the contagion began to change into black or livid blotches, which showed themselves in many [first] on the arms and about

the thighs and [afterward spread to] every other part of
the person.

After the plague had passed, the Church was left with a weakened
clergy to do its work. In one year alone, twenty-five archbishops and 207
bishops died. The priests who were victims were beyond numbering.
Two-thirds of the universities that were stricken ended up closing their
doors. The men ordained in the years that followed did not have the same
educational or formational opportunities, and they may have been hurried
through. It is likely the Church suffered from this decline in quality of its
clergy.

Lay people were deeply affected by the experience, and historians note
a change in devotional literature—an emphasis on emotions, a preoccu-
pation with mortality, and a keen awareness of the effects of sin.

This is the golden age of meditation upon the Passion of Jesus—in
the Stations of the Cross, in the sculpting of the *Pietá*, in the portrayal of
Christ on the cross, and in the crosses that were buried with one's children,
parents, siblings, neighbors, and friends.

For More

Warren H. Carroll. *The Glory of Christendom, 1100–1517*. Front Royal, VA: Christendom
    Press, 2004.

Barbara Tuchman. *A Distant Mirror: The Calamitous 14th Century*. New York: Random
    House, 1987.

A document seal from Antipope John XXIII. From the collection of Fr. Richard Kunst, Papal Artifacts. Photo by John Latour.

48

An Antipope's Seal

This is a *bulla*, or "seal," from the early fifteenth century. It has not weathered the years well, and its details are faded. But most people would rather forget the life of its owner. The *bulla* belonged to Baldassarre Cossa, a man who claimed to be pope in the years 1410–1415.

He took the name John XXIII. John had, till then, been the most popular name taken by popes as they began their reign. But Cossa tainted the name so badly that more than five hundred years would pass before another pope would choose to be called John.

For most of his life, Baldassarre Cossa was not a clergyman. Born into shabby gentility, he rose to prominence in the military, then studied law and entered government. He showed himself to be an able administrator, savvy with money. He was also a notorious womanizer. Rising high in the papal curia, he was made a cardinal in 1402, even though he remained a layman.

The Church was at that time thrown into confusion by the existence of two, and then three, claimants to the papal throne. There were "popes" in Avignon, Pisa, and Rome. Cardinal Cossa had associated himself with Alexander V, who was a genuinely good man and possibly a legitimate pontiff (the Church has never declared on the matter). But Alexander died in 1410 after less than one year in office—and, coincidentally, while he was in the care of Cardinal Cossa, whom many people suspected of poisoning his guest.

In any event, Cardinal Cossa immediately summoned a "conclave," poorly attended, at which he was elected pope. So, on successive days, he was ordained a priest and then crowned as pope.

Cossa was an *antipope*—a false claimant to the office of the papacy. He was, sad to say, not the first in the Church's history. There were two in the third century, Novatian and Hippolytus. Hippolytus thought the popes of his time were encouraging laxity by extending absolution to those who confessed mortal sins. He set up a rival faction in the city and had himself elected pope in opposition to the legitimate office holder. He continued his opposition through the reign of three popes.

According to tradition, he reconciled with the last of these popes, Pontian, while both were condemned to hard labor. Novatian's story is almost the same, involving most of the same issues, but without any evidence of a final resolution.

In the following century, the Emperor Constantius II deposed a pope whose doctrine he disliked—and then replaced him with a candidate more congenial to the Arian heresy.

The story of every antipope is a tragedy and a scandal. It was, however, not a scandal that affected most ordinary Catholics—or even most clergy—in real time. Communications were primitive in antiquity and the Middle Ages; and most people, most of the time, may have been only dimly aware of the name of the current occupant of St. Peter's chair.

The antipope's seal, such as we see in this photo, was not binding over time; most have suffered far worse corrosion than this one. They represent a kink, not a link, in the chain of papal succession.

For More

Eamon Duffy. *Saints and Sinners: A History of the Popes*. New Haven, CT: Yale University Press, 2006.

J. N. D. Kelly. *The Oxford Dictionary of Popes*. New York: Oxford University Press, 1986.

The statue of St. Catherine of Siena, near St. Peter's Basilica. Photo by Jim Luptak.

49

St. Catherine Monument

An enormous modern statue of Catherine of Siena stands between Vatican hill and the Tiber River. It rises high from the flower gardens, where it was placed in 1961. Four marble carvings on the front tell stories from the saint's life. The statue stands as a warning, perhaps, in case a pope should forget his place.

Catherine's life was brief—she died at age thirty-three—and her circumstances hardly encouraged ambitions in the realm of geopolitics. She was a woman. She came from a large family. She lived an unusual and socially unacceptable form of life. She couldn't write, and she came to reading late in life.

Catherine was born in an age of extreme anxieties. The Black Death was wiping out the population of towns and cities. The popes had abandoned Rome for the pleasant climate of Avignon in France. From early childhood she had visions of God, and at age seven she dedicated her life to his service. Her parents wanted her to marry, but she resisted, cutting her hair short and fasting to make herself unattractively thin. Yet she was not drawn to the convent, which was the acceptable alternative to marriage in her day. Instead she chose to serve God as a Third Order Dominican. She spent her days doing ordinary work at home and then tending the poor in her city.

Increasingly she became involved in civic life, led there, she said, by the expressed wish of Jesus Christ. She counseled secular leaders about alliances. She dictated letters to the kings of France and Hungary. She

203

strove to negotiate peace between warring parties. She even survived an assassination attempt.

She began corresponding with the pope, Gregory XI, urging him to return to Rome. She addressed him in the most affectionate terms, calling him "Daddy" and "our sweet Christ on earth," but she was uncompromising. She appealed to his conscience. She also seemed to know his secrets. She knew, for example, that he had made a private vow to God that, if he attained the papacy, he would move to Rome. She reminded him of that fact, and he was shaken. She even traveled to Avignon to meet with him as an official ambassador of the government in Florence.

By that time, seven legitimate popes had reigned from Avignon. Gregory would be the last. He returned to Rome, visiting Catherine on his way there in 1377. When Gregory died, his successor, Urban VI, called Catherine to Rome for support as he defended his title against claimants in Avignon. She carried on this diplomacy until shortly before her death in 1380.

Antipopes would continue to make noise in Avignon—and both the pope and the antipope continued to name cardinals. A synod met in Pisa in 1409 to sort out the problem, but instead of sorting it out it added a third claimant to the papacy, who took the name John XXIII—a man of questionable morals and unquestionable greed. For the next few years, the world was in an uproar. Finally the Council of Constance threw out all three popes (only Gregory, who really does seem to have desired the peace and unity of the Church, abdicated voluntarily). In 1417, Martin V was made pope, and the century-long incident known as the Great Schism was over.

In the centuries since then, the popes who procrastinated and obstructed have faded from popular memory. Catherine, however, remains a leader. In 1970 Bl. Paul VI named her a Doctor of the Church.

For More

Eamon Duffy. *Saints and Sinners: A History of the Popes*. New Haven, CT: Yale University Press, 2006.

Mary O'Driscoll, O.P. *Catherine of Siena: Passion for the Truth—Compassion for Humanity*. Hyde Park, NY: New City Press, 2005.

Crusaders carved crosses into the wall at the Church of the Holy Sepulchre in Jerusalem.
Photo by ywoolf / iStockphoto.com.

50
Graffiti *at the* Church *of the* Holy Sepulchre

These are the marks they made, those who achieved the goal of their pilgrimage—those who took up the cross and arrived in Jerusalem. They made these particular marks on a stairway leading to a lower chapel in the Church of the Holy Sepulchre.

Their pilgrimage of the cross was known as a *crusade*; the pilgrims were known as *crusaders*. The cross was the mark they chose to make in their graffiti.

Through most of subsequent history, the crusaders have been remembered with honor. "Crusade" was a metaphor for the passionate advocacy of a good cause. More recently, however, crusaders have been cast as greedy opportunists foreshadowing the later colonial powers.

The Crusades were a popular Christian movement that lasted five hundred years. Thousands made the voyage. So it is certainly possible to find examples of crusaders who went astray and perpetrated crimes. But they were never the norm—and they were always condemned by their fellow Christians and by legitimate Church authorities. To portray the crusaders as adventurers, profiteers, or proto-colonialists is unjust, untrue, and anachronistic.

The Crusades were a defensive action. Muhammad had conquered all of Arabia by AD 632. His successors pressed on with his war, and within a century two-thirds of the lands once Christian had been Islamized, with the practice of Christian faith severely restricted.

The native Christian communities endured. In the eleventh century, however, the situation changed as the Holy Land came under control of powers bent on active persecution. First Egyptians and then Turks enslaved Palestine's Christians—and many pilgrims from Europe as well. By 1095 it was clear that, unless Christians united to halt the aggression, the remaining Christian territories in the East would soon be overrun and Europe would be vulnerable.

The Byzantine emperor begged Pope Urban II for help. So the pope summoned churchmen and statesmen to an unusual council at Clermont, in France. There he issued a call for action that would be simultaneously military and spiritual, a campaign to defend Christendom against Muslim aggression, to help persecuted Christians in Eastern lands, and to reclaim the Holy Sepulchre. Christian soldiers would take a vow and wear a red cross. As they strove to fulfill their vow, they would receive a plenary indulgence from the Church—a remission of the temporal punishment due to their sins. The council received Urban's preaching enthusiastically, crying "*Deus vult!*"—"God wills it!"

From this first summons onward, the Crusades were taken up for religious reasons—as penance for one's own sins and in solidarity with persecuted Christians in the East. There was no money to be made. In fact, there was much to be spent and lost. The voyage itself would cost a fortune—close to a quarter of a million dollars in today's money. Many crusaders borrowed or bankrupted themselves to do it. It was an investment they would never recoup in any material sense. Those who departed on crusade knew, moreover, that there was a good chance they would never return home. Travel was dangerous in normal circumstances; it was deadly in times of war. Yet thousands went, and they left their mark on history and on the walls of Jerusalem.

The papal calls were renewed many times over the centuries. Not all the Crusades were directed toward the East or toward Muslims. Some focused on European locales controlled by heretics.

Since crusading was a penitential exercise and a personal choice, only God can judge its success, in total or in each individual case. We can say that the Crusades failed, ultimately, in their original objectives of recovering the Holy Land or saving the Byzantine Empire.

They succeeded, however, in holding off Muslim incursions long enough for Europe's societies to grow up and be ready for the direct attacks that inevitably came.

For More

Thomas F. Madden. *The New Concise History of the Crusades*. Lanham, MD: Rowman and Littlefield, 2005.

Jonathan Riley-Smith. *What Were the Crusades?* San Francisco: Ignatius Press, 2002.

Artwork damaged during the 1453 invasion of Constantinople. Photo by ihsanylidizil / iStockphoto.com.

51

Damaged Artwork
in Constantinople

The mosaic tiles have been scraped away as high as a weapon could reach—as high as a long sword could hack when wielded by a soldier on foot. The image adorns a wall of the south gallery in the preeminent church in Eastern Christendom, Hagia Sophia, in the city formerly known as Constantinople. The composition follows the traditional iconic representation known as the Deësis: Christ in glory, flanked by the Virgin Mary and John the Baptist. The mosaic was defaced by the invading Ottoman army in May of 1453.

Constantinople had long been in a weakened state. At the end of the Fourth Crusade, in 1204, a band of crusaders sacked the city. In doing so, they violated their vows and incurred automatic excommunication. But they didn't care about that. In fact, they had detoured to Constantinople against the expressed wishes of the pope—enticed there by a Byzantine prince who later reneged on his promises, leaving them stranded and broke.

Infuriated and trapped, the crusaders laid siege to the city, captured it, and even ruled over it for a time afterward. Neither the capital nor the empire ever recovered.

Yet Constantinople still had one more burst of greatness in her. Byzantine culture, in the aftermath, burst into a renaissance of the arts—as glorious as the one that was beginning in Italy at the same time. Such beautiful murals as the Deësis (the word in Greek means "supplication") were completed even as the remains of the empire crumbled.

The Turks advanced city by city, until nothing was left of the empire but Constantinople itself. Finally the emperors were reduced to acknowledging themselves vassals of the Turkish sultan. But that wasn't enough for the sultan, who was bent on making Constantinople his capital.

In 1452 the Byzantine emperor, Constantine XI, tried valiantly to rouse the interest of the West. But by then the Eastern and Western churches were riven by mutual excommunication. And nothing in the two hundred years since 1204 had repaired the distrust of either the Latins or the Greeks. Constantine managed to forge an alliance, but it was superficial. It lacked support from his people, many of whom said they'd rather be ruled by the sultan than the pope.

The little support the emperor received from the West was not enough to stop the sultan's momentum.

After two months of siege, the Turks breached the walls of the capital. On the night of May 28, 1453, the emperor received last rites. Then he rode out to die in a final heroic defense that he already knew was doomed. The next morning, the sultan rode over his mangled body without even recognizing him.

Hagia Sophia filled up with panicked citizens. They believed God would protect his people in his own church. Then came a horrible pounding at the doors.

All at once the church was filled with Turkish soldiers. They bound up the helpless refugees to be hauled off into slavery. In the days that followed, the Turks destroyed or defaced every Christian symbol in Hagia Sophia—including this one.

When all the mosaics had been whitewashed and all the icons destroyed, the building was dedicated as a mosque.

For More

Thomas F. Madden. *Istanbul: City of Majesty at the Crossroads of the World.* New York: Viking, 2016.

John Julius Norwich. *Byzantium: The Decline and Fall.* New York: Knopf, 1995.

Renaissance *and* Reformations

The saints had long been clamoring for renewal. Now world events forced the moment. It was an age of exploration and discovery. European powers discovered a New World. Philosophers, pastors, and artists renewed the traditional Christian emphasis on human dignity. The sciences and technology raced forward with inventions such as the printing press, which radically changed the way individuals and societies interact. The Church experienced—within a few years—the challenge of reform from within, the mass defection of nations, and the sudden conversion of peoples. Great men and women arose to purify old forms of community and propose new ones.

The famous printing press of Johannes Gutenberg. Photo: Josse / Scala / Art Resource, NY.

52

Gutenberg's New Machine

It wasn't exactly a novelty. For years similar machinery had been used to produce wines. But Johannes Gutenberg came up with a "secret" assembly that gathered the same components into something more useful even than a winepress. It was a printing press with movable type.

Other men had made printing presses, but theirs were block presses. Each surface was a single wooden slab, painstakingly carved, which represented a single page. Block presses were most useful for picture books, but long text proved an impossible burden for the carvers. And, after the press run, the blocks were useless as anything but firewood.

Gutenberg was a smith by trade, and his innovation was movable type made of an alloy of several metals. It could be positioned on blocks for the printing of a book—and then disassembled for repeated reuse. He also developed oil-based inks for permanence and clarity.

He had developed a method of movable type that enabled the affordable mass production of books.

He had launched a revolution in the way people think, learn, and live.

But he wasn't a revolutionary. He was an entrepreneur. His goal was to make books for the market he knew was ready—and that was the Catholic Church. The business of religion required many books—books of scripture, books of commentary, books of rites and blessings, books of instruction for confessors, books of the lives of the saints. Then there were books for higher study and more refined tastes: theology, philosophy, and the writings of the Church Fathers. All of these works had, till now, to be copied out by scribes. Each book was a project that could take months or even years to complete.

That was indeed to be Gutenberg's market. With help from a financier named Johann Fust, he launched his business in the city of Mainz, Germany. Among the earlier items to roll off his press were a papal letter and thousands of certificates of indulgences. He printed a grammar for ecclesiastical Latin. His masterwork, of course, was his "Forty-Two-Line Bible" in Latin—the Gutenberg Bible—printed between 1452 and 1454.

In 1456 he had a falling out with his backer, who fired him. Gutenberg set up shop in another town. The presses were proliferating. He had once referred to the printing press as his secret, but now the secret was out. The first books—*ever*—had been printed at mid-century, and by the end of the century more than twenty million books were in print. By 1500 there were press operations in more than 250 European cities.

The earliest vernacular Bibles began to appear around 1460, in High German and Low German. Also printed were books of hours and other prayer books, psalters, and pious travelogues.

The first religious reformer to exploit the new technology was the firebrand Girolamo Savonarola, an Italian friar and (for three years) ruler of Florence. Enterprising printers made booklets of his sermons and sold them in the streets. Since Savonarola was politically and religiously controversial, his booklets drove his opponents to print responses. By the time of his death by hanging in 1498, he had more than a hundred and fifty works in print.

Gutenberg had been right about his invention's utility for the Church. Catholic institutions were among the most ardent promoters of the new technology, and it was missionaries who established the first presses in Asia.

Books, repositories of knowledge, had formerly been accessible only to a few. But with movable type it was possible to get word out to hundreds or thousands of literate persons in a matter of days. Arguments could be conducted publicly. Responses could be made instantly. Discipline could be enforced (theoretically, at least), around the world, in a uniform way.

Now the word was made print and dwelt everywhere.

For More

A. Hyatt Mayor. *Selected Writings and a Bibliography*. New York: Metropolitan Museum of Art, 1984.

Michael F. Suarez, S.J, and H. R. Woudhuysen, eds. *The Book: A Global History*. New York: Oxford University Press, 2014.

*The great explorer's compass at the Museum of Christopher Columbus, Las Palmas,
Spain. Photo: Album / Art Resource, NY.*

53

Christopher Columbus's Compass

Christopher Columbus owned this compass and used it, no doubt, in one of his voyages to the New World—the half of the world he "discovered."

The lands that came to be known as the Americas had been visited by Christians long before 1492. As early as the tenth century, the Norse had explored and even set up small colonies in the northeast. The Viking Leif Erikson is the first known European to have made the trip. A convert to Christianity, he was on his way to bring the faith to Greenland. Blown off course in a storm, he found his way to a land he called Vinland—probably what we know today as Newfoundland and New Brunswick. This was almost five hundred years before Columbus sailed.

But over those centuries, none of the Viking trading settlements developed into a permanent presence.

Columbus was not out to discover a new world. What he wanted was a westward route to the Far East. Europe's ongoing conflict with the Muslim Turks had made trade with the East troublesome. Europe wanted India's spices and China's silks, but danger and extortion were driving up the prices.

Mariners of the fifteenth century knew that the world was round and that there must be a more direct way to reach India. But was it navigable?

Columbus believed it was and that such a route should be found. The voyage of discovery, however, needed a sponsor. For the better part of a decade he shopped the idea to European monarchs but raised little interest. Eventually he attracted the attention of Ferdinand and Isabella, the first rulers of a united Spain and Portugal. They had just completed the reconquest of the Iberian Peninsula; after seven hundred years, Spain's Christians were free from Muslim domination. The royals were eager to develop trade with the East, especially if they could bypass any Muslim involvement. For years they kept the conversation with Columbus going but delayed making a decision. Finally in 1492 they agreed to terms, and Columbus and his crew set off as agents of the Spanish crown.

Ferdinand, Isabella, and Columbus—and undoubtedly all the men on his ships—had a strong economic interest in the venture. But that wasn't all they wanted. The king and queen had a keen desire to evangelize and so did Columbus. The Spaniards had known life under Muslim rule, and they did not want to return to it. They wanted to bring the world to Christian faith.

Columbus's piety and motives are clear from the first pages of his diary. It begins with a dedication "in the Name of Our Lord Jesus Christ." It ends with the words "Thanks be to God." Throughout the log he shows an awareness of his religious mission. He interprets a storm that almost killed him as just punishment for his sins. Once he arrives and encounters the native people, he forbids his men "to do any unjust thing to the Indians." He refers to his crew as "the Christians."

As Columbus traveled, he exercised an Adam-like prerogative of naming everything he saw. Most bodies of water and expanses of land he named for saints, the mysteries of faith, and the Divine Persons of the Trinity. He addressed his patrons directly with counsel about any future exploration: "Your Highness ought not to consent that any foreigner set foot or trade here except Catholic Christians, since the beginning and end of the enterprise was the increase and glory of the Christian religion." He further specified that later explorers should be *good* Catholics.

He foresaw the day, he said, when all the native peoples would eagerly embrace Christianity. Though he was troubled by the cannibalism of some tribes, he observed that they had no strong attachment to idols, and he believed that this would make conversion easier for them.

Columbus made four transatlantic voyages and served as colonial governor in the New World, and he soon discovered the particular challenges of ruling. His subjects complained of his harshness, his patrons recalled him and revoked his benefits, and he spent his remaining years tangled in lawsuits with the crown. He believed his achievements to be the fulfillment of biblical prophecy. But such claims drew an ambivalent response, and they still do.

For More

Christopher Columbus. *The Four Voyages: Being His Own Log-Book, Letters, and Dispatches with Connecting Narratives.* New York: Penguin, 1992.

Oliver Dunn and James E. Kelley Jr., trans. *The Diario of Christopher Columbus's First Voyage to America 1492–1493.* Norman: University of Oklahoma Press, 1989.

The miter of Cardinal Cisneros, now in the collection of the Metropolitan Museum of Art (17.76).

54

The Miter *of*
Cardinal Cisneros

This miter, symbol of the office of bishop, belonged to Francisco Ximénez de Cisneros. Though it was his by right, it was a long time in coming.

As a young lawyer, Cisneros, a Spaniard, worked in Rome. He was spectacularly gifted and won notice among the most prominent leaders in the Church, including Pope Pius II. The pope sent him home with an appointment to the next available bishopric in his region. Cisneros dutifully went, but the archbishop there refused to recognize the pope's letter, wanting instead to bestow the see on a man of his own choosing. Cisneros insisted upon his right to the office and was promptly thrown into prison, where he endured six years of confinement rather than renounce his right. When the archbishop relented, Cisneros accepted an offer to trade his original assignment for another. He served as vicar general for a large diocese for a time before deciding, at age forty-eight, to enter the Franciscan order.

The decision shocked many people. It was late in life to be making such a decision. And he would have to give up his possessions in becoming a Franciscan. He would also give up his freedom, vowing obedience to his superiors. That seemed tantamount to relinquishing a brilliant career.

He took the name Francisco in religion. Afterward, he lived Francis's life of renunciation. He refused even to sleep on a bed. Under the robes of a friar, he wore a cilice, a garment of rough cloth and wire, so that he would always be penitentially uncomfortable. He asked to be assigned to a remote place. Even so, his reputation followed him and remained strong.

In time he was summoned to serve as Queen Isabella's confessor and then was nominated by the pope to become archbishop of Toledo. He tried to run away, but he was overcome by the queen's guards and forced to accept.

He made the most of the opportunity. He founded the university that is today known as the Complutense University of Madrid, and he made it into a great research institution. He commissioned the production of a polyglot edition of the Bible. He promoted scripture study and encouraged devotional reading of the Bible in the vernacular.

He reformed his own order and then the other mendicant orders as well, insisting that friars had to give up their mistresses and live the celibacy they had vowed. This led to an all-out rebellion. In protest, four hundred friars emigrated to North Africa with their mistresses and converted to Islam.

Cisneros is most controversial for his cooperation with the expulsion of Muslims and Jews from Spain. He did not think religious pluralism was workable, and he did not believe non-Christians would be converted by slow, gradual exposure to the Gospel. The country had been plagued by rebellions of Muslims since the reconquest. With Cisneros's consent, the king and queen made the decision a stark one for religious minorities: convert or leave.

On the other hand, he emerged as a defender of the native peoples in the Americas. He was appalled by reports of the burgeoning slave trade and horrified to find that Columbus was complicit. He carefully selected the early missionaries to be sent to the New World, so that none would be infected by greed. He took an active part in the first attempts to establish just government in the "Indies" and even published a directory for proper treatment of native peoples.

These directives, like many such, were roundly ignored. When commercial interests began to complain, Cisneros found himself increasingly alienated from the crown. He was semi-politely dismissed and died shortly afterward.

For More

John C. Olin. *Catholic Reform from Cardinal Ximenes to the Council of Trent, 1495–1563.* New York: Fordham University Press, 1990.

Hugh Thomas. *Rivers of Gold: The Rise of the Spanish Empire, from Columbus to Magellan.* New York: Random House, 2013.

Symbol of the Inquisition in a façade in the village of La Alberca, Spain. Photo: Album / Art Resource, NY.

55

A Sign *of the* Inquisition

A cross, a sword, and a palm appear on the façade near a doorway in the tiny village of La Alberca in the province of Salamanca, Spain. The elements in the seal represent the possible results of the inquisitors' interrogation: the sword, the rigors of justice; the palm, the honor of those who are vindicated after being falsely accused. The cross stands for the inquisitor himself.

Even in a community of fewer than a thousand people, inquisitors had a presence. The Spanish crown made sure of it.

Their Catholic Majesties—a title Ferdinand and Isabella received from the pope in 1494—were determined that Spain should never lapse again from the Catholic faith. After so many centuries of resistance, they saw unity as imperative. Moreover, they knew from their own experience that a stubborn minority could wear away its opponents. So from the start, the king and queen took every measure to build up a pure faith in Spain, and that meant giving no refuge to infidels and heretics.

To accomplish these goals, Ferdinand and Isabella used the means that were considered normal in governments of their time. The modern idea of the separation of church and state would never have occurred to rulers in the fifteenth and sixteenth centuries. National unity, national security, and public order depended ultimately on religious unity. Thus, the German princes and Swiss theocrats enforced national unity in religion, whether Protestant or Catholic.

Spain's history presented the rulers with unique problems. A mixture of Muslims, Jews, and Christians lived in the formerly Muslim parts of Spain. As Isabella and Ferdinand reconquered town after town, they inherited this diverse mix. In 1478, Pope Sixtus IV gave Ferdinand and Isabella authority to set up an Inquisition in their realm, and they took to it with the same enthusiasm that marked everything they did.

In the beginning, the Inquisition in Spain, as elsewhere in Europe, was a relatively quiet thing. It was not until 1483 that the Spanish Inquisition became something more. That was when Tomás de Torquemada took the office of Grand Inquisitor.

Torquemada's ancestors were Jewish, and perhaps because of that he had no tolerance for unconverted Jews or for insincere converts. It was Torquemada who persuaded Ferdinand and Isabella to offer all Jews in Spain a choice: convert, leave, or die. Faced with that choice, thousands chose exile. But some chose to convert and were baptized.

Some of those conversions were sincere. But many were not. Some Jews simply made a show of Christianity but kept up their Judaism in secret at home. This seems to have shocked Torquemada. Ferreting out these insincere converts turned into the Inquisition's main business.

In Torquemada's hands, the Inquisition caught thousands of supposed infidels—and a large number of innocents.

Catholics in Spain and elsewhere were appalled by this, and many complained to the pope. Sixtus IV made official protests to the Spanish government but to no avail. No one in Spain knew what it would take to preserve Spain's unity and independence; no one was willing to place the reconquest at risk.

Torquemada, though, was as mortal as any of his victims. His rule of terror lasted only a decade and a half, but it was long enough to leave a black mark on history.

The Spanish Inquisition is singularly notorious, but Torquemada is not. He was no more ruthless than many of his contemporaries and near-contemporaries—Luther, Calvin, and Elizabeth I, to name just a few. His Inquisition was, however, made the subject of a popular fiction in England, a propaganda leaflet that spoke of hooded fiends who closed their victims into Iron Maidens. It was the first volley in a propaganda campaign that would last centuries. Spaniards call it the Black Legend, and for many years, the English-speaking world called it history.

For More

Henry Kamen. *The Spanish Inquisition: A Historical Revision*. New Haven, CT: Yale University Press, 1998.

Edward Peters. *Inquisition*. Berkeley: University of California Press, 1989.

Even bad popes have valid seals. From the collection of Fr. Richard Kunst, Papal Artifacts. Photo by John Latour.

56

Alexander VI's Seal

Good popes, bad popes, even (as we've seen) antipopes, issued documents marked by leaden seals. A papal bull is named for the lead pendant (*bulla*) used to seal it. The seal makes the document official. This particular *bulla* bears the name of Alexander VI.

Alexander ranks high on any list of the Church's bad popes. The conclave that elected him in 1492 was probably the most corrupt in history. Italian Rodrigo Borgia used his family's ample fortune to buy the cardinals' votes, and on election he chose the name Alexander.

As pope, his main goal was to make his son Caesar master of as much of Italy as he could get his hands on—Caesar, who murdered his own brother and his brother-in-law. Alexander VI had no scruples about going out in public with his mistress.

This scandal roused the rage of the Florentine friar Girolamo Savonarola, who thundered publicly against the pope's vices. Pope Alexander came up with a scheme to silence Savonarola. He arranged for the French to march into Italy and occupy Florence. They did—but once there, the French made friends with the Florentines who were allied with Savonarola. The friar ended up acting as chief consultant to the new government, and his popularity grew as he rooted out corruption in the city.

It might have been good for Savonarola's place in history if he had been martyred then. So far he had shown only good, orthodox enthusiasm for reform. But now he had power, and it went to his head. His pronouncements took a turn for the extreme. An army of boys and girls became his spies, seeking out real or imaginary vice in every house so that parents lived in fear of their own children. Soon he was seeing visions. He prophesied. He began to act less like a zealous reformer and more like an unhinged fanatic.

All things considered, Pope Alexander had been remarkably tolerant of Savonarola. But at last, in May 1497, the pope excommunicated him. By then, Savonarola was too far gone to be frightened by a bull of excommunication. He responded by challenging the legitimacy of Alexander's papacy.

Enough was enough. The pope sent the city of Florence an ultimatum: either arrest Savonarola or the whole city will be placed under interdict—denied the sacraments and made a pariah in the world.

Savonarola's megalomania knew no bounds. He called for a general council of the Church to depose Alexander. But it was too late for that. Florence had begun to doubt Savonarola. There were riots, with casualties, and the government of Florence arrested Savonarola. The pope was happy, then, to lift his sanctions.

In prison, Savonarola was subjected to torture, and he confessed to numerous heresies, but when the torture stopped he repudiated his confession. Finally he was strangled and burned in 1498.

In later centuries, some tried to hail Savonarola as a hero, casting him as an early Catholic reformer or proto-Protestant. But he wasn't a hero; he might have been if he had died earlier, but power drove him mad. Nevertheless, the reaction to him in Florence proved one thing: Christians were willing to practice a demanding faith, and they wanted to hold their clergy to a high standard.

While faith was reviving, the wicked were fading. In 1503, Alexander VI fell victim to poison. He died a horrible death, his body blackened all over. But grace came even through the horrid Alexander VI. His instinct was always to promote peace and tolerance, which were good for Borgia business. Though he was responsible for wars and murders in Italy, he also was responsible for peace between Spain and Portugal, and he saved many Jews from the excesses of the Spanish Inquisition.

Even Alexander's notorious immorality ultimately was an instrument of grace. His illegitimate son had a son, and that son had a son, and *that* son grew up to be St. Francis Borgia.

For More

Mike Aquilina. *Good Pope, Bad Pope: Their Lives, Our Lessons.* Ann Arbor, MI: Servant Books, 2013.

The Pietà, the most recognizable piece of sculpture from the Renaissance. Photo by Fr. Gaurav Shroff.

57
Michelangelo's *Pietà*

The *Pietà*, now the centerpiece of a chapel in St. Peter's Basilica, is the only work of art to be signed by Michelangelo.

Michelangelo completed the *Pietà* in 1399, before his twenty-fifth birthday. Cardinal Jean de Bilhères commissioned the work to appear beside his mausoleum. He went to Michelangelo, who was already recognized as preeminent in his field. It was unveiled to much acclaim.

According to the artist's friend and biographer, Giorgio Vasari, Michelangelo one day mingled in the crowd, listening eagerly to the praise of his work from so many strangers. He heard one man ask his companion the name of the artist who had made the sculpture. The answer came: "Our Gobbo from Milan" (another stone-carver).

Michelangelo said nothing. But he returned at night, shut himself in, and with hammer and chisel carved his name on Mary's sash. In Latin he wrote: "Michelangelo Buonarroti made this."

Since he never signed another work, it seems he came to regret this outburst—or he never considered another work so worthy.

The *Pietà* does rather perfectly embody the ideals of the period known as the Renaissance. A cultural movement of the fourteenth through seventeenth centuries, it was manifest in many arts and sciences. The Renaissance represented a fundamental shift in perspective—a new humanism—a placement of man at the center of everything. In sculpture and painting, the human form was presented in ways simultaneously more real and more ideal. Artists portrayed men and women with physiological exactness, placing bones, muscles, and veins exactly where they are in life. Yet the human figures themselves often represent an idealized beauty, the perfection of youth.

These qualities are evident in the *Pietà*, where Jesus is, even in death, the perfect form of masculinity. His mother seems no older than he is; young and beautiful; she is, even in sorrow, the very model of feminine beauty.

Historians sometimes portray the Renaissance as a period of increasing secularization. That's not quite true. Intellectuals of the time based their turn to humanism on Christian principles. The book of Genesis presents man and woman, after all, as the crowning achievement of God's creation. The Eternal Word entered history in no other physical form but the human. No less an authority than St. Irenaeus, in the third century, proclaimed that the glory of God is man fully alive.

The Renaissance marked a distinctive change in emphasis, and it brought about a great recovery in classical forms from ancient Greece and Rome. It was not anti-Christian or neo-pagan. It was, in fact, funded mostly by the Church. Michelangelo himself was a professed member of the Secular Franciscan Order.

Even the most immoral of the "Renaissance popes" were great patrons of the arts. It was seen as a duty of office. It was a cardinal who commissioned the *Pietà*. It was a pope who invited Michelangelo to paint the Sistine Chapel. And it was yet another pope who hired Michelangelo to take over the design of St. Peter's Basilica.

With his contemporary Leonardo da Vinci, Michelangelo represents the ideals of the Renaissance. He lived a long life, dying at eighty-eight, and was phenomenally productive as sculptor, painter, poet, and architect. In every medium he produced at least one masterpiece.

In his lifetime, however, he faced critics who scoffed at the impossible beauty of his subjects. His pupil Ascanio Condivi put the question to him about Mary's excessive youth in the *Pietà*. Michelangelo's response was passionate and theologically astute. He said that chaste women keep their good looks longer than those who are unchaste. The principle, he added, would apply in the highest degree to the immaculate Virgin.

And that's only the beginning—of his defense and of the Renaissance.

For More

Elizabeth Lev and Jose Granados. *A Body for Glory: Theology of the Body in the Papal Collections.* Rome: Edizioni Musei Vaticani, 2016.

Giorgio Vasari. *Lives of the Artists.* New York: Oxford University Press, 2008.

The dome of St. Peter's. Photo by Fr. Gaurav Shroff.

58

Dome *of* St. Peter's

As artifacts go, St. Peter's Basilica is on the large side. It is an "object" in the same way that the moon is an object. For the whole earth it reflects light shone from long ago. It effects the tides of history. It has gravitational pull.

St. Peter's is the largest church in the world (163,200 feet inside), and its dome is taller than any other (448 feet). It's designed to hold 60,000 people indoors; with overflow into the piazza outside, capacity is almost 400,000.

Within St. Peter's are monuments of some of history's most significant moments: the porphyry stone that commemorates Charlemagne's imperial coronation; the *Pietà* that stands as the pinnacle of Renaissance art; and of course, the bones of St. Peter resting directly beneath the church's high altar.

Individual design elements are themselves recognized as architectural marvels: the colonnade, whose 284 individual pillars are each sixty-six feet tall; the obelisk that rises 135 feet into the air; the dome, of course; and the matching fountains created by two titans of Renaissance art.

St. Peter's is a singularity. The current church is constructed on top of the basilica built by Constantine in the fourth century. By the 1400s it was showing signs of serious disrepair. While the popes enjoyed the pleasant weather in Avignon, Rome suffered neglect. Earthquakes had made St. Peter's walls unstable, and centuries of battles had left their marks. In 1506, Pope Julius II decided it should be entirely replaced.

Julius was a man of colossal ambitions; on his election to the papacy, the cardinals had tasked him with restoring discipline in the Church and continuing the war with the Turks. He also wanted to unify Italy and make it great again, freeing its fractured regions from the dominance of foreign powers. He was intensely competitive and bellicose. He would do nothing by half-measures.

Thus, the new basilica—his basilica—would be the most magnificent church ever built, peerless in might and beauty. It would send a clear message that Christianity remained triumphant and still ascendant, even though Constantinople had fallen. (It would also include a monumental tomb for Julius himself, decorated with sculptures by Michelangelo.)

The pope sponsored a competition and invited the greatest architects of his day to submit their designs. Donato Bramante was the winner.

Julius laid the cornerstone of St. Peter's in 1506 and encouraged its progress till his death in 1513. The project lasted more than a hundred years, through the reign of twenty popes, and was overseen by thirteen chief architects in succession—among them, Bramante, Michelangelo, and Bernini. The design would undergo significant changes along the way, but none that made the plans less grand or less expensive. Some elements, such as Bernini's bell towers, went up, were found to be defective, and were soon torn down.

The difficulty at every stage, of course, was to pay for such a project. This difficulty would soon lead to far greater difficulties.

For More

James Lees-Milne. *Saint Peter's: The Story of Saint Peter's Basilica in Rome*. New York: Little, Brown, 1967.

Christine Shaw. *Julius II: The Warrior Pope*. Cambridge, MA: Wiley-Blackwell, 1997.

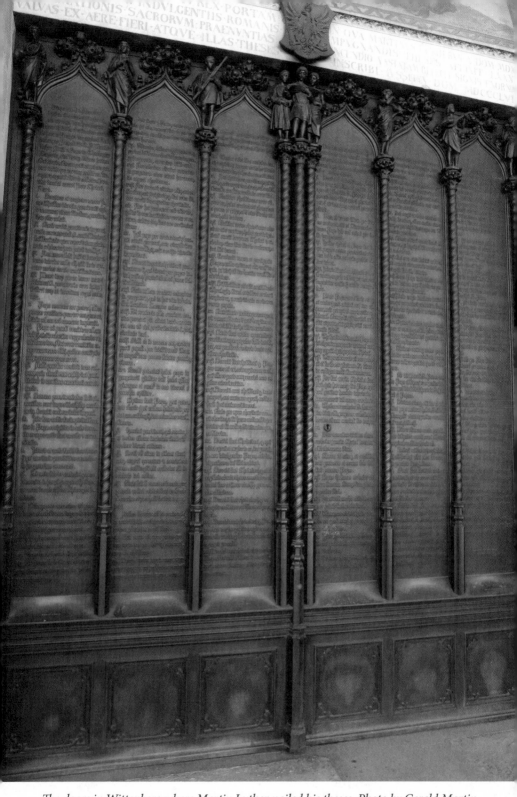

The doors in Wittenberg where Martin Luther nailed his theses. Photo by Gerald Martin.

The Wittenberg Doors

Here he stood, on October 31, 1517, and here, on the doors of All Saints Church in Wittenberg, Germany, Martin Luther nailed his Ninety-Five Theses.

Called the "Castle Church," All Saints served as the chapel of the university where Luther taught theology. The wooden doors that took his nails are long gone, burned in a fire in the eighteenth century. These bronze doors, their eventual replacement, bear the full text of Luther's original protest. All the standard histories mark the doors of All Saints—and the posting of the theses—as the starting points of the Protestant Reformation. Luther is forever identified with this place. His body is even buried inside.

The occasion of Luther's protest was an indulgence granted by Pope Julius II. Eager to fund the monumental new St. Peter's, Julius granted a plenary indulgence to anyone who contributed money to the cause. Now, an indulgence, properly understood, grants the remission of the temporal punishment due for a sin that has been forgiven. But preachers simplified the doctrine and exaggerated in their eagerness to gather contributions. Their listeners sometimes went home with the impression that they could buy a dead person's way out of purgatory.

Luther was horrified by that suggestion. In his theses he took aim not only at the abuses but also at the tradition of granting indulgences, as well as its theological underpinning. He rejected the very notion of a "treasury of merit," which had been a constant in biblical religion. He denied, furthermore, that the clergy's power of "binding and loosing" should or could be exercised in indulgences.

He posted his theses at the university, and he likely expected them to provoke a debate on campus. But the printing press, then a rather new invention, soon spread Luther's challenge all over Germany. It was no longer an academic discussion.

Pope Julius was hesitant to discipline Luther. They shared some common allies. But amid silence from the Church, Luther's popularity increased, and the reformer became more stridently rebellious. When the pope finally excommunicated him in 1521, he burned the bull of excommunication. Soon afterward, at an imperial council (the Diet of Worms), the emperor, Charles V, declared that he would defend the Catholic faith against Luther's attack. Luther refused to back down, and he fled just before the Diet declared him a criminal.

The German princes immediately saw the political potential in the situation. They used the controversy as an occasion to gain power, seize lands, and settle old scores. Those who aligned themselves with Luther placed themselves outside the Catholic Church. The movement gained momentum. In the lands of his allies, Lutheran mobs raided convents and carried nuns off for marriage. Luther, who seemed to remain devout in his rebellious faith, married a former nun to make a point.

Luther invoked the Holy Spirit as his "Council" as he opposed the authority of all the popes and councils that had gone before. In rejecting papal and episcopal authority, he assumed that the authority of his own interpretation would be self-evident. But it wasn't. Luther's movement inspired counter-movements, whose doctrine was an even more radical departure from tradition. Zwinglians denied the efficacy of the sacraments. Anabaptists rejected all rites and human authority.

Luther urged the secular authorities to act decisively against such anarchy. When the peasants revolted, he addressed a tract to the princes, saying, "Kill them, strangle them. . . . Strike, throttle, stab, secretly or openly." The princes took this as their license. Years later, Luther took credit for the slaying of more than a hundred thousand peasants.

Later reformers were like Luther in their eagerness to throw off the yoke of tradition. But once they succeeded and assumed authority themselves, they learned the value of establishment and discipline. John Calvin imposed a social order of his own devising in Geneva. Yet from his deathbed, he said to his ministers, "I beg of you make no changes, don't bring in anything new . . . because all changes are dangerous and sometimes harmful."

The situation in Germany devolved into a horrible religious war that lasted until the Peace of Augsburg in 1555. That settlement divided Germany into Catholic and Protestant zones.

For More

Warren Carroll. *The Cleaving of Christendom, 1517–1661*. Front Royal, VA: Christendom Press, 2004.

Christopher Dawson. *The Dividing of Christendom*. San Francisco: Ignatius Press, 2009.

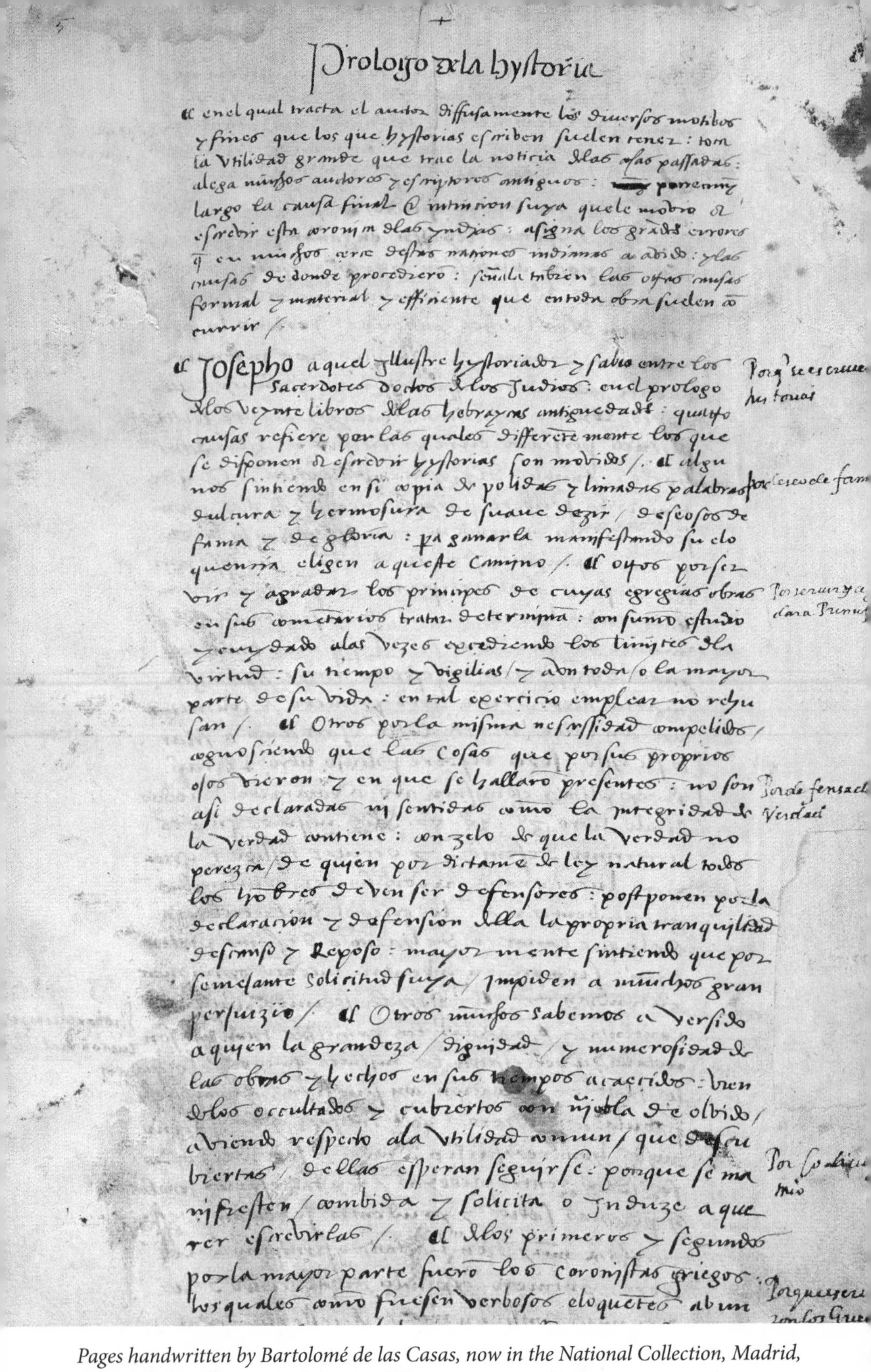

Prologo dela hystoria

en el qual tracta el auctor diffusamente los diuersos motiuos
y fines que los que hystorias escriben suelen tener: toma
la vtilidad grande que trae la noticia delas cosas passadas:
alega muchos auctores y escriptores antiguos: y ponen en
largo la causa final e intencion suya quele mouio a
escreuir esta coronica delas yndias: asigna los grandes errores
q en muchos series destas naciones indimos a ados: y las
causas de donde procedieron: señala tambien las otras causas
formal y material y efficiente que en toda obra suelen oc-
currir /

Josepho aquel illustre hystoriador y sabio entre los
sacerdotes doctos delos Judios: enel prologo
delos veynte libros delas hebraycas antiguedades: qualro
causas refiere por las quales differente mente los que
se disponen de escreuir hystorias son mouidos /. el algu-
nos sintiendo en si copia de policia y limadas palabras
dulcura y hermosura de suaue dezir, deseosos de
fama y de gloria: pa ganarla manifestando su elo
quencia eligen aqueste camino /. el otros por seruir y agradar los principes de cuyas egregias obras
en sus comentarios tratar determina: con sumo estudio
y cuydado alas vezes excediendo los limytes dela
virtud: su tiempo y vigilias / y aun todo la mayor
parte de su vida: en tal exercicio emplear no rehu-
san /. el otros por la misma necessidad compelidos,
conosciendo que las cosas que por sus proprios
ojos vieron y en que se hallaro presentes: no son
asi declaradas ny sentidas como la integridad de
la verdad contiene: con zelo de que la verdad no
perezca, de quien por dictame de ley natural todos
los hombres deven ser defensores: postponen por la
declaracion y defension della la propria tranquilidad
descanso y reposo: mayor mente sintiendo que por
semejante solicitud suya, impiden a muchos gran
perjuyzio /. el otros muchos sabemos a ver sido
a quien la grandeza / dignidad, y numerosidad de
las obras y hechos en sus tiempos acaescido: bien
dellos occultados y cubiertos con nyebla de olbido,
aviendo respecto ala vtilidad comun / que desu
biertas / dellas esperan seguirse: porque se ma
nifiesten / combida y solicita o induze a que-
rer escreuirlas /. el delos primeros y segundos
por la mayor parte fuero los coronistas griegos:
los quales como fuesen verbosos eloquetes a bun

[marginal notes, right side:]
Porq' se escriue historias

Por seruir y dar Precio...

Por de sensa de verdad

Por lo qual el mio

Porq seri... son los Grie...

Pages handwritten by Bartolomé de las Casas, now in the National Collection, Madrid, Spain. Photo: Album / Art Resource, NY.

60

Bartolomé's Manuscript

This page of scrawl was set down in 1542 by the impassioned hand of Bartolomé de las Casas, a Dominican friar who had taken part in Columbus's early adventures in the New World. His manuscript was eventually published with a curious title: *A Short Account of the Destruction of the Indies*.

Destruction? Columbus's voyages had been a triumph for Spain. The explorer returned and paraded through towns amid displays of gold and accompanied by exotic natives. What could Las Casas mean by "Destruction"? In his many works, Friar Bartolomé said exactly what he meant. He himself had gone to the New World as an active participant in the conquest—but he was gradually horrified by what he saw.

The men who colonized the New World were soldiers, not farmers. They had little notion of how to work the ground they now claimed as their own. For that work they exploited the native population. The Spaniards took the peoples of sophisticated civilizations and reduced them to slave labor. Some Spaniards even discouraged the Indians from converting to Christianity because conversion would disqualify them as slaves and reduce their economic value.

Young Bartolomé may have been the first man to be ordained a priest in the New World. He was then a secular priest, serving as chaplain to the soldiers who conquered Cuba. He retained his share in his family's property and his personal stake in the ownership of slaves.

One day, however, he was stopped short by a passage in the Old Testament book of Sirach: "The bread of the needy is the life of the poor;

whoever deprives them of it is a man of blood. To take away a neighbor's living is to murder him; to deprive an employee of his wages is to shed blood" (Sir 34:21–22). Fr. Bartolomé knew immediately that he was guilty of those very crimes.

The passage, moreover, was preceded by the line, "If one sacrifices from what has been wrongfully obtained, the offering is blemished; the gifts of the lawless are not acceptable." So whatever good he did as a priest was nullified by his participation in the slave trade.

He renounced his stake in the family's slave holdings and began to preach against the practice, urging others to follow his example. His efforts were futile. So he returned to Spain to bring his case before the king and many bishops. He found a powerful ally in Cardinal Cisneros, who would soon serve as guardian and regent for the heir to the throne.

Fr. Bartolomé helped the cardinal draft new regulations for the treatment of Indians in the New World. The cardinal gave him the title "Protector of the Indians" before sending him back to the colonies.

Once there, he took part in an experiment in peaceful colonization in Venezuela. But his group met constant opposition from profiteers. The venture ended in tragedy with the massacre of the Indians involved. The priest blamed himself. He afterward sought refuge in religious life, entering the Dominican order. There he worked quietly for a decade before returning to advocacy and protest. He wrote steadily, seeking to influence the monarchs and bishops in Europe. Eventually, his work reached the pope, who used it as the basis for the first major papal statement against slavery, the bull *Sublimis Deus* published in 1537. King Charles of Spain also enacted laws ensuring the rights of the Indians. Unfortunately, all of these were roundly ignored by the conquistadors.

Las Casas came to occupy more prominent pulpits as he became vicar of the Dominicans in his region and then bishop of Chiapas in Mexico. But the opposition continued, and eventually it became clear that his life was endangered. Eventually he concluded that he could accomplish more for the Indians by returning to Europe and lobbying there on their behalf.

He lived long and wrote much. Many powerful people sought to have him silenced and retired to a monastery. Some said he should be charged with treason. But he always enjoyed the favor of the crown. Las Casas exercised a profound influence on the way later generations spoke of universal human dignity and human rights. He died in 1566.

For More

Ulrich Lehner. *The Catholic Enlightenment: The Forgotten History of a Global Movement.* New York: Oxford University Press, 2016.

Rodney Stark. *Bearing False Witness: Debunking Centuries of Anti-Catholic History.* West Conshohocken, PA: Templeton Press, 2016.

The miraculous image of Our Lady of Guadalupe. Photo by abalcazar / iStockphoto.com.

61

The Miraculous Image *of* Our Lady *of* Guadalupe

The image appeared first, miraculously, on this rough garment called a *tilma*. It is made from cactus fiber, worn by the poor, and usually worn out quickly. It was not made to last. Nor was it designed to hold an image.

Yet there it is, after almost half a millennium. The image and the medium have not merely lasted—against all odds—they have remained beautiful. Devotees have made duplicates, using the same materials, and those images have decayed. Paint that has been added to decorate the image has shown signs of deterioration. But the image never fades. And it draws several million pilgrims each year to the shrine in Mexico City where it is on display.

When the Spaniards, led by Hernán Cortés, entered Mexico in 1519, they encountered a people enslaved by the worship of many gods, chief among them the snake-god, Quetzalcoatl. The Aztecs believed their gods were bloodthirsty, demanding massive human sacrifice. Thousands upon thousands of people were offered up—a quarter of a million per year, according to the natives' chronicles. Even if we allow for exaggeration, we can be sure that many were dying in the temples.

Ordinarily, the black-robed Aztec priests would tear the still-beating hearts from their terrified victims. Often the victims were members of tribes that had been subjugated by the Aztecs.

With the Spanish conquest, the practice of human sacrifice was forbidden, and the Aztec temples were razed. Yet the problem persisted. Native people continued their carnage, believing that an increase in sacrifices might rid them of their humiliation by the Spanish. Their failure made them more desperate and more zealous.

Colonial law proved impotent. The Spanish missionaries had little success in converting the Aztecs.

Then, in 1531, a convert, who had taken the Christian name Juan Diego, was hurrying to Mass one day when he encountered the Blessed Virgin Mary. She gave him a message to deliver to his bishop. Juan Diego relayed the message, but the bishop was skeptical. As Juan Diego returned home, he met the Blessed Virgin again, and she gave him another message for the bishop. This time, the bishop asked for a sign.

But Juan Diego could not return to the hill the next day. His uncle had taken sick and seemed to be near death. The family asked Juan Diego to summon a priest to administer the last sacraments. Juan Diego set off for the city—but he avoided his usual route, so that he would not be delayed by the Blessed Virgin. But as he rounded a corner, he found her waiting for him. She told him his uncle had been cured, and she instructed him to gather flowers—in winter—to give to the bishop. Juan Diego looked and saw roses growing in abundance. He gathered them into his tilma, and he hurried to the bishop. When he presented the roses to the bishop, they saw that the tilma now bore the miraculous image of the Virgin.

The effect of the apparition was immediate. Word spread about "Our Lady of Guadalupe," and pilgrims began making their journey to the site where Juan had received his gifts. In just a few years, more than nine million Aztecs embraced the Catholic faith.

While the Church in Europe was torn apart by wars of religion, the people of Mexico were finding their way into the fold. Before too many centuries passed, Mexico would be home to one of the largest Catholic populations on earth.

For More

Paul Badde. *Maria of Guadalupe: Shaper of History, Shaper of Hearts*. San Francisco: Ignatius Press, 2009.

Eduardo Chavez. *Our Lady of Guadalupe and Saint Juan Diego: The Historical Evidence*. Lanham, MD: Rowman and Littlefield, 2006.

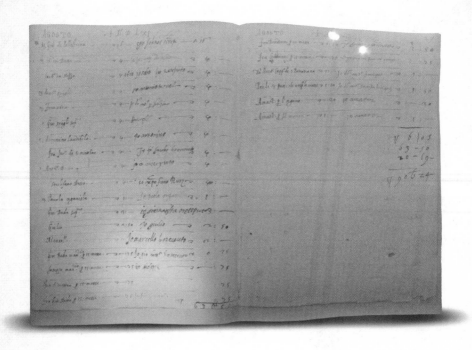

Accounts payable to the composer Palestrina, among others. Photo by Fr. Gaurav Shroff.

62

A Ledger Book

This ledger book records payment to Giovanni da Palestrina for services rendered to the church of St. Mary Major in Rome.

Palestrina didn't introduce polyphonic music to Italy. The compositions of northern Europeans had been making their way to Rome for decades. They were performed. They were imitated. But not until Palestrina did Italy produce a composer of genius to produce polyphonic music for worship.

Baptized Giovanni, the great composer grew up in the town of Palestrina, about twenty miles east of Rome. He showed such promise, however, that he was sent to the city at a very young age. At age twelve his name appears among choir members at one of Rome's major basilicas.

While still a teenager he was chosen to be organist at the cathedral church back home. Palestrina began composing settings for the Mass, and his works made a powerful impression on his bishop. It was the young musician's good fortune when his bishop was elected pope, as Julius III.

Julius invited his countryman to direct the choir at St. Peter's Basilica. Giovanni spent most of his remaining years as maestro at various Roman churches. As with the visual arts, so with music: the Church was the sponsor and the incubator of the Renaissance. The Church made it pay to be an artist or composer.

Palestrina was very much aware that he was, as he put it, "writing in a new manner." Until his time, polyphonic music—music with harmony—was viewed as inappropriate for worship. Chant was the only proper way to present the words of the liturgy. But the quality of Palestrina's work was undeniable in its effect on congregations.

Patrons and critics complained that other polyphonic compositions obscured the words of the prayers when they rendered them in harmony. But Palestrina placed a premium on intelligibility.

He also had a deep and intuitive understanding of the action of the liturgy. This is evident in his music, which always complements and never interrupts or distracts from the Mass. The music of Palestrina fosters contemplation.

His most enduringly famous melody is his setting for *O Filii et Filiae*. In English it is used for the Easter hymn "Alleluia! The Strife Is O'er!"

Palestrina lived a long life, dying in 1594, just shy of his seventieth birthday. By that time he had composed more than a hundred settings for the Mass as well as hundreds of other works, sacred and secular.

His collected compositions fill thirty-four volumes.

For More

Zoë Kendrick Pyne. *Giovanni Pierluigi da Palestrina: His Life and Times*. London: John Lane, 1922.

R. J. Stove. *Prince of Music: Palestrina and His World*. Sydney, Australia: Quakers Hill Press, 1990.

Receiving room at the Sanctuary of Loyola in Spain. Photo by Jacqueline Poggi,
Meyrargues, France.

63

Iñigo's Bookshelves

These shelves held nothing that Iñigo de Loyola wanted to read. He was an avid consumer of novels about chivalry—romances about bravery in battle and bloodshed in honor of a forbidden love. From such stories he had drawn inspiration as he pursued a life of knighthood. Romances served up models of machismo. Their heroes were violent and sometimes adulterous. Like his literary models, Iñigo fought many duels and had many affairs.

Now, having been injured in battle, he faced a long convalescence in a room with books selected by someone with far more pious tastes than his own. What lined the shelves? A biography of Jesus Christ and some legends of the saints.

Iñigo was addicted to high adventure. He had stood with the few last defenders of the Spanish city of Pamplona as they faced a force of twelve thousand French soldiers. As the French finally breached the city walls, he was struck by a cannonball, which passed through his legs, tearing open his left calf and breaking his right shin. The injuries could have killed him. Instead, it seemed, they had consigned him to months alone with books that were not to his taste.

The alternative, though, was utter boredom. So he took down a book and began, reluctantly, to read. And he continued reading what was at hand, although they held little that was interesting to him. When he put down the books, his thoughts would return to worldly achievement.

But he noticed a pattern. After reading the spiritual books, he enjoyed a sense of peace. After thinking about knightly exploits, he felt agitated and discontented. The thought occurred to him: "Suppose that I should do what St. Francis did, what St. Dominic did?"

He began to see great adventure in the lives of the saints. Iñigo put aside his dreams of battlefield glory and chose to pursue holiness instead. He stopped dressing and grooming like a dandy, and he took up the habit of poverty. He set out as a pilgrim to find the way that God intended for him. Iñigo traveled Spain, begging alms as he went. He battled with temptations to despair of his salvation. He ventured to the Holy Land but was turned back. He made his way to Paris, where he took up theological studies and became known as Ignatius.

Ignatius's happiness was evident, though his chosen life was hard. He began to attract many disciples. They shared their master's way of life, by now embodied in his book of *Spiritual Exercises*. Ignatius was ordained a priest in 1537. Eventually, he and his companions became known as the Society of Jesus—and colloquially as the Jesuits.

The Jesuits soon earned renown for their intelligence, obedience, discipline, drive, and holy ambition. One historian has called them "the most vibrant, most provocative" religious order the Church has produced. They would be the frontline of the Counter-Reformation, fearlessly facing the Catholic Church's new opponents and responding with ingenious arguments and tireless action. Their numbers grew rapidly.

By the time of their founder's death in 1556, the Jesuits had already established prodigious missions around the world (as far away as Japan to the east and America to the west) and dozens of schools. Many of the men of that first generation have been canonized: Francis Xavier, Peter Faber, Peter Canisius. Ignatius himself was declared a saint on March 12, 1622.

The home from which Ignatius first set out on pilgrimage is, today, a pilgrim destination. The Casa Santa is a shrine within the Sanctuary of Loyola in the municipality of Azpeitia, in Spain's Basque Country.

The books that sparked his conversion—books left for him, casually, by his sister—still sit on the shelves: *The Life of Christ* by Ludolph of Saxony and *The Golden Legend of the Saints* by Jacobus de Voragine.

For More

José Ignacio Tellechea Idígoras. *Ignatius of Loyola: The Pilgrim Saint*. Chicago: Loyola Press, 1994.

Ignatius of Loyola. *St. Ignatius' Own Story: As Told to Luis Gonzalez de Camara.* Chicago: Loyola Press, 1998.

A slipper worn by St. Pius V. From the collection of Fr. Richard Kunst, Papal Artifacts.
Photo by John Latour.

64

St. Pius V's Shoe

Who knew that Renaissance popes wore prescribed uniform shoes for indoors? This red slipper belonged to St. Pius V, who reigned as pope from 1566 to 1572. His outdoor shoes were made of leather, but this one's velvet, adorned by a white cross and a gold braid tie.

If he endured luxury in these trappings of office, Pope Pius denied himself in every other way, living a monk's life amidst the fantastic wealth of the Vatican. It's the ascetic life that made the difference.

His predecessors, for a hundred years or more, had known that the Church needed reform. Even the immoral popes tried their hand at restoring discipline to the bishops and parish clergy. But Pius's predecessors had been ineffectual, continually distracted by wars and intrigues. Meanwhile, the Church was losing souls to the Protestant Reformation, still facing a continental threat from the Muslim Turks, and grappling with new problems associated with colonialism.

Michele Ghislieri, a Dominican priest, was engaging the issues with intensity, first as a theology teacher and then as an inquisitor, diocesan bishop, and curial cardinal. He won renown for his justice and intelligence. He refused to allow even the pope to use the Inquisition for settling scores. He proved to be an immovable obstacle when Pope Pius IV tried to make a cardinal of a thirteen-year-old boy from the Medici family. That particular refusal cost him his job—all his jobs, in fact—and he was about to return to his diocese when he received news of the death of the pope.

As the cardinals entered the conclave, the influential Cardinal Charles Borromeo urged them to elect Ghislieri, and they were happy to do so. His resistance in the Medici affair had impressed them all. On coronation, Ghislieri took the name Pius V.

He changed his wardrobe for the office but little else. He continued to observe the demanding fasts and vigils that had been his habit since his teen years. As gifts poured in from princes and prelates currying favor, he directed all of it to be distributed among Rome's poor. In his rule of the city, he insisted that good morals be strictly enforced. He shut down the brothels and directed the hit men and thieves to leave town. He drained the swamps and improved the sewer system. He raised standards in the universities and in the instruction of children.

Yet he is most famous not for his cleanup of Rome but rather for his cleanup of the Church. He launched the movement known as the Catholic Reformation, or Counter-Reformation, by completing the Council of Trent, which had been summoned many years before but was proceeding only by fits and starts.

With the documents of the council, he produced genuine reform. He set demanding requirements for the seminary system and for candidates for the office of bishop. He published a catechism. He standardized the liturgy. He promoted the doctrine of St. Thomas Aquinas by naming him a Doctor of the Church.

One of his most impressive feats was the creation of the Holy League, a military alliance comprising many states that had long been rivals. Pius saw that their disunity was suicidal. The Ottoman Turks were dominating the seas and beginning to snatch up the eastern colonies of the western powers. The Turks took Cyprus in July 1570, and it was clear that they would soon be advancing on the European mainland. Pius's leadership gave cohesiveness to the coalition, and he called upon the whole Church to support the naval force in prayer. The Holy League turned back the Turkish fleet in the Battle of Lepanto in October of 1571.

His list of accomplishments seems too long for a man who held office for only six years. He could do it all because he himself observed the disciplines he imposed on others. He himself strove for the personal holiness he urged upon the Church.

For More

Robin Anderson. *Saint Pius V: His Life, Times, and Miracles*. Charlotte, NC: TAN Books, 2009.

John W. O'Malley. *Trent: What Happened at the Council*. Cambridge, MA: Harvard University Press, 2013.

Rosary beads, the most common Catholic aid to prayer. Photo by Susan Brown.

65

Rosary Beads

These beads have become the universal sign of Catholic prayer. Film directors use their presence as a distinguishing mark, a shorthand to advance the drama. If a character is holding a rosary, the character is Catholic and praying.

The popes hand out rosaries at their private audiences. They promote the prayer in their preaching and official documents.

The beads are simple counters for the person praying. They are strung in five sets of ten (decades), each set punctuated by a single bead. On each bead in the decades, a Hail Mary is prayed; on each of the punctuating beads, an Our Father. In recent centuries, Catholics typically begin a Rosary by reciting the Apostles' Creed and some preliminary prayers: one Our Father and three Hail Marys. There are many different ways to end a Rosary.

The prayer, in its most basic form, consists of the five decades and five Our Fathers. During each decade, the person praying focuses on a single "mystery"—an event from the biblical accounts of the lives of Jesus and Mary. Traditionally, there are fifteen mysteries: five Joyful, five Sorrowful, and five Glorious. (St. John Paul II proposed a fourth set, the Luminous Mysteries, in 2002.)

Since the dawn of Christianity, believers have used such devices to count prayers. The Desert Fathers did it. St. John Cassian and other early Christian writers attest to it. St. Paul the Hermit used to pick up a pebble every time he said a prayer. His goal was to have three hundred pebbles by the end of the day. Others used knotted ropes to count off their devotions.

Monks followed the custom of reciting all one hundred and fifty psalms—either every day, every week, or every month. People who couldn't read would simply substitute a common prayer and recite it a hundred and fifty times.

The Rosary, as a Marian prayer, seems to have emerged this way, developing gradually over time.

According to a popular legend, St. Dominic Guzmán received the Rosary directly from the Blessed Virgin in an apparition in 1214. But there is ample evidence that Christians were praying the Rosary in the century before. In any event, St. Dominic and his religious order played a major role in promoting the devotion. The Rosary served as an effective remedy to the heresy of the Albigensians, who despised human flesh. After all, the Mysteries of the Rosary focus on Jesus' earthly life, his life in the flesh. Every mystery of the Rosary showed how Christ, by his Incarnation, made human flesh holy.

Rosary confraternities became extremely popular throughout Europe. By the end of the fifteenth century, in Germany alone, at least 100,000 people had joined one.

That was a large market, and the printers met demand with a wide variety of devotional aids. Before Gutenberg invented the printing press, block printers published simple picture books illustrating the fifteen mysteries. With the advent of movable type, the books became more sophisticated, including scripture and meditations.

St. Pius V was a Dominican friar and true to his formation. As pope, when he solicited prayers for the success of the Holy League at the Battle of Lepanto, he specified that people should pray the Rosary. On the day of the battle, he led Rosary processions in the city of Rome.

Immediately after learning of the victory, he ordered that a commemoration of the Rosary should be made on the first Sunday of October every year.

For More

Patricia Ann Kasten. *Linking Your Beads: The Rosary's History, Mysteries, and Prayers.* Huntington, IN: Our Sunday Visitor, 2011.

Anne Winston-Allen. *Stories of the Rose: The Making of the Rosary in the Middle Ages.* University Park, PA: Penn State University Press, 2005.

Reliquary with sketch by St. John of the Cross. Photo by Matthew Leonard.

66

A Sketch *by* St. John *of the* Cross

Friar John, the chaplain at the Monastery of the Incarnation in Avila, was praying in the loft above the sanctuary chapel. As sometimes happened, he received a vision, and he sketched what he saw. It was the crucifixion of Jesus but from an unusual angle—not the view of those who watched from the ground nearby. John saw the Son's last agony from the perspective of the Father in heaven. Jesus' body is inclined toward the earth, which the Father is willingly saving.

John made the sketch at some point during the years 1574–1577, and today it is venerated at the monastery. He was Fray Juan, then. *Fray* is Spanish for "brother" or "friar." Since the seventeenth century, this sketch has been displayed in a monstrance, as a relic of the saint John became.

St. John of the Cross and his friend St. Teresa of Avila have been called by "clear consensus . . . the pre-eminent authorities of the Western Church" in matters of prayer and spirituality.

Both John and Teresa are known for the extraordinary spiritual phenomena they experienced: visions, locutions, foreknowledge, and miracles. But these were relatively rare, and they take up just a small portion of their collected writings. In fact, both saints discouraged any fascination with, or desire for, mystical gifts. As directors and as authors, they were eminently practical. They wrote about the stages of prayer, the typical obstacles to prayer, and the moral challenges along the way. They used homely examples for illustration. Teresa asked people to imagine the soul as a castle with seven dwellings, each a stage along the way to union with God. John compared the spiritual life to the ascent of a mountain.

Both were members of the Carmelite order, whose institutional origins are lost in the mists of legend. It likely began with the community life of hermits on Mount Carmel, in the Holy Land, in the twelfth century. But hermits don't usually keep good records. Members of the order trace their spirit, however, back to the prophets Elijah and Elisha, who lived and worked wonders on Mount Carmel (1 Kgs 18:19 and 2 Kgs 2:25).

The early Carmelites lived austere lives removed from contact with the world. They wore rough clothes and went about barefoot in all weather. They dedicated their lives to prayer and contemplation.

Over the centuries, however, members—and entire communities— had slackened in their observance of the rule. Teresa and John sought to return their monasteries (Teresa for women, John for men) to the order's primitive simplicity and rigor.

These were the days when the Protestant Reformation was sweeping through Europe's Germanic lands, and so any talk of reform was suspect. Mystical phenomena, too, roused suspicions of occult activity. Nor were many of the more relaxed Carmelite communities eager to change their ways. So Teresa and John were often denounced to the Inquisition as heretics or sorcerers. Both were subjected to ostracism and isolation. John was beaten and locked in a dark cell. Both were vindicated by the purity of their witness.

Their lives were not all ecstasy and visions. Teresa suffered well over a decade of dryness in prayer without any consolations from God. John, for his part, introduced the world to the phrase "Dark Night of the Soul" (the title of one of his works).

In spite of many obstacles they succeeded in their reform, essentially refounding their order in Spain—and then beyond. They also established terms by which subsequent generations would systematically study and discuss the experience of prayer and spirituality. They taught Christians a way to experience the grace of transcendence, to see the world and redemption from a God's eye view.

With the lives of Teresa and John, Ignatius of Loyola, Pius V, and Thomas More (and many others), the Church in Europe began to see its long-awaited period of renewal. History calls this age the Catholic Reformation, since it was in no way a reactionary movement.

For More

Jordan Aumann. *Christian Spirituality in the Catholic Tradition*. San Francisco: Ignatius Press, 1985.

Cheslyn Jones et al. *The Study of Spirituality*. New York: Oxford University Press, 1986.

A document testifying to an untruth. Photo by Fr. Gaurav Shroff.

67

The Acquiescence *of* Walsingham

By this document, the prior and other canons at Walsingham acknowledged their acceptance of the Act of Supremacy of 1534. In signing, they recognized King Henry VIII by the title he had claimed for himself: the supreme head of the Church of England. To deny the king's right was considered treason and punishable by death.

The Act of Supremacy was Henry's decisive break from the unity of the Catholic Church—his rejection of papal authority. The pope had denied Henry's request for an annulment of his first marriage. Henry was eager to marry a younger woman and produce a male heir. If the pope would not cooperate with Henry's plans, Henry would bestow a national papacy upon himself.

The canons at Walsingham sought to preserve the shrine, which was a popular pilgrim destination. Henry had once made pilgrimage there, as had his first wife and his putative second wife.

Signing didn't save the shrine. In 1537 one of the canons was found to be plotting against the king, and he was hanged in sight of the priory. In 1538 Henry ordered the confiscation of all the monastery's holdings and treasures—and then the place was demolished. The shrine's artistic treasures were consigned to flames. And the prior who had signed his acceptance of the act also, in time, consented to the priory's destruction.

Vows and loyalties meant something different now that Henry was the final religious authority in the land for Henry could be volatile. He would marry six times, legitimizing his divorces even after he obtained the son he had wanted. He would vacillate between Protestant principles and Catholic forms of worship, trying to create a form of Christianity that suited his tastes as well as his immediate needs.

Henry dissolved the monasteries because he needed their money—and he considered their popularity an implicit threat to his program.

He did the same to his friends and once-trusted advisors. The renaissance humanist Thomas More, author of the novel *Utopia*, was Henry's Lord Chancellor, given the post when his predecessor had failed to obtain Henry's annulment. But Thomas could not, in good conscience, consent to Henry's self-proclaimed supremacy in the Church. He resigned quietly and retired to his estate. But Henry had him charged with treason anyway, and Thomas was beheaded for his loyalty to Christian tradition.

Henry died at age fifty-five, morbidly obese after a life of constant self-indulgence. According to one account, he was tormented on his deathbed with guilt for his actions. His last words were reportedly, "Monks! Monks! Monks!"

Henry's son, Edward, died young and was succeeded by Mary, Henry's daughter with his first wife. She restored Catholicism as the religion of the empire and earned the nickname "Bloody Mary" by executing three hundred Protestants, many of them prominent men.

Mary died in 1558 and was succeeded by her half sister Elizabeth, a Protestant. Elizabeth took no chances. She established the first police state in history, and her agents worked to eradicate Roman Catholicism from the realm. Clergy, once captured, were subjected to gruesome, humiliating public tortures and execution. More than six hundred men and women died as martyrs for the Catholic faith in the time of the English Reformation.

It was a choice—for them as for the monks at Walsingham—to lose everything or try to preserve what they might.

For More

Eamon Duffy. *The Stripping of the Altars: Traditional Religion in England 1400–1580.* New Haven, CT: Yale University Press, 1992.

John Guy. *A Daughter's Love: Thomas More and His Dearest Meg.* New York: Houghton Mifflin, 2009.

The Age *of* Revolutions

An unintended consequence of the Protestant Reformation was to make religion subservient to the state. In the centuries that followed, philosophers of the Enlightenment openly challenged Christianity's public influence and moral authority. Challenge turned to mockery, and with the revolutions of the eighteenth and nineteenth centuries, mockery turned to active persecution. Catholic intellectuals and clergy were sidelined, silenced, and killed. The Church faced new questions in its relations with secular states and democracies. Even so, God sent great saints to propose revolutions in the spiritual order—in the ways of prayer and moral life.

Devotional image of Jesus' Sacred Heart. Photo by Godong / Alamy Stock Photo.

68

The Sacred Heart
of Jesus

This image of the heart of Jesus is radiant above the incorrupt body of St. Margaret Mary Alacoque. The motto in the arch preserves the words that Jesus spoke to her in a vision: "I constitute thee heiress of my heart."

From 1673 to 1675, Margaret Mary, a nun of the Visitation order, experienced visions of Jesus in her convent in Paray-le-Monial, France. He encouraged her to share the dispositions and sentiments, the sufferings and humiliations of his own heart. He taught her to meditate upon his Sacred Heart and urged her to spread such devotion to the world.

Hers was not the first encounter in which Jesus appeared with his heart exposed to view. In the thirteenth century, three mystics—St. Lutgarde, St. Mechtilde, and St. Gertrude—reported such visions. Great saints, such as Bonaventure and Francis de Sales—had written moving reflections on the heart of Jesus.

The seventeenth century, however, was the right moment for the flourishing of the devotion. And France was the right place. It was then and there that, historians say, the foundations were laid for modern spirituality.

In seventeenth-century France the Jansenists were deeply influential. They followed the posthumously published doctrine of a Dutch bishop, Cornelius Jansen, who promoted extreme asceticism to atone for human depravity.

Opposed by the Jesuits—and declared heretical by the pope—the Jansenists found an eager defender in the brilliant mathematician Blaise Pascal. His *Provincial Letters* are a satire of Jesuit life in France at the time.

His *Pensées* are now considered a classic, although they are just notes he wrote in preparation for a book he never finished.

Standing in contrast to the Jansenists are the writers that came to be known as the French School of spirituality. The best known are Cardinal Pierre de Bérulle, Jean-Jacques Olier (founder of the Sulpician order), St. John Eudes, and St. Louis de Montfort.

The French School is noted for its focus on the humanity of Jesus and the necessity of adherence to him in love. St. John Eudes summed everything up in devotion to the Sacred Heart of Jesus. In Jesus' heart St. John found an abundance of love, compassion, and mercy, poured out upon the earth.

But the doctrine reached the world most effectively through the reports of St. Margaret Mary's apparitions. She wasn't much of a publicist. Her spiritual director, St. Claude de la Colombière, a Jesuit, instructed her to write an account of her visions. She did. And he discreetly shared it with friends. He kept a copy for himself and annotated it carefully. It was found among his papers when he died, and it became a manifesto for Sacred Heart devotion, which the Jesuit order promoted zealously.

The emphases of the French School remain in Catholic piety today. Its authors were deeply Christ-centered and scriptural. Their devotions were Marian and eucharistic. They often emphasized the affective quality of devotion. They promoted profound reverence for the sacramental priesthood.

If Margaret Mary was Christ's "heiress," we are her heirs.

For More

Raymond Deville, S.S. *The French School of Spirituality: An Introduction and Reader.* Pittsburgh, PA: Duquesne University Press, 1990.

William M. Thompson. *Bérulle and the French School: Selected Writings.* Mahwah, NJ: Paulist, 1989.

A cradle in the childhood home of St. Junípero Serra in Spain. Photo by Gregory Orfalea.

69

St. Junípero's Cradle

This cradle still rocks in the childhood bedroom of Miguel Serra, whom the world knows now as St. Junípero. He was baptized on the day he was born, November 24, 1713. His two older siblings had died in infancy, and his parents were taking no chances.

The Serras were a hard-working farming family on the Spanish island of Mallorca. Miguel accompanied his father in the fields from the time he was seven. He also received an education from the local Franciscan friars.

His parents would greet him, as was the local custom, with a blessing: "May God make a saint of you."

On Mallorca, saint must have seemed synonymous with missionary. The island was a leading center of training for the mission fields. And the New World was still very new, and many of its native people had not heard the Gospel.

Miguel was an outstanding student. At fifteen he went away to study in the island's capital city, Palma. A year later he entered the Franciscans and was given the name Junípero. Once ordained a priest, he was assigned to teach philosophy, a task he dutifully carried out for years, though his secret desire was to follow his students into the distant missions. At age thirty-five he applied for such an assignment, and it was granted. In leaving, he knew he would never see his family again.

Arriving in Mexico, he refused the horse provided for him and began his journeys on foot, with no possessions, relying on the kindness of strangers. He soon contracted an infection in his foot, which caused him trouble for the rest of his life.

Nonetheless he moved forward. He took as his motto *Siempre adelante*, "Keep moving forward." He would, in time, found nine missions in California and one in Baja California.

Within his missions he would establish a structured religious life and provide regular work for the people. He always spoke of them with affection, emphasizing their virtues. While the colonial government referred to the native population as "savages" or "barbarians," Fr. Junípero used the term "gentiles," the biblical word for those who are waiting to know God.

He rode circuit from one mission to the next, and he repeatedly came to his people's defense. He raised his voice against the military's sexual exploitation of native women and even moved a mission to protect Indians from Spanish soldiers.

He defended the Indians even when some of them wronged him. When his assistant was killed in an ambush, Fr. Junípero was sure that he, too, was about to die. But he prayed to God that the faith would be victorious and not a single soul would be lost.

In 1775, when a local tribe burned his San Diego Mission, warriors tortured and killed his close friend and fellow missionary, Fr. Luís Jayme. Yet afterward, Fr. Junípero pleaded with the colonial government to show mercy to the killers.

He had ongoing conflicts with the military commander in California. Finally he went to appeal his case to the viceroy in Mexico. There, in 1773, he drafted the thirty-two articles of his *Representación*, a "Bill of Rights" for the Indians.

Fr. Junípero lived long enough to see the beginnings of the movement for independence in North America. In 1783, the year before he died, he took up a collection in the missions—for the benefit of General George Washington and his troops.

For More

Ulrich L. Lehner. *The Catholic Enlightenment: The Forgotten History of a Global Movement*. New York: Oxford University Press, 2016.

Gregory Orfalea. *Journey to the Sun: Junípero Serra's Dream and the Founding of California.* New York: Scribner, 2014.

In CONGRESS, July 4, 1776.

The unanimous Declaration of the thirteen united States of America

Four names below the highly visible John Hancock is the signature of Charles Carroll, the only Roman Catholic signer of the Declaration of Independence. Photo by selimaksan / iStockphoto.com.

70

The Declaration *of* Independence

It is easy to find the signatures of Maryland's members of the Second Continental Congress. They signed the Declaration of Independence just below John Hancock, the man whose name, for its prominence here, became synonymous with the word "signature." The Maryland delegation is notable, too, because one of its signers, Charles Carroll, was the only man to include the town of his origin. He identifies himself as "Charles Carroll of Carrollton."

He was also the only Roman Catholic to sign the document.

The Carrolls had already lived in Maryland for more than a century. The first Carroll to arrive there, Daniel in 1659, served as the colony's first attorney general. Maryland had been founded as a refuge for Catholics from England. But a 1704 law, designed to "prevent the growth of Popery in this Province," denied Catholics the right to vote, practice law, or hold government office. The family turned to business and made a fortune and grew numerous. Charles Carroll included his hometown in his signature because he was proud of his origins (the town was named after his family) but also because he had to distinguish himself from other prominent relatives who shared his name.

As a Catholic, Carroll felt the sting of injustice more keenly than most of his neighbors. Very early on, he became involved in the cause of independence. His religious affiliation occasionally made him valuable to his compatriots. He was chosen to accompany Benjamin Franklin on a mission to persuade the Québécois to join the lower colonies in rebellion. But the Continental Congress had earlier chided King George III for allowing the Catholics in Québec to enjoy free exercise of religion. Of course the mission failed.

By the time of the Revolution, anti-Catholicism was already, as historian Robert Lockwood puts it, part of North America's "cultural inheritance." The very first line in *Of Plymouth Plantation*, written by William Bradford in 1630, speaks of "the gross darkness of popery which had covered and overspread the Christian world." Almost all the colonies had laws restricting the practice of the Catholic faith.

After the Revolution, Rome assigned Charles Carroll's cousin John Carroll to serve as the new nation's first bishop. John was extremely sensitive to his countrymen's suspicions about Catholicism. For that reason, among others, he petitioned Rome in 1787 to allow US Catholics to celebrate Mass in English. The request was denied.

The new archbishop's patriotic credentials should have been unquestionable. He had been associated with the cause of independence from the beginning. His brother was the only man to sign both the Constitution and the Articles of Confederation. And his cousin Charles was one of his closest friends.

But the prejudice persisted. John Carroll regularly had to speak up against movements to establish Protestantism as the United States' official religion. In the century that followed there would even arise an anti-Catholic political party, the Know-Nothings, and occasionally its members would foment riots and destroy Church property. As late as 1960, presidential candidate John F. Kennedy had to persuade voters that he could indeed be a faithful Catholic and loyal American.

For More

Robert P. Lockwood. *Anti-Catholicism in American Culture*. Huntington, IN: Our Sunday Visitor, 2000.

Russell Shaw. *Catholics in America: Religious Identity and Cultural Assimilation from John Carroll to Flannery O'Connor*. San Francisco: Ignatius Press, 2016.

Eighteenth-century model of a guillotine, now at the Musée Carnavalet in Paris. Photo by LindaMarieB / iStockphoto.com.

71

The Guillotine

Beheading machines had been in use for centuries, but the guillotine was by far the simplest, most efficient, and most mercifully quick. It was designed as a response to a proposal by physician Joseph Ignace Guillotin for reform of the methods of capital punishment.

Dr. Guillotin wanted the death penalty to be administered in a more humane way. Before the French Revolution, the sentence was carried out differently depending on the criminal's social class. Nobles were beheaded, and ordinary people were hanged. Either method, though, could take a long time. Since beheadings were carried out by executioners wielding a sword or an ax, the force of the blow depended upon the strength of the individual. It might take several attempts before the executioner cut through. Hanging, similarly, was unpredictable.

Guillotin wanted the experience to be uniform and dispassionate. If death was to be the object, then it should be accomplished as quickly as possible, without torture. All criminals should be treated uniformly, regardless of social class. And the criminal's family should not be humiliated in any way.

The intentions were noble, though they could be most ignobly applied. At the height of the post-Revolution Reign of Terror (1792–1794), it's likely that more than a hundred thousand died this way. Daily executions became spectacles of mass entertainment as great crowds gathered. Vendors sold programs with the names of scheduled victims. Others sold refreshments.

At the start of the Revolution, no one would have predicted that the guillotine would be used for the extermination of Catholics. Most of France was at least nominally Catholic, and the country—known as the "eldest daughter of the Church"—had negotiated special privileges from the pope.

But the revolutionaries wanted absolute assurance of loyalty, and Catholics, especially the clergy, were suspect because of their fealty to authorities other than the state. In November 1790 France's National Constituent Assembly required all members of the clergy to swear an oath of loyalty to the new constitution. Around half of the priests complied with the Assembly. The other half was removed from their positions. Later laws identified clergy as "enemies of liberty" and treasonous. In 1794, almost a thousand priests were penned up in a filthy prison camp on the Ile Madame in the River Charente, where they were fed starvation rations. Hunger and typhus killed 254 of them.

The most famous martyrs of the Revolution were the Carmelite nuns of Compiègne. Sixteen of them were beheaded in July 1794. At the guillotine they renewed their vows and sang hymns.

Just two weeks later, the Reign of Terror would effectively come to an end when its mastermind, Maximilien Robespierre, was himself ushered to the guillotine, a victim of the climate of fear he himself had created.

The revolutionaries' program of de-Christianization continued, but without success. The replacement religions proposed by the state fell flat. The most sophisticated was Theophilanthropism, a religion based on goodness, niceness, and (of course) loyalty to the state. It seems silly now. But for a brief time, the great Cathedral of Notre Dame was dedicated to its cause.

For More

William Bush. *To Quell the Terror: The Mystery of the Vocation of the Sixteen Carmelites of Compiègne Guillotined July 17, 1794.* Washington, DC: ICS Publications, 1999.

Henri Daniel-Rops. *The Church in an Age of Revolution, 1789–1870.* New York: Image Books, 1967.

A brooch pin from the time of Pope Pius VII. From the collection of Fr. Richard Kunst,
Papal Artifacts. Photo by John Latour.

72

Symbols *of the* Papacy

This ordinary brooch bears a tiny mark—not to identify its maker but to celebrate an event. Pressed into the smallest space are two symbols of the pope's office: the crossed keys and the papal tiara. Artists and jewelers in the Papal States used this as their mark, beginning in 1814, when Napoleon Bonaparte finally released Pius VII, the *second* pope he had abducted.

After the disaster of the French Revolution, the reign of Napoleon in France was seen by Catholics as a liberating improvement. He rose to prominence as a military leader, as France, in the midst of its own Revolution, declared war on many nations, first in Europe but then stretching to Egypt.

Napoleon's power grew with his victories. He seemed to be the unifying leader who could restore order to France's post-revolutionary chaos.

He cared little for religion, but he recognized its social value. Nuns do a better job of staffing hospitals and orphanages than state employees do, and they do it much more cheaply.

But geopolitics was another matter. Pope Pius VI had aligned the Papal States with France's enemies—a category that, by then, included many of the nations of Europe. When a French diplomat was murdered in Rome, Napoleon seized the moment and invaded, imposing humiliating terms on the pope. When the pope refused to accept the terms, the French took him prisoner and carted him off over the Alps to France. Pius was eighty-two years old and in poor health. He died, and his body was embalmed but not buried for months. It was returned to Rome in 1802 and finally received a Catholic funeral, attended by his successor, Pius VII.

The new Pius seemed better able to negotiate with Napoleon. They came to agreement on procedures for naming bishops and the regularizing of the French clergy, which had been in disarray since the Revolution.

But business was business, and Napoleon remained peevish about Rome's relations with France's adversaries and the pope's refusal to recognize Napoleon's authority over Rome. The pope insisted that his office necessitated independence from external control.

The situation infuriated Napoleon, but he recognized that he needed the Church for peace at home. The rural peasants had been much more cooperative with the military draft since Napoleon had distanced himself from the policies of the blasphemous revolutionaries. It was a delicate operation.

But in 1809 Napoleon took the Vatican, and his men decided it would be a good idea to kidnap Pius VII. What followed was slapstick comedy. French soldiers snuck into the Vatican in the wee hours guided by a disgruntled ex-employee. He showed them the pope's bedroom window, and the men positioned their ladder—but it cracked and broke, loudly, under the weight of the kidnappers. This roused the guard on duty, who fled when he saw the size of the kidnapping cohort. The French soldiers went on a spree and tore up the place. The pope somehow retained his dignity, dressed, and flanked by cardinals, walked to his audience hall to receive the visitors officially—before they led him off as their captive.

Napoleon saw this as his great opportunity. He would have the imprisoned pope crown him as emperor, evoking the long-ago precedent of Charlemagne. Pius refused, so Napoleon crowned himself.

Napoleon held him captive till 1814, when the pope returned to Rome, amid great rejoicing—evident even in the city's jewelry and stickpins.

When eventually Napoleon fell, as emperors often do, Pius gave shelter in the Vatican to members of the Bonaparte family, including Napoleon's mother, brothers, and uncle. When Napoleon asked to see a priest, it was Pius who sent one.

For More

Lewis Rayapen and Gordon Anderson. "Napoleon and the Church." *International Social Science Review* 66, no. 3 (Summer 1991): 117–127.

Andrew Roberts. *Napoleon: A Life*. New York: Penguin, 2015.

This rock marks the foundation of the US Catholic school system, as it was favored by St. Elizabeth Ann Seton for her catechetical instruction. Photo courtesy Seton Shrine, Emmitsburg, Maryland.

73

Seton Rock

The rock itself sits on Catoctin Mountain in Emmitsburg, Maryland. Upon this rock once sat St. Elizabeth Ann Seton. A marker nearby tells the story: "Here on Sunday afternoons Mother Seton 'seated on a rock known as hers,' taught Christian doctrine to the children of the mountain parish." The marker then eulogizes her with a verse from scripture: "They that instruct many to Justice shall Shine as the Stars for all Eternity" (Dn 12:3).

St. Elizabeth is often called the founder of the US parochial school system, and that system is one of the marvels of history. At its peak in the 1960s the system served more than 5.2 million students in almost 13,000 schools (according to the National Catholic Education Association).

There had always been some form of Catholic education in America. Spaniards who colonized with Columbus brought priests and tutors for their children's schooling. In 1606, Franciscans opened a school in what is now St. Augustine, Florida. A parish school opened in Philadelphia in 1783. But by founding a religious order whose mission was education, Mother Seton introduced the possibility of a far greater program.

She started with one school. A widow and a mother of five, Elizabeth was looking for a way to support her family. By her conversion to the Catholic faith, she had alienated herself from her family and social circle. She considered moving to French Canada, where Catholics were dominant and opportunities greater, but a Sulpician priest invited her to start a school near the newly founded Mount St. Mary's College in Maryland. In 1810 the St. Joseph's Academy and Free School opened its doors. Elizabeth established a religious order for the running of the school and called them the Sisters of Charity of St. Joseph's. It was the first order for women to be founded in the United States, so she soon received interest from many women who had been waiting for such an opportunity.

Meanwhile, in nearby Baltimore, an African-American woman, Mary Elizabeth Lange, was helping to found a school for the children of Haitian immigrants. The school opened in 1813; in 1829 Mary Elizabeth founded a religious congregation, the Oblate Sisters of Providence, for the purpose of educating black children.

Soon many parishes were establishing schools, and other groups of sisters appeared, some arriving from Europe while others founded new orders to fill the need. The success of Catholic schools was evident in the lives of alumni—of all races and ethnic backgrounds, including Native American tribes. Anglo-Americans who were disposed to anti-Catholicism saw these new schools as cause for alarm. By mid-century, Know-Nothing (see chapter 70) mobs were burning convents and tarring and feathering priests.

But the school system continued to grow. The Catholic bishops encouraged its growth because US public schools used the Protestant King James Bible for instruction and otherwise favored Protestant customs and doctrine. In 1866 the bishops, at the Plenary Council of Baltimore, pledged to organize effective Catholic schools in every diocese. In 1884 the Third Plenary Council of Baltimore went further still, saying, "All Catholic parents are bound to send their children to the parochial schools," when parochial schools are available. They went on to add that every parish should strive to establish a school.

The anti-Catholic opposition persisted, and in the twentieth century tried even to make public school education mandatory. Cases went to the Supreme Court, and Catholic schools managed to survive. So what began with Mothers Seton and Lange became an educational force unprecedented in history.

For More

Thomas C. Hunt et al., eds. *Handbook of Research on Catholic Education*. Westport, CT: Greenwood, 2001.

Timothy Walch. *Parish School: A History of American Catholic Parochial Education from Colonial Times to the Present*. New York: Crossroad, 1995.

The confessional where St. John Vianney spent much of his adult life. Photo by Cardinal Sean O'Malley.

74

A Confessional

This sturdy piece of church furniture—a wooden confessional booth—was as much a home to St. John Vianney as any room in his parish rectory. Every year, tens of thousands of people traveled to his remote rural parish to make their confession there.

John was born just before the French Revolution, in 1786, and in the social upheaval that followed his education was spotty at best. His parents hoped he would grow up to do his share of farm work as they had done. Yet he discerned a vocation to "win souls for the good of God" and to do so as a priest.

Getting into seminary was a long shot. He had difficulty with learning and memorizing. His Latin was abysmal—and the seminary courses in theology were taught in Latin. His studies were also interrupted by a draft notice. Summoned to serve in Napoleon's army, when he missed the appointment to leave with his military unit he had to go into hiding to avoid punishment as a deserter.

He somehow made it through minor seminary and was sent on, but the major seminary dismissed him in short order for poor grades. The vicar general of the diocese intervened, however, and had John reinstated. He was ordained a priest on August 12, 1815.

The bishop played it safe. He assigned John to be sole priest at a remote rural parish in the village of Ars. His church had 230 members and was notable only for its religious indifference. The bishop warned the young priest: "There is not much love of God in that parish."

John rose to the occasion. He labored over his homilies, preparing each one by exhaustively researching the theological and spiritual issues involved. He worked long into the night. He taught catechism classes.

But it was in the confessional that he shone. People went to Ars, said St. John Paul II, for the opportunity of "meeting a saint, amazing for his penance, so close to God in prayer, remarkable for his peace and humility in the midst of popular acclaim, and above all so intuitive in responding to the inner disposition of souls and in freeing them from their burdens, especially in the confessional."

First, word spread through his little parish. Lives were changed, and homes grew happier. Then word spread beyond and then far. Pilgrims came from all over France, first a few and then very many. Eighty thousand came in 1858 alone. The trains had to accommodate the priest's popularity by adding a stop in the middle of nowhere. The local government had to accommodate the trains by building a new station. People sometimes waited for days in line to go to his confessional.

Fr. John Vianney established Ars as a pilgrim destination. In the following century he would be declared patron of parish priests.

His life stands as a symbol of what God can do with apparently meager gifts. From the bottom of the seminary graduating class came the model for all the parish priests of the world. From the ashes of the French Revolution came a Church that was vibrant and ready for mission.

For More

George William Rutler. *The Curé D'Ars Today: St. John Vianney*. San Francisco: Ignatius Press, 1988.

John Paul II. *Letter to Priests for Holy Thursday 1986: The Curé of Ars*. Vatican City: Libreria Editrice Vaticana, 1986. http://w2.vatican.va/content/john-paul-ii/en/letters/2004/documents/hf_jp-ii_let_20040406_priests-holy-thursday.html.

A writing table at the house of Bl. John Henry Newman. Photo by Fr. Gaurav Shroff.

75

Cardinal Newman's Desk

This writing table rests by a window in a cottage in the village of Littlemore, near Oxford, England. Bl. Domenic Barbieri offered the Holy Sacrifice of the Mass at this table. But it was, most of the time, consecrated to another sacred work.

The table belonged to John Henry Newman, a most prolific author. His collected works fill thirty-one volumes, and they hardly account for all of his writing.

Newman was involved in controversy from when he was very young. Born in 1801, he was raised in a devout home in the Evangelical (or "Low Church") Anglican tradition. While in graduate school at Oxford, however, he met intellectuals who challenged his Evangelicalism. Eventually, he came to embrace the sacramental and ecclesiastical views of the "High Church" wing of Anglicanism. With his friends he established the Oxford Movement, which promoted doctrines and practices associated with the ancient Catholic faith. Newman undertook an exhaustive study of the Greek and Latin Fathers.

The Oxford Movement drew intense opposition. Their theological battles often began on campus and spilled over into the more popular newspapers and magazines. Eventually, Newman was pressured to stop teaching. But that left him more time for writing.

In 1832 he went with friends on a tour of southern Europe and became gravely ill. In Sicily he came close to dying. Recovery gave him a renewed sense of mission. He believed God had preserved him for some special purpose.

Once home, he and his associates launched a series of provocative tracts. Their arguments became much more impassioned—and more public. Newman continued his studies of the early Church and gradually came to the conclusion that the great Fathers would not have tolerated the kind of doctrinal deviation that had taken place among England's Christians since the Reformation. For a while he toyed with the idea that Anglicanism was a "middle way" between Protestantism and Roman Catholicism. But in 1845, as he finished his massive *Essay on the Development of Christian Doctrine*, he felt compelled to conclude that "of all existing systems, the present communion of Rome is the nearest approximation in fact to the Church of the Fathers. . . . Did St. Athanasius or St. Ambrose come suddenly to life, it cannot be doubted what communion he would take to be his own."

He was received into full communion by an Italian Passionist priest, Dominic Barberi, in 1845. This turned out to be the midpoint of his life. He had many productive years ahead as a priest and the founder of an oratory but especially as a writer and a friend. He kept close ties with his former colleagues and maintained a letter-writing apostolate that was best described by author George William Rutler:

> [Newman] dipped an unfettered pen in his inexhaustible well of charity and wrote kindly of friend and foe, esteeming the merits of his former allegiance and his adopted Catholicism with elegant judiciousness; and when he laid down his pen forty-five years later, it is roughly estimated that his personal contact had converted 636 noblemen, 700 clergymen and 1100 of their children and wives, 700 professionals, 800 writers and artists, 612 young men who became priests, 164 young women who became nuns, besides the numberless worker to whom he devoted so much of his attention as teacher and confessor.

His influence on Catholic thought is incalculable. His ideas about doctrinal assent, Catholic education, and historical theology shaped the minds of great theologians of the twentieth century, not least Pope Benedict XVI, who declared Newman "Blessed" in 2010.

For More

Ian Ker. *John Henry Newman: A Biography*. New York: Oxford University Press, 2010.

George William Rutler. *Beyond Modernity: Reflections of a Post-Modern Catholic*. San Francisco: Ignatius Press, 1987.

Marble statue of Bl. Pius IX at prayer. Photo by TasfotoNL / iStockphoto.com.

76

The Marble Figure *of* Bl. Pius IX

It is a larger-than-life-sized statue in a confined space, so this marble figure of Bl. Pius IX, sculpted by Ignazio Jacometti, dominates the crypt chapel of Rome's Basilica of St. Mary Major. Pius was a man of intense Marian devotion, and it was he who commissioned the construction of the chapel to be dedicated to the relics of the manger of Jesus' birth.

In worldly terms, Pius IX was a man much diminished by the events of his lifetime. In political and military terms, he was defeated and reduced, withdrawn into his small remaining territory as a "prisoner of the Vatican." And yet he had an outsized effect on subsequent history.

At thirty-one years, his pontificate was the longest since that of the Apostle Peter. He served from 1846 until his death in 1878. In Europe and abroad, it was a time of revolutions and resurgent nationalism. Italy itself—sharply divided by region—was experiencing a strong popular movement toward unification: *Il Risorgimento*, it was called, "The Resurgence." As ruler of the Papal States, Pope Pius was at first warm to the idea, and he worked to reform the government of his territories. But eventually he grew suspicious of revolutionary movements. Still, *Il Risorgimento*, led by Giuseppe Garibaldi, surged on and eventually, in 1870, captured Rome.

By then, Pius had already astonished Catholics with his boldness. In 1854 he defined as dogma the Immaculate Conception of the Virgin Mary. It had long been enshrined in devotion and endorsed, implicitly or explicitly, by saints and theologians. But it had also been challenged by no less an authority than St. Thomas Aquinas. Pius consulted the world's bishops on the matter, and some advisors told him the time was not right for such a provocative statement. But he pressed on.

He also convened the ecumenical council Vatican I, which defined the doctrine of papal infallibility:

> We teach and define as a divinely revealed dogma that when the Roman Pontiff speaks *ex cathedra*, that is, when, in the exercise of his office as shepherd and teacher of all Christians, in virtue of his supreme apostolic authority, he defines a doctrine concerning faith or morals to be held by the whole Church, he possesses, by the divine assistance promised to him in blessed Peter, that infallibility which the divine Redeemer willed his Church to enjoy in defining doctrine concerning faith or morals. Therefore, such definitions of the Roman Pontiff are of themselves, and not by the consent of the Church, irreformable. (*Pastor Aeternus* 4.9)

Again, this was bold language—though the power it described was strictly limited.

Pius was not afraid of provocation; and neither, apparently, were his bishops. In 1864, he issued yet another bombshell: his *Syllabus of Errors*, a document condemning various propositions from then-current political and philosophical thought.

In the eyes of the world, Pius lost his shoving match with modernity. Garibaldi inexorably took the Papal States and installed the king who would rule all of Italy from the ancient capital of Rome. The council was suspended, and Pius withdrew. He made no public appearances outside the Vatican.

Most Catholics looked upon these events as a catastrophe. Temporal power, they believed, was the pope's guarantee of freedom. As long as popes had ruled central Italy, they were subject to no one and—theoretically, at least—free from undue influence by worldly concerns.

But a strange thing happened. Now that the popes were no longer associated with geopolitical strategies, their moral stature increased. Their voice became more credible. They were, in fact, more free than they had been before.

For More

E. E. Y. Hales. *Pio Nono: A Study in European Politics and Religion in the Nineteenth Century.* New York: P. J. Kenedy, 1954.

James J. Hennesey. *The First Council of the Vatican: The American Experience.* New York: Herder and Herder, 1963.

Bottles used to transport water from Lourdes, France. Photo courtesy University of Notre Dame Archives.

77

Holy Water Bottles

Construction workers found these glass bottles in 2016 while digging a utility trench at the University of Notre Dame. Archivists called to the scene saw the great number of bottles, all intact and carefully buried, and knew the likely story. They had been used in the late nineteenth century to transport holy water from Lourdes, France. Once emptied of their contents, they could not be thrown out with ordinary trash. Like any blessed item, they had to be destroyed or buried. They were buried on campus, to bear their witness more than a hundred years later.

"Lourdes water" was something new at that time but already in great demand because of its reputed healing power. Pilgrims were making their way to the little village and reporting miracles when they bathed in the spring there or drank from its waters.

Lourdes had—in just a few years' time—become the third most popular Catholic pilgrim destination in the world after Rome and the Holy Land.

In 1858, a poor fourteen-year-old girl named Bernadette Soubirous was pasturing sheep when she had a series of visits from a woman beautifully dressed in white. The woman identified herself as "the Immaculate Conception." Bernadette had no social standing or influence. Nonetheless, the woman told her to "go and tell the priests to build a chapel here" and "have the people come here in procession."

It seemed an outrageous request and not only because of Bernadette's poverty and ignorance. The pasture was used by villagers as a trash dump.

But there was a groundswell of response from villagers and the nearby countryside, and soon pilgrims came from far away. The local bishop bought the land in 1861, three years after the visions, and official Church approval came the following year.

Soon afterward came reports of miraculous cures experienced by people who bathed in or drank water from a spring on the land—a spring the Virgin had led Bernadette to discover.

Soon great throngs were visiting Lourdes every year. Since 1858 almost a quarter of a billion pilgrims have made the journey to Lourdes. Probably tens of thousands have claimed to be cured. Around 7,000 have submitted their cures for rigorous investigation by the Medical Bureau of Lourdes. Of those, only sixty-nine have been certified as miracles by the Church.

The twentieth-century novelist Flannery O'Connor, who suffered from lupus, made pilgrimage to Lourdes and experienced some relief. She was even able to put aside her crutches for a while. But she thought the real miracle of Lourdes was the charity it inspired. She said she was inclined there not to pray for herself but for the others she saw, who were much worse off than she was.

For those who have not been able to come to the water, the water has been brought home or shipped out in bottles. Today's containers are more likely to be plastic than glass.

For More

Kerry Crawford. *Lourdes Today: A Pilgrimage to Mary's Grotto*. Ann Arbor, MI: Servant Books, 2008.

Jacques Perrier. *Lourdes for Today and Tomorrow*. Hyde Park, NY: New City Press, 2008.

A page-turner and its case, for use with Pope Leo XIII's revised Roman Missal. From the collection of Fr. Richard Kunst, Papal Artifacts. Photo by John Latour.

78

A Parchment Page-Turner

This is no ordinary bookmark. It was crafted to hold and turn the heavy parchment pages of the Roman Missals that belonged to Pope Leo XIII. Its use was a matter of ceremonial dignity but also a practical consideration. The acids in human sweat could cause the deterioration of the pages. It was better to leave all contact to the ivory instrument.

The books were newly revised, after all. In the years 1884–1886 Leo instituted a few minor changes to the liturgy. He added what would be called the Leonine Prayers to the end of every Mass. At the foot of the altar, the priest (sometimes joined by the congregation) would recite three Hail Marys, a Salve Regina, and prayers to the Sacred Heart of Jesus and St. Michael the Archangel. These prayers were the prescribed ending for all Masses from the 1880s until 1965.

When first mandated, these prayers were to be offered for a special intention: the temporal sovereignty of the Holy See, which had been severely challenged during the reign of Leo's predecessor, Bl. Pius IX.

After thirty-two years of Pius, some of the cardinals wondered whether it was a good thing for a pope to rule so long. So they elected a man already quite old at sixty-eight, and they elected a man quite different from Pius.

But they failed in their prognostications. Leo would reign for a long time—a quarter-century, until his death at ninety-three. Though Pius remained the longest-reigning pope since Peter, Leo would finish his years in second place.

Leo did not suffer the distractions of invading armies as Pius did, and so he was free to concentrate on teaching and administration. He issued eighty-five encyclical letters during his pontificate. Often, his encyclicals focused on particular social issues. He advocated for the universal abolition of slavery. He spoke up about the plight of Italian immigrants to other countries. He wrote letters on religious freedom, socialism, the family, education, dueling, and human liberty, among many other topics. He revived the study of St. Thomas Aquinas as the Church's quasi-official theologian, and he ordered the production of a complete edition of the great Dominican's works.

Leo was the first pope to publish memoirs. In the United States his book was issued in 1887 by Samuel Clemens and sold door-to-door by peddlers.

He was the first pope in centuries *never* to have ruled over the Papal States, and he showed how much a pope could accomplish once free from the burdens of secular government.

Leo was a more cerebral man than his predecessor. He took a keen interest in emerging trends in social thought. In his first class of cardinals (1879) was the Englishman John Henry Newman, a convert and a leading-edge intellectual. Where Pius tended to withdraw, Leo was likely to engage.

Still, he was not naïve about the dangers afoot in his day. He promoted devotion to St. Michael the Archangel, heaven's warrior in the battle against Satan, and Leo himself composed several prayers to St. Michael. Leo died in 1903; afterward rumors abounded that he had once received a vision of the twentieth century, and he saw it as a time of unprecedented evil.

If the story is true, he never spoke of it publicly, and there is no evidence he did so privately, though he did live to turn the calendar page to a new century.

For More

Bernard O'Reilly. *Life of Leo XIII: From an Authentic Memoir*. New York: Charles L. Webster and Co., 1887.

Robert Quardt. *The Master Diplomat: From the Life of Leo XIII*. Staten Island, NY: Alba House, 1964.

Union membership pin, 1903. Photo by Susan Brown.

79

Union Membership Pin

This pin proclaims membership in the United Textile Workers of America. It was still a risky thing to wear a union pin in public in 1903 when this was made, but a growing number of Americans were doing it—and Catholics among them did so with encouragement from their Church.

In 1903, this particular union was only two years old, born from the merger of several earlier collectives. Even with that combined negotiating power, it failed to draw membership that was truly representative of the industry. Most textile laborers then were immigrants to the United States; the union, however, never succeeded in claiming more than 10 percent foreign-born membership.

Unions were a tough sell. Laborers didn't enjoy working in dangerous conditions for low wages, but they didn't want to take the chance of alienating their employer by joining a union. A dangerous job was better than no job. Sometimes, too, factory owners resorted to violent intimidation.

Societies were trying to figure out how to adjust to the Industrial Revolution. It began, in the eighteenth century, with advances in the efficiency of mining methods. Metals and coal were suddenly available in abundance. Resourceful minds figured out how to harness those resources for machinery of mass production. Overnight, it seemed, certain trades became obsolete. All of a sudden, it seemed, other skills were increasingly in demand to make the machines—along with "unskilled labor" to work the machines. In search of work, families moved from farms to cities and from one country to another. Workdays could run as long as the machines could run.

Since so many Catholics were in the burgeoning American workforce, parish priests and bishops were intensely aware of the problems faced in the mines, fields, and factories. Parishioners were strongly attracted to groups such as the Knights of Labor, an early attempt to unionize, but some members of the hierarchy were put off by its secrecy. The bishop of Québec suspected the Knights were just another brand of Freemasonry and so should be off limits to Catholics. Cardinal James Gibbons of Baltimore petitioned Rome in defense of the Knights, explaining that their secrecy was necessary for the safety of members. He won a hearing with Pope Leo XIII.

The pope, in time, produced a landmark text, the encyclical letter *Rerum Novarum* (1891), affirming the rights of workers to form unions—and yet rejecting ideologies such as Communism, just emerging, which encouraged strife between social classes.

By encouraging Catholic participation in unions, *Rerum Novarum* helped to make possible the phenomenal growth of the labor movement in the decades that followed. Many union leaders of the twentieth century—Cesar Chavez, for example, and Lech Wałęsa—would cite the profound influence of Leo XIII.

Other "social encyclicals" would follow, often released on significant anniversaries of *Rerum Novarum*. Leo's manifesto remains a landmark in social thought, critical of both socialism and capitalism but positive and synthetic in its vision and presentation.

For More

Mike Aquilina. *The Social Doctrine of the Catholic Church*. Chicago: Midwest Theological Forum, 2013.

Kevin E. Schmiesing. *Within the Market Strife: American Catholic Economic Thought from Rerum Novarum to Vatican II*. Lanham, MD: Lexington Books, 2004.

The Global Village

Catholic thinker Marshall McLuhan coined the term "Global Village" to describe how the world has been shrunk by communications technology and motor travel. The process began with the telegraph and newspapers and still moves forward by way of social media and the World Wide Web. Media have brought about instant communication among distant peoples. Technology has raced forward, working near-miracles in medicine. And yet the same technology has made possible horrific efficiencies in genocide and warfare. In the Global Village, wars were no longer local; they were world wars. The Church shared the joys and the hopes, the griefs and the anxieties of this age.

Locks of love: hair shorn from St. Thérèse as she entered the Carmelites. Photo by Fr. Gaurav Shroff.

80

St. Thérèse's Curls

Thérèse left these long blond curls behind to become a Carmelite nun. Her hair had been her pride and joy. As a small child, her father loved to see her in curls, and so her older sisters combed and dressed her hair every single day. They loved grooming Thérèse so much that she reached the age of eleven and was still unable to use a comb.

When she was fourteen, she told her father of her desire to enter the convent, as three of her sisters had already done. She petitioned for early admission but was refused. On pilgrimage to Rome, she begged Pope Leo XIII to allow her to enter, but he said the decision belonged to the Carmelite superiors. Thérèse had to be carried away, still pleading, from the pope's presence.

Later, she met with her local bishop. Preparing for the meeting, she put up her hair, trying to make herself look older. The bishop eventually gave the Carmelite superiors permission to receive Thérèse as a postulant.

Ordinarily, a young woman's hair would have been cut upon her entering the convent. But her superiors chose not to do this. Because she was so young, they thought she might not persevere and so should be left unshorn for her possible return to the world.

Soon afterward she persuaded her sister Pauline, who was also a nun in the convent, to cut her hair off as a "sacrifice for Jesus." The hair is on display today in the bedroom where Thérèse slept as a child.

Thérèse did persevere in the Carmel of Lisieux, and hers was an ordinary, uneventful life, from all appearances. She worked in the refectory. She recited and sang her prayers. She followed the rules.

She tried to offer small sacrifices throughout the day. She tried to befriend sisters who were socially awkward and whom she found, actually, to be off-putting. She wrote letters of encouragement to missionaries in far-off places.

She tried to do all these little things with extraordinary love. In a memoir she wrote toward the end of her life, she explained her approach.

> For me to become great is impossible . . . but I will seek out a means of getting to heaven by a little way. . . . We live in an age of inventions; nowadays the rich need not trouble to climb the stairs, they have elevators instead. Well, I mean to try and find an elevator by which I may be raised up to God, for I am too tiny to climb the steep stairway of perfection.

She found many confirmations of this idea in her reading of scripture, both the Old Testament and the New. She found it confirmed as well by her experiences, which she wrote about in her memoir, published many years later as *Story of a Soul*.

In 1896, when she was twenty-three years old, she contracted tuberculosis. She continued writing during her illness, which lasted a year and a half. She died in 1897, unnoticed by the world and found unremarkable by most of the nuns in her convent.

Her sisters preserved her *Story* and edited it. The book was first published in 1898 and soon sold millions of copies. It influenced most of the spiritual leaders and movements in the century to follow, from Josemaría Escrivá and Opus Dei to Dorothy Day and the Catholic Worker. Thérèse's "little way" became the "invention" she wished it to be, a spiritual technology accommodating a great, diverse, and very modern crowd.

For More

John Clarke, trans. and ed. *Story of a Soul: The Autobiography of St. Thérèse of Lisieux.* Washington, DC: ICS Publications, 1996.

John Clarke, trans. and ed. *St. Thérèse of Lisieux: Her Last Conversations.* Washington, DC: ICS Publications, 1977.

R. Morul
R. Langénieux
R. Gibbons
R. Rampolla ///////////////////////////// (29
R. Richard
R. Goossens
R. Gruscha
R. Di Pietro)
R. Logue
R. Vaszary
R. Perraud
R. Kopp
R. Lécot
R. Sarto //////////// (10
R. Sancha y Hervás
R. Svampa
R. Ferrari
R. Gotti ///////////////// (17
R. Casañas y Pagés
R. Manara

Counting votes in the 1903 papal election. From the collection of Fr. Richard Kunst,
Papal Artifacts. Photo by John Latour.

81

A Ballot *from* *the* Conclave *that* Elected Pius X

This ballot and scrutiny sheet should have been destroyed. Papal conclaves—the meetings of the cardinals to elect a pope—are carried out in utmost secrecy; all papers are required to be burned. But somehow these sheets survived and reside today in a private collection. The tallies clearly show that the man who became pope in 1903, Cardinal Giuseppe Sarto, the Patriarch of Venice, was actually a distant second in the voting. Cardinal Mariano Rampolla, the Vatican secretary of state under Leo XIII, was the clear winner.

Church law at that time granted certain monarchs veto power in papal elections—and, to everyone's surprise, a Polish cardinal exercised the veto on behalf of the Austro-Hungarian emperor Franz Joseph. In the ballots that followed, the cardinals abandoned Rampolla and turned to the man from Venice.

It was a decisive turn. Cardinal Sarto was a man of peasant stock. He held no advanced degrees. He differed in significant ways from his aristocratic predecessors. In style, in emphases, and in expression, he would distinguish himself from his predecessor. He took as his unofficial motto "To Restore All Things in Christ," an echo of Acts 3:21 and a theme that appears often in the letters of St. Paul. And he did see his work as a recovery of things that had been lost.

Pius X was especially concerned about religious ignorance and about the heresies emerging from modern thought.

Even as pope he took time to teach catechism to children, and he required such instruction to be established in every parish. He believed that doctrine should be taught in simple, everyday language. He himself published a catechism to serve as a model.

But he worried about certain new trends in theology and philosophy. His predecessors, for many years, had expressed similar concerns. Bl. Pius IX issued the *Syllabus of Errors*; Leo XIII identified the heresy of "Americanism," a certain indifference and individualism in matters of religion. Pius came to consider many recent trends under the common heading of "modernism." And modernism, he said, was more than just another heresy. It was "the synthesis of all heresies."

Some prominent thinkers were willing to accept the label. A French priest and scholar, Fr. Alfred Loisy, wrote that modernists were united by "the common desire to adapt Catholicism to the intellectual, moral and social needs of today." To some, modernism seemed more a mood than a movement—a smug dismissal of tradition, authority, and the supernatural and an exaltation of political theory and scientific hypotheses over holiness.

In 1907, with the encyclical *Pascendi* and subsequent decree *Lamentabili*, Pope Pius X officially condemned modernism. Before long, Fr. Loisy was excommunicated, as was the Irish priest George Tyrell, who had been expelled from the Jesuit order. Others charged with modernism—Baron Friedrich Von Hügel, Maurice Blondel, and Fr. Henri Brémond—remained in the Church's graces, though with lingering suspicion from the hierarchy.

A group of overly zealous anti-modernists established an informal network of censors called the *Sodalitium Pianum*—the Pius Society. Its members carried out cloak-and-dagger investigations of teachers, writers, prelates, and simple priests who had the misfortune to fall under someone's suspicion. They would denounce people anonymously without a fair hearing. Pius had no oversight of the *Sodalitium*, but he never acted to curtail it, either.

Intellectual histories tend to emphasize the "Modernist Crisis" in their treatment of Pius's pontificate. This is not altogether just: it was important to him but not defining. His aspirations were ambitious and his achievements rather remarkable. (See more in the following chapter.) Pius brought about sweeping reforms in canon law. He had a warm personality and was beloved by Catholics worldwide. His cause for sainthood was launched shortly after his death in 1914, and he was canonized in 1954.

For More

Raphael Merry del Val. *Memories of Pope Pius X*. Westminster, MD: Newman Press, 1951.

Marvin R. O'Connell. *Critics on Trial: An Introduction to the Catholic Modernist Crisis*. Washington, DC: Catholic University of America Press, 1995.

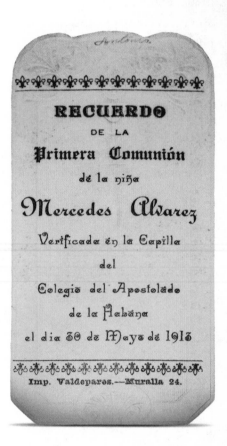

A card commemorating a little girl's First Communion from Havana, Cuba, in 1913. Photo by Susan Brown.

82

First Communion Card

"Here is the gift of God's tenderness," reads the front of this card; "here is the response of Jesus' love to our love."

The card is a "remembrance of the First Communion of the little girl Mercedes Alvarez" in Havana, Cuba, on May 13, 1913.

The card, the sentiments, and the youth of the girl as she went up for Holy Communion probably struck some people as a novelty. Not even three years had passed since Pope Pius X published his decree on First Communion.

In *Quam Singulari*, in 1910, he urged parents and pastors to admit children to the sacrament at an early age; in doing this he was bucking the trend of centuries. Parishes had, in fact, been taking an increasingly cautious approach, delaying First Communion till the later teens or early adulthood.

Pius dismissed these measures with the strongest language. "Such precautions," he said, "proceed from the errors of the Jansenists, who contended that the Most Holy Eucharist is a reward rather than a remedy for human frailty." He also urged that pastors "should announce and hold a General Communion of the children once a year or more often."

Pius intended to recover the ancient Church's understanding of the Eucharist as nourishment and medicine. Not only did he advocate an early initiation but also he encouraged frequent Communion—even daily, if possible. In the decree *Sacra Tridentina* (1905) he confidently expressed "the desire of Jesus Christ and of the Church that all the faithful should daily approach the sacred banquet."

He blamed any countervailing scruples, again, as ill effects of "the widespread plague of Jansenism."

These were bold and radical changes, with profound implications that caused no little anxiety among those who had erred on the side of caution. These were mostly clergy, who feared that familiarity with the Eucharist would breed contempt—or at least carelessness. Pius, on the contrary, hoped that early and frequent Communion would inspire people to make even greater efforts to avoid sin and give them the grace they needed to succeed.

In intellectual circles, Pius would be remembered (with rue or with approval) as the anti-modernist pope (see previous chapter). But among ordinary people he was "the pope of early communion" and "the pope of frequent communion."

In some countries, these changes marked a seismic shift in the Church's practice—and certainly a great difference in individual lives.

Then came the small-sized suits and ties, the dresses and veils, the cards of remembrance, like that of Mercedes Alvarez in Cuba—and the great festivities.

For More

Josef Andreas Jungmann. *Handing on the Faith: A Manual of Catechetics*. New York: Herder and Herder, 1962.

John Wright. *First Confession and First Communion*. Vatican City: Congregation for the Clergy, 1980. http://www.vatican.va/roman_curia/congregations/cclergy/documents/rc_con_cclergy_doc_07121980_fconf_en.html.

A pen belonging to Pope Benedict XV, who became known as the "Pope of Peace." From the collection of Fr. Richard Kunst, Papal Artifacts. Photo by John Latour.

83

Pope Benedict XV's Fountain Pen

He used this pen often as he advocated for peace.

It was Cardinal Giacomo della Chiesa's cross to be elected pope at the onset of the First World War. The electors chose a relatively young man, at fifty-nine, strong enough to weather the storm that everyone saw coming.

More importantly, they chose an experienced diplomat who had worked for years in the Holy See's State Department.

He chose the name Benedict XV and declared from the start the Holy See would remain neutral—in spite of tremendous pressure to follow the lead of newly unified Italy. Nonetheless, the predominantly Protestant nations suspected him of favoring the Catholic nations—and the Catholic nations resented his meddling.

In his first encyclical letter, *Ad Beatissimi Apostolorum*, he described in most moving terms "the sad conditions of human society . . . perhaps the saddest and most mournful spectacle of which there is any record."

> On every side the dread phantom of war holds sway: there is scarce room for another thought in the minds of men. The combatants are the greatest and wealthiest nations of the earth; what wonder, then, if, well provided with the most awful weapons modern military science has devised, they strive to destroy one another with refinements of horror. There is no limit to the measure of ruin and of slaughter; day by day the earth is drenched with newly-shed blood, and is covered with the bodies of the wounded

and of the slain. . . . Yet, while with numberless troops the
furious battle is engaged, the sad cohorts of war, sorrow
and distress swoop down upon every city and every home;
day by day the mighty number of widows and orphans
increases, and with the interruption of communications,
trade is at a standstill; agriculture is abandoned; the arts
are reduced to inactivity; the wealthy are in difficulties;
the poor are reduced to abject misery; all are in distress.

This was the first large-scale war to employ weapons of large-scale
destruction: bombs, tanks, machine guns, and mustard gas. Benedict saw
the most advanced nations tumbling after one another into barbarity—
returning, he said, to paganism in their lust for power.

He proposed a peace plan in 1917 that was favored by some nations
but rejected by Germany and the United States, two principal opponents
in the conflict. Several elements of his plan, however, were included in the
war's eventual settlement.

Though he failed to achieve his primary aim, he succeeded in other
major efforts. He brokered exchanges of severely wounded prisoners of
war, especially those who were left crippled by mustard gas. He also negotiated the safe transport of civilians who were trapped behind battle lines.

Most importantly, Benedict succeeded in demonstrating the true neu-
trality of the Church in international relations. With no territory to lose
or gain by war, he was free to speak only for justice. He established what
would be the Church's role in a new, emerging world order.

Benedict worried about the stockpiling of arms and foresaw that the
situation would lead, in the future, to the proliferation of hostilities. He
called the Great War a "useless massacre" and "the suicide of civilized
Europe."

He blamed the situation not on world leaders but on the ineffectiveness
of the Church's preachers, who had failed to communicate a sense of the
supernatural and the desirability of virtue.

He set his pen down for the last time in January 1922.

For More

Ashley Beck. *Benedict XV and World War I: Courageous Prophet of Peace.* London: Catholic Truth Society, 2014.

John F. Pollard. *The Unknown Pope: Benedict XV (1914–1922) and the Pursuit of Peace.* London: Bloomsbury, 1999.

Blunderbuss pistol owned by Armenian leader Garo Sassouni and taken with him into exile. Photo courtesy Chris Sassouni.

84

A Weapon *against* Genocide

It was already an antique when he first held it, a powder-loading flintlock used for hunting game in Armenia's mountains. But Garo Sassouni carried this ancient pistol with him as he fought the genocidal squads sent out by the Turks. He carried it when he fled the Soviets. Even when he reached safety in Lebanon, he kept it in his apartment.

Though he was born into a wealthy family, he gave his life to service, first teaching in village and regional schools and then going on to study law in Constantinople. His passion was for the Armenian people, their cultural identity, their Christian religion—all of which the Turks systematically tried to destroy.

The Armenian Genocide (1894–1923) was part of the Ottoman Empire's program to achieve racial and religious purity within its vastly shrunken borders. The empire had become coterminous with Turkey, and the Armenians represented the largest non-Turkish, non-Muslim population in the land. Once the Armenians had been reduced, their lands to the east could easily be annexed.

The Turks began with military raids on Armenian villages in 1894–1896, but the program began in earnest in 1915 with a purge of Armenian intellectuals and leaders. Garo Sassouni was exiled, but he eventually made his way back to his homeland. He would serve the Independent Republic of Armenia as a member of parliament and a provincial governor.

But the Turkish genocidal program was now in full force. The government emptied prisons to create special "butcher squads" for the liquidation of Christians. Armenians were raped, crucified, starved, and made to march naked. Garo's mother was burned alive in a cage. Other members of his family were shot at point-blank range.

The Armenians pushed back as they could. Garo's political party, the Armenian Revolutionary Federation, met in churches with the encouragement of the bishops. Most of the people were members of the Armenian Apostolic Church, but there were many Catholics as well as Protestants. They all fought together.

In a sense, they fought alone. World War I was raging all through Europe, and Western nations were not eager to take part in yet another "local" conflict. Armenian diplomats issued repeated pleas for assistance—or even simple recognition of what was happening. The newspapers hardly took notice. The nations were silent.

Against the might of the Ottoman military, and with no assistance from abroad, the Armenians could put up little in the way of defense. The Turks were relentless, and by the middle of the 1920s more than a million and a half Armenians were dead. Millions more were living in exile. The Armenian Catholic patriarch has, since then, governed from Beirut, Lebanon.

Decades later, when German dictator Adolf Hitler was planning his own genocidal program, he looked to the Armenian Genocide as a model. And he expressed admiration for the thoroughness of the Turks. He asked, rhetorically, "Who, after all, speaks today of the annihilation of the Armenians?" Hitler wanted to be as "successful" in purging the Jews as the Turks had been in eliminating Armenian Christians.

Until 2010 the United States government gave no official recognition to the Armenian Genocide. Turkey has never acknowledged responsibility. When Pope Francis made reference to the genocide in 2015, Turkey withdrew its envoy to the Vatican. That year Pope Francis marked the centennial of the twentieth century's "first genocide" with a Mass at the Vatican. At the same time he named St. Gregory of Narek, a tenth-century Armenian monk and poet, as a Doctor of the Church.

For More

Peter Balakian. *The Burning Tigris: The Armenian Genocide and America's Response.* New York: Harper, 2004.

Ronald Grigor Suny. *"They Can Live in the Desert but Nowhere Else": A History of the Armenian Genocide.* Princeton, NJ: Princeton University Press, 2015.

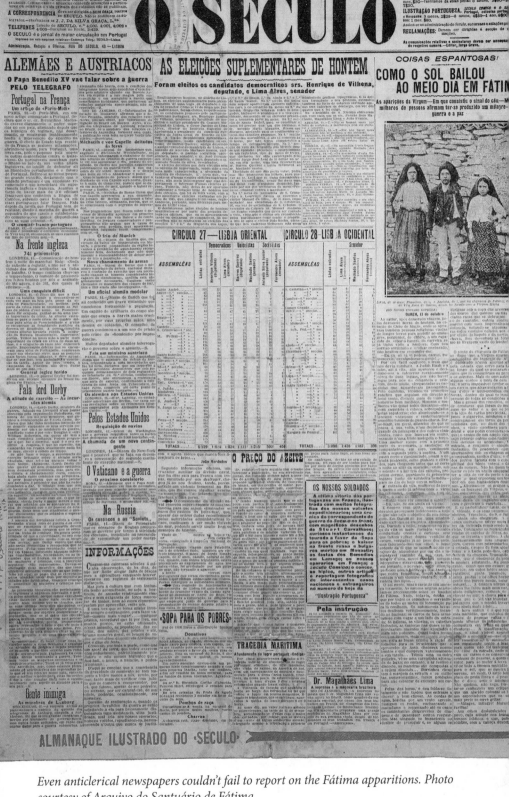

Even anticlerical newspapers couldn't fail to report on the Fátima apparitions. Photo courtesy of Arquivo do Santuário de Fátima.

85

A Newspaper Headline

The editors at Lisbon's daily *O Século* had a reputation for being anticlerical, but they knew a good story when they saw one. The apparitions of the Blessed Virgin Mary, reported in nearby Fátima, were front-page news. Three children—Lúcia dos Santos and her cousins Jacinta and Francisco Marto—had, since May, claimed to see the Virgin and speak with her on the thirteenth day of every month.

People were skeptical. Even the children's parents punished them severely. But they reported in July that the Virgin would vindicate them in October with a miracle that would be visible by all.

When the day arrived, tens of thousands of people gathered at the field where the children reported meeting the Virgin. It was raining, the sky was thick with clouds, and the ground was mud. Then, according to the testimony of many witnesses, the clouds parted to reveal the sun, which "trembled" or "danced." The phenomenon was seen from twenty-five miles away.

Few events of the twentieth century would have so profound an impact on the popular imagination of Catholics worldwide. A preacher could speak the name "Fátima" and evoke the entire content of the messages in his hearers. The words of the Virgin were apocalyptic. She made predictions shrouded in symbolic language that invited multiple interpretations. She spoke of current events—the world war and the revolution in Russia. And she seemed to forecast a century of horrors. She also told the children three "secrets," which they would not reveal to the public but only to their bishop (and later the pope).

The nature of these revelations excited the popular imagination. And events afterward seemed to bear out the accuracy of the Virgin's predictions. The two younger seers, Jacinta and Francisco, died in an epidemic the year after the events, just as the Virgin had said they would. The third, Lúcia, entered a Carmelite convent of the strictest observance, dying there at age ninety-seven. Since none of the children ever profited from their celebrity—or ever retracted a word of their claims—their lives and deaths seemed to confirm the authenticity of their visions.

The Church provided confirmation, too, but slowly. The local bishop approved the visions after thirteen years of investigations. Pope Pius XII approved them for the universal Church in 1940 and afterward invoked Our Lady of Fátima in his own public statements.

Speculation about the meaning of Fátima—and the content of the "secrets"—grew more feverish as the century wore on, and its wars and weapons grew more monstrous. As the turn of the millennium approached, conspiracy theories abounded, and Fátima was fast becoming a cottage industry for fear-mongers. In order to dispel the widespread speculation, the Vatican, in June 2000, released the four-page text of Sister Lúcia's account of the third secret, the only one that remained unrevealed. Appended with the document was an official interpretation by the head of the Vatican's Congregation for the Doctrine of the Faith, the man who would later be Pope Benedict XVI. He assured the public that many of the terrifying predictions had come to pass and there was no extraordinary cause for alarm.

The message of Fátima, he said, was a call not to spectacles, secrets, and fear but to conversion, prayer, and penance—none of which, alas, make for front-page news.

For More

Andrew Apostoli. *Fátima for Today: The Urgent Marian Message of Hope.* San Francisco: Ignatius Press, 2012.

Joseph Ratzinger. *The Message of Fátima*. Vatican City: Congregation for the Doctrine of the Faith, 2000.

Soviet propaganda poster from the early 1920s. From the collection of Fr. Douglas Grandon.

86

A Poster *of the* Russian Revolution

This poster, first hung in 1920, proclaims in Russian, "Comrade Lenin Cleans the World of Filth." And there he is: Bolshevik leader Vladimir Lenin sweeping away two monarchs, an industrialist, and a priest, all of them grown fat by stealing from the poor.

Communism may have been godless, but it had its demons, and religion ranked high among them. Karl Marx, who cowrote *The Communist Manifesto*, called religion "the opium of the people." He looked forward, he said, to its abolition.

Marx called for a thoroughgoing "criticism of religion," which would lead people to "give up a condition that requires illusions."

After the Russian Revolutions of 1917 (there were two, not one), Lenin undertook that work of criticism, using the tools of propaganda: slogans and caricatures. Posters typically portrayed the clergy in an unflattering light. But they also mocked Jesus—shown blessing the guns of murderous troops. They depicted bishops conspiring with capitalists to enslave the working class. They showed Christian believers as frumpy old biddies lighting candles while attractive young atheists smirked at them. "Religion is poison," declared one poster, "Protect children from it."

But religious people were the ones who would need protection under communist regimes. When government criticism didn't work—when the people proved reluctant to give up their "illusions"—the Soviets turned to active persecution. And as more client states were added to the constellation of communist lands, the repression became more severe.

The Soviets shut down the Eastern Catholic Churches in Ukraine, Czechoslovakia, Poland, and Romania. They executed hundreds of thousands of clergy and millions of lay people. It is often difficult to tell whether an individual was killed for his religious or political views. Christians presented the most effective arguments against Communism, and such arguments could be prosecuted as treason. Conservative estimates place the number of Christians martyred by the Soviets at fifteen to twenty million.

Lenin's successor, Joseph Stalin, did not bother denying the mass killings. Nor did he deny the substance of his propaganda campaigns. In a now-famous public speech he laid out his rationale in a series of dogmatic statements:

> We conduct propaganda and we shall conduct propaganda against religious prejudices. . . . The party cannot remain neutral with respect to religion . . . because it stands for science, and religious prejudices go against science, for all religion is contrary to science.

Later propaganda regularly portrayed religion as the *opposite* of science: the strong young cosmonaut beside a hunched old priest dressed in black or a shiny new health clinic beside a crumbling old church. In a poster from 1965 a woman drops her religious icons into the trash as she watches a rocket on her television screen. The caption beams: "The bright light of science has proven there is no God!"

Sixty years after the revolution, it was clear to everyone that the economic experiment had failed. In 1979 a pope, for the first time, visited a communist country, Poland. At the capital, Warsaw, more than a million people crowded the public square to see Pope John Paul II. Someone shouted, "We want God!" And soon the chant was taken up by the million voices: "We want God. We want God. We want God."

Within fifteen years, the people at last could truly give up a condition that required illusions. It wasn't religion.

For More

Paul Froese. *The Plot to Kill God: Findings from the Soviet Experiment in Secularization.* Berkeley: University of California Press, 2008.

Robert Royal. *The Catholic Martyrs of the Twentieth Century: A Comprehensive World History.* New York: Crossroad, 2006.

The view from the radio-transmission booth of Old St. Patrick's Church in Pittsburgh, Pennsylvania. Photo by Derris Jeffcoat.

87

A Hole *in the* Wall

From this rectangular slot, a sound engineer watched the progress of the Mass and quietly narrated for those tuning in at home.

In 1925 the radio was a new invention. Sets were expensive, and relatively few people owned them. It had only been five years since KDKA, the world's first commercial radio station, had first begun broadcasting from Pittsburgh, Pennsylvania.

The owners of WJAS, a station based in Johnstown, Pennsylvania, reasoned that Catholic listeners would appreciate a regularly programmed Sunday Mass for shut-ins. So they asked Fr. James Renshaw Cox, a Pittsburgh priest, for permission to install equipment for the transmission of his regularly scheduled liturgy.

Fr. Cox did more than okay the idea. He saw its potential for evangelization. He carefully crafted homilies that would reach people who could not see the posture, gesture, or facial expressions of the preacher. He recognized that everything depended on his voice.

The response was tremendous. WJAS's signal reached far and donations poured in to Fr. Cox from all over the United States—and from Catholics, Protestants, and Jews. A year later, another priest, Fr. Charles Coughlin, began to broadcast from WJR in Detroit.

Fr. Cox's fame grew. His on-air homilies reflected his interests. He was a World War I veteran who worried about the plight of his fellow vets. He held a master's degree in economics, and he voiced urgent fears about an impending crash. When the crash came in 1929, thousands of people, including many veterans, found their way to his parish, Old St. Patrick's in Pittsburgh's warehouse district, and camped on his property. Fr. Cox became the unofficial mayor of the city's "Hooverville"—the slang term for a homeless camp, named for then-president Herbert Hoover.

In 1932 Fr. Cox led 25,000 unemployed men, gathered through radio appeals, in a march on Washington, DC. Soon he was nominated as a presidential candidate in the election that year.

Fathers Cox and Coughlin were not the only Catholics to predict the evangelistic power of the new medium. Radio as we know it was based on the patents of another Pennsylvania priest, Fr. Jozef Murgaš of Wilkes-Barre, Pennsylvania, who made the first wireless voice transmissions in 1905. As early as 1925, the Vatican began drawing up plans for its own wireless station. Radio's inventor, Guglielmo Marconi, a convert to the Catholic faith, arranged and personally introduced the first radio broadcast of a pope, Pius XI, in 1931. In his discourse, the pontiff punned wildly from scripture: "Listen, O heavens, to that which I say; listen, O Earth, listen to the words which come from my mouth. . . . Listen and hear, O peoples of distant lands!"

Marconi then established Vatican Radio, which the pope eventually entrusted to the Jesuit order. In the decades to come, it broadcast hope— and uncensored news—to people suffering in lands dominated by Nazism and Communism.

For More

Alan Brinkley. *Voices of Protest: Huey Long, Father Coughlin, and the Great Depression.* New York: Knopf, 1982.

Kenneth J. Heineman. *A Catholic New Deal: Religion and Reform in Depression Pittsburgh.* University Park: Pennsylvania State University Press, 1999.

Tools of the auto-repair trade, embossed in the glass at the tomb of Bl. Salvador. Photo by Rafael Piña Valdez.

88

Bl. Salvador Huerta
Gutiérrez's Tools

He is known for dying as a martyr. But Bl. Salvador Huerta Gutiérrez earned his *living* with tools—wrenches, pliers, and screwdrivers—like these etched on his tomb. He was an automobile mechanic when automobiles were still a new invention. He had a reputation for the excellence of his work—and for his honesty. His employees knew that he could tolerate behavior that was rough but never blasphemy. His tomb today displays the tools of his trade encased in glass.

Salvador lived in the midst of an undeclared war, and the souls of his countrymen were the battlefield. Mexico's constitutions had been anti-Catholic, and especially anticlerical, since the 1850s. In the revolution that raged from 1910 to 1920, the dominant parties came to resent and fear the challenges of the Catholic Church. In successive constitutions, the laws regarding religion became increasingly restrictive. Mexico became an officially atheist state.

At first Mexican Catholics tried nonviolent resistance and civil disobedience. In 1926, Catholic groups circulated a petition for constitutional reform and got two million signatures. When that didn't work they began a boycott against the government and refused to use public transportation or attend movies and plays. But their peaceful efforts were met with violence, and nothing changed. So they decided it was time to fight back. They took up what weapons they had and began to capture smaller towns one by one.

The government did its best to scare the inexperienced volunteer soldiers—*Cristeros*, "Christ's army," they called themselves. Priests were executed, and as many as 30,000 Cristeros were killed. They weren't given an easy death, either. Rebels were often tortured, either to obtain information or in an attempt to get them to renounce their faith.

One day Salvador returned home to find policemen waiting for him. They brought him back to the station, under the pretense that they needed him to fix a car. Once there, they tortured him by hanging him by his thumbs and demanded that he tell them the whereabouts of certain priests. Salvador refused to betray his comrades, and the next day he was executed. Even as they prepared to shoot him, he called out praise to God and the Blessed Mother.

Salvador Huerta Gutiérrez was one of many ordinary Catholics who became soldiers and martyrs during the Cristero war. They were not professionally trained for combat. They took up what weapons they could find and even found ingenious ways to make weapons of their own. The women of the Feminine Brigades of St. Joan of Arc made grenades out of tin cans and also smuggled secret messages by writing them on strips of silk and hiding them in their shoes.

Although the rebels weren't strong enough to overcome their adversaries, their constant fighting became a strain on the government. Eventually, restrictions on public worship were relaxed and the Church was promised its buildings and schools back.

The Mexican government was spotty at best in keeping its promises. Some churches and schools were returned, but not all. Every now and then there would be another execution. Cristero veterans were still being killed into the 1950s. The anticlerical laws remained almost to the end of the twentieth century. A new constitution in the 1990s restored to the clergy, among other things, the right to vote and the freedom to wear clerical garb in public.

For More

David C. Bailey. *¡Viva Cristo Rey! The Cristero Rebellion and the Church-State Conflict in Mexico.* Austin: University of Texas Press, 1974.

Jean A. Meyer. *The Cristero Rebellion: The Mexican People between Church and State, 1926–1929*. London: Cambridge University Press, 1976.

Souvenirs from a celebration: the liberation of the pope and the creation of Vatican City State. From the collection of Fr. Richard Kunst, Papal Artifacts. Photo by John Latour.

89

Mussolini-Era Ribbons *and* Pins

Italians, especially in Rome, wore these pins to celebrate. The pin at the top right bears the images of Fascist dictator Benito Mussolini, Pope Pius XI, and Italy's King Victor Emmanuel III. Another displays only the image of the pope. A third features the pontiff's coat of arms and the colors of the Italian flag (now a bit faded).

There was plenty of cause for celebration that year. It was the fiftieth anniversary of Pius's ordination to the priesthood. More importantly, it was the year of the ratification of the Lateran Treaty, the agreement that created the Vatican City State as an independent country existing within the city of Rome.

Since 1870 the popes had claimed sovereignty, but that claim went unrecognized by the country that surrounded the Apostolic Palace. Thus the popes were trapped—essentially prisoners of the Vatican. With the treaty of 1929 the popes could begin to celebrate Mass again in the Roman churches. Pius celebrated his anniversary with Mass at St. John Lateran on December 20 that year. It was the first time a pope had openly set foot in Rome since 1870.

In his newly crafted sovereign state, the pope ruled over 530 subjects in the 356 acres surrounding St. Peter's Basilica. But the creation of the city-state raised questions in the minds of anti-Catholic bigots abroad. In the United States, some Protestants raised again the question of the loyalty of Catholic citizens. Would they now owe dual allegiance to the foreign monarch? Since there were now twenty million Catholics in America, should this be cause for alarm? Catholics urged Congress to settle the question by recognizing the sovereignty of the Vatican. Others lobbied for Congress not to recognize the Vatican. The United States did not have official diplomatic relations with the Holy See until 1984.

Pius XI reigned amid the tumult of the Great Depression and the rise of totalitarian ideologies that were hostile to religion. Catholics were persecuted, to varying degrees, in Germany, Mexico, Spain, and the Soviet Union. His strategy was to use diplomacy to ensure the safety and guarantee the rights of his flock in every country. His concordat with Italy worked to the Church's advantage. After difficult negotiations, he arrived at terms with Nazi Germany as well. Hitler, however, routinely disregarded the agreement, and in 1937 Pius wrote an encyclical letter, *Mit Brennender Sorge*, detailing the abuses. It was read aloud from German Catholic pulpits on Palm Sunday that year. Hitler's secret police, the Gestapo, raided all the churches the following day.

An early challenge to the Italian concordat came in 1938 when the Fascist government enacted laws forbidding marriage between Jews and non-Jews. The Vatican objected, citing the Lateran Treaty and claiming the exclusive right to regulate Catholic marriages. The Italian government backed down and agreed to recognize the validity of any marriage witnessed by Catholic clergy.

Pius's strategy is debated to this day. Is it right and is it useful to negotiate with despots? The pins and ribbons, which celebrate Pius and Mussolini together, have proven to be bad for public relations. Pius's reputation has suffered, and anti-Catholics have used the concordat to accuse the Church of giving a virtual imprimatur to dictatorships.

But the concordats—and the freedom they negotiated—made possible the survival of thousands who found refuge in the Vatican in the years that followed.

For More

Frank J. Coppa. *Controversial Concordats: The Vatican's Relations with Napoleon, Mussolini, and Hitler*. Washington, DC: Catholic University of America Press, 1999.

Peter Eisner. *The Pope's Last Crusade: How an American Jesuit Helped Pope Pius XI's Campaign to Stop Hitler.* New York: William Morrow, 2013.

*The security gate at Auschwitz extermination camp. Photo by YMZK-photo /
iStockphoto.com.*

90

A Concentration Camp Sign

Polish political prisoners made this sign in 1940. Its motto, *Arbeit macht frei*, means, roughly, "Work sets you free."

The sign is wrought iron, sixteen feet long, and it arches over the gates of the notorious concentration camp run by the Nazis at Auschwitz, Germany.

The slogan was first raised up in another camp, at Dachau, and later copied at other sites. It was taken from a nineteenth-century moralistic novel about redemption through work. The camps, after all, were built for labor, places where prisoners could be rehabilitated for a useful life in Hitler's Reich.

But soon after construction, most of the facilities at Dachau and Auschwitz were repurposed for mass extermination. The signs stood as a cruel joke to those who were brought there to die. An estimated 1.5 million people died at Auschwitz, most of them Jews. Auschwitz was only one of many sites—a total of 42,500 camps and ghettos—where between fifteen and twenty million people were imprisoned and killed during Hitler's regime.

Hitler intended to rid the world of his enemies—the Jews first of all but then many others. Baptized a Catholic, he had little religious upbringing and no use whatsoever for the Church. He considered Christianity in general to be a religion that was fading away. Yet the most effective resistance he encountered came from Catholics. The fuhrer was infuriated by Pius XI's orchestrated effort to have his anti-Nazi letter read from German pulpits. A Catholic aristocrat, Claus von Stauffenberg, organized an assassination plot that nearly succeeded. Pius XII also used his weekly radio addresses to hammer away at Nazi ideology. Hitler, like many totalitarians, suspected Catholics because of their international ties and networks—and what seemed to him a divided allegiance. He doubted their readiness to put the Fatherland first, before the concerns of their religion.

Many of his victims were conscientious Christians. The Nazis hanged Dietrich Bonhoeffer, a Lutheran pastor and dissident. Bl. Franz Jägerstätter, an Austrian Catholic, was beheaded for refusing to serve in the military. Many priests and religious were interned. Bl. Odoardo Focherini, an Italian Catholic, was caught smuggling Jews over the Swiss border; he died in the camps. In Dachau alone, 2,720 clerics were imprisoned and 1,034 died. Bl. Titus Brandsma, a noted Dutch Carmelite and journalist, died there.

Among the most famous Christian martyrs of the Reich are a priest and a nun: St. Maximilian Kolbe and St. Teresa Benedicta of the Cross (known in the world as the philosopher Edith Stein). Both died at Auschwitz.

In the aftermath of World War II, the Catholic Church generally—and Pius XII particularly—received praise. Pinchas Lapide, Israel's consul in Italy, said, "The Catholic Church saved more Jewish lives during the war than all other churches, religious institutions, and rescue organizations put together." He added, "The Holy See, the nuncios, and the entire Catholic Church saved some eight hundred thousand Jews from certain death." The World Jewish Congress donated about $20,000 to Vatican charities in thanks for the pope's rescue efforts. Golda Meir, the future prime minister of Israel, told the United Nations, "When fearful martyrdom came to our people in the decade of Nazi terror, the voice of the Pope was raised for the victims. The life of our times was enriched by a voice speaking out on the great moral truths above the tumult of daily conflict."

In spite of all the evidence, the Soviet Union made a concerted effort, in its propaganda, to cast Pope Pius as Hitler's willing accomplice. The smear was remarkably successful, influencing the pontiff's depiction in plays, movies, novels, and even academic histories.

Recent years, however, have seen Pius's vindication among historians. In 2004 David G. Dalin, a rabbi and historian, published a collection of "responses to the critics of Pius XII." In 2016 the BBC apologized for airing a documentary that charged the Church and Pius with "silence" in the face of the Holocaust. After reviewing the matter, the BBC released a statement admitting that its reporter "did not give due weight to public statements by successive popes or the efforts made on the instructions of Pius XII to rescue Jews from Nazi persecution, and perpetuated a view which is at odds with the balance of evidence."

Pope Benedict XVI declared Pius XII venerable in 2009.

For More

Mark Riesling. *Church of Spies: The Pope's Secret War against Hitler.* New York: Basic Books, 2015.

Ronald J. Rychlak. *Hitler, the War, and the Pope*, rev. ed. Huntington, IN: Our Sunday Visitor, 2010.

French medal honoring philosopher Jacques Maritain. Photo by Susan Brown.

91

The Maritain Medal

The French mint Monnaie de Paris struck this bronze medal in the 1970s to honor one of the country's great men of the twentieth century.

Jacques Maritain was not a typical hero. He never fought in a war or ruled in a government. He was a philosopher—a trade that presents a particular challenge for a medallic artist, whose "canvas" is very small and who must traffic in easily recognized symbols.

Maritain appears here as a strikingly handsome man, youthful but with aged eyes. The prominent eyes, with the high forehead and the hint of a beard, signify wisdom.

The Latin inscription on the reverse makes the connection explicit. It is, in fact, from the Bible's book of Wisdom: *in se ipsa manens innovat omnia*—"remaining in herself, she [wisdom] renews all things" (7:27).

White-haired and dapper, Maritain cut a striking figure on the world scene in the mid-twentieth century. He ranged in his work across disciplines, producing theoretical works on art, politics, history, and knowledge itself. The home he shared with his wife, Raïssa, became a salon—attracting great cultural figures such as the filmmaker Jean Cocteau, the painter Marc Chagall, and the novelist Julien Green.

Maritain and his wife converted to Catholicism in 1906 and were fervent in their faith. They evangelized not through proselytizing but through friendship. The English title of Raïssa's memoir is *We Have Been Friends Together*.

By the outbreak of World War II, Maritain had achieved the rare status of celebrity intellectual. Since Raïssa's background was Jewish, the couple was especially vulnerable when the Nazis occupied France. They fled as refugees to the United States, where Maritain taught at Columbia

University, Notre Dame, and finally at Princeton's prestigious Institute for Advanced Study, where his colleagues were Albert Einstein and Kurt Gödel, among others.

He cared intensely about France, Europe, and what he saw as the rapid disintegration of social order in his lifetime. He lectured widely and published many books. In the years following World War II, world leaders called upon Maritain as they met to form the United Nations. He served as an influential advisor during the drafting of the UN's Universal Declaration of Human Rights.

John Humphrey, the man who prepared the first draft of the UN's Universal Declaration of Human Rights, later recalled that Maritain helped provide the theoretical foundation for the document, introducing the traditional Catholic notion of the natural law that dictates natural rights. It was Catholicism's conceptual framework that enabled people from vastly different perspectives to converge and come to an agreement.

Maritain also exercised a strong influence on the Catholic intellectuals who applied themselves to the problems of European reconstruction after the war. Of the seven men usually called "Founders of the European Union," five were Catholic.

These statesmen, like their mentor, promoted neither laissez-faire capitalism nor communism. Their aim was to create a peaceful and tolerant society, based upon Europe's Christian heritage, but respectful of those who adhered to other religions. Their philosophy provided the intellectual core of the Christian Democratic movement. The influence of these men also shows in the governing document of the European Union, the Treaty of Maastricht, which uses the language of Catholic social thought—terms such as *solidarity* and *subsidiarity*, which entered political discourse by way of the social encyclicals of popes.

As the bronze medal declares, wisdom like Maritain's, rooted in divine truth, has the power to renew all things. The passage from the book of Wisdom says still more: "In every generation [wisdom] passes into holy souls and makes them friends of God, and prophets."

The twentieth century marked an age of ideology and war—a time when political theories predominated and small points of theory could claim millions of human lives. Against such an age, Maritain arose indeed as a prophet and a friend of God.

For More

Jean-Luc Barré. *Jacques and Raïssa Maritain: Beggars for Heaven.* Notre Dame, IN: University of Notre Dame Press, 2005.

Raïssa Maritain. *We Have Been Friends Together.* South Bend, IN: St. Augustine's Press, 2016.

The Second Vatican Council was the first ecumenical council that offered parking passes such as the one above. From the collection of Fr. Richard Kunst, Papal Artifacts. Photo by John Latour.

92

Vatican II Parking Pass

From October 1962 to December 1965, this was one of the most valuable items in Rome. The streets were not built to accommodate the automobile traffic they had to endure while the Second Vatican Council was in session. At a typical session, 2,200 bishops were in attendance. Some of them came with a retinue of *periti* (experts) to advise them on theological matters. Almost a hundred observers attended from other Christian communities. And then there was the press. Everyone needed a parking space.

Vatican II, as the council was popularly known, was the first held in an age of mass media. Never before in history had commentators been able to provide real-time analysis of the discussions of bishops in session. Never before could Catholics in Taiwan or San Francisco hear daily news of a council as it happened.

From car traffic to press coverage, Vatican II was like no council that had gone before. For one, it had the largest attendance—with nearly three times the number of bishops who had attended Vatican I in 1870. Air travel made it easy for bishops from far-off lands to come and go.

The council was unique also because it was not provoked by a crisis. Most previous councils were called to deal with an emergency or a catastrophe—a heresy, a schism, a political upheaval. Vatican II was not. In fact, its agenda was first proposed in 1948 to Pius XII, who intended to follow up but never made it a priority. Other matters required more urgent attention. His successor, Bl. John XXIII, announced shortly after his coronation that he would convene the council.

The sessions were portrayed in the popular press as a death match between liberals and conservatives, who lined up on easily identifiable teams. But the truth is more complicated, more intricate, and more beautiful. If it must be broken down to two components, they could be identified as *ressourcement* and *aggiornamento*.

Ressourcement is the French term used to describe the trend in theology, in the decades leading up to Vatican II, to return to the sources. The biblical movement promoted interest in the scriptures. The patristic movement examined the early Church Fathers. And the liturgical movement studied the variety of the Church's rites through history and throughout the world. All of these movements exerted a profound influence at the council.

Aggiornamento was a word introduced to the discussion by Pope John. Literally, it means "todaying," and it suggests an openness to new intellectual currents in the world. Many theologians were trying to engage modern thought on its own terms—to speak in a language people today could understand.

But it's not as if *ressourcement* and *aggiornamento* represented different factions. Some of the most influential thinkers of the period—Henri de Lubac, Yves Congar, Hans Urs von Balthasar—were profound scholars of the early Church and yet at the forefront of the movement called *nouvelle théologie* (new theology). They wanted to make sure it was truly the ancient faith they were bringing into the language and categories of life today. The result was a stunning synthesis of new and old.

Alas, that's not what made the headlines. And it's not what most people noticed in the aftermath. Ordinary Catholics fixated on the changes they could see. The council had called for a reform of the liturgy, and the men charged with implementation took "reform" to mean an overhaul. So the Mass suddenly looked and sounded very different. The priest was facing the people. The prayers were in the vernacular, not Latin. New hymns sounded a lot like the songs on the radio. To some folks this was invigorating; to others it was horrifying.

There were overhauls, too, of the Church calendar, the feasts, and the lectionary of readings for the Mass. And these got some notice in the press.

The real message, however, was often obscured. One of the youngest bishops participating in the council was Karol Wojtyła of Krakow, Poland. From the time he was elected pope in 1978, he returned repeatedly to the documents of Vatican II. He boiled its message down to one radical phrase: "the universal call to holiness" (see John Paul II, *Christifideles Laici* 16 and Vatican II, *Lumen Gentium*, chapter 5). God calls everyone, without exception, to be a saint.

For More

Matthew L. Lamb and Matthew Levering. *Vatican II: Renewal within Tradition.* New York: Oxford University Press, 2008.

Joseph Ratzinger. *Theological Highlights of Vatican II.* Mahwah, NJ: Paulist, 2009.

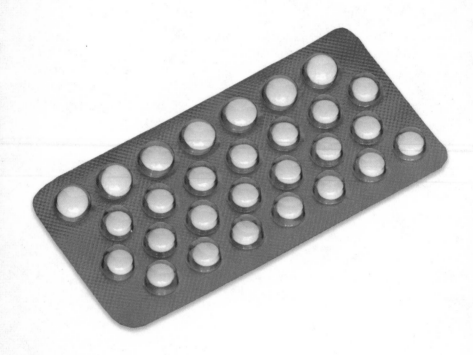

The Pill altered body chemistry, changed the family, and helped bring on a "demographic winter." Photo courtesy Christina Dickerson.

93

The Pill

These tiny pills pack a lot of power—and not only hormonal power. The oral contraceptive popularly known as "The Pill" has the power to change society and culture and ignite a revolution more sweeping than those of the French and Russians combined.

The Sexual Revolution has deeper roots. Sexologists and advocates such as Margaret Sanger and Havelock Ellis were, in the early 1900s, promoting the idea of sex removed from its traditional setting. Societies had universally, if tacitly, understood sex to be best reserved for lifelong marriage between a man and a woman. The permanence of the bond ensured a stable setting for raising the children that normally follow after sexual relations.

Like other revolutions, this one began with declarations of independence. The sexual liberation movement sought to dissociate sex from procreation. It sought to dissociate both sex and procreation from marriage. By accomplishing these goals, it would radically redefine marriage.

Sanger institutionalized the sexual liberation movement with her founding of the American Birth Control League in 1921. The organization became Planned Parenthood in 1946. Its work went beyond the provision of contraceptives. It also campaigned for changes in law and sponsored the development of pharmaceutical methods of birth control.

Sanger found an ally in the obstetrician-gynecologist John Rock, a Catholic and daily communicant. Despite the Church's firm and constant condemnation of birth control, Rock publicly promoted it. He was more useful to the cause as he joined the faculty of Harvard Medical School in the 1940s. He wrote pamphlets and a book on the subject. But the

Church didn't budge; eventually Rock reported that he had lost his faith and stopped attending Mass altogether.

Pope John XXIII convened a special commission to study the morality of the new methods of birth control. The Second Vatican Council, meanwhile, affirmed what the Church had always taught (see *Gaudium et Spes* 51). Indeed, one of the members of Pope John's commission, Fr. John Ford, S.J., conducted exhaustive research on the subject and demonstrated that the Church had "constantly and emphatically taught that contraceptive acts are objectively grave violations of the law of God." Still, a majority of the commission's members recommended change.

Pope Paul VI took all the data into consideration in the years that followed. In 1968 his long-awaited answer appeared in the encyclical letter *Humanae Vitae*. It granted no change. It argued instead, and with clarity, for the integrity of the tradition of sexual marriage—for the place of sex within marriage—and for the great good of openness to new life.

The encyclical was met by protests from academics in the United States. Even cardinals criticized the letter publicly. At least one auxiliary bishop resigned in protest.

But seen from fifty years later, Paul's predictions read like prophecy. He warned that widespread contraception would "lead to conjugal infidelity and the general lowering of morality." He said it would increase the number of divorces, abortions, unplanned pregnancies, and sexually transmitted diseases. He said that men would objectify women and consider them to be mere instruments of pleasure. And he warned that contraception would be a "dangerous weapon" in the hands of public authorities—as would be seen, for example, in China's "one child" policy and the industrialized nations' imposition of contraceptive programs as a condition of international aid.

Many countries with high rates of contraception use, moreover, are now facing a "demographic winter," with too few children born while the elderly live longer. The little pill has proven its power—which was evident since the first clinical trials among the poor in Puerto Rico. Two of those young women, both seemingly healthy, died from strokes. The Pill remains a frequently prescribed drug in spite of its correlation with an increased risk for blood clots and stroke, breast cancer, liver cancer, cervical cancer, and depression.

Named to Pope John's original birth control commission was a young bishop from Poland who had recently published a philosophical study of sex. His name was Karol Wojtyła, and his book was *Love and Responsibility*. Two decades later, as Pope John Paul II, he would present the Church's vision of sex in a positive, holistic way in a series of addresses collectively known as the Theology of the Body.

For More

Sue Ellen Browder. *Subverted: How I Helped the Sexual Revolution Hijack the Women's Movement.* San Francisco: Ignatius Press, 2015.

Mary Eberstadt. *Adam and Eve after the Pill: Paradoxes of the Sexual Revolution.* San Francisco: Ignatius Press, 2013.

Cassette tapes were a lifeline to understanding and a sense of community. Photo by Father Richard Simon.

94

Catholic Conference Tapes

Cassettes and conferences were a spiritual lifeline for members of the Catholic Charismatic Renewal in the 1970s. They had experienced something new, and they wanted to understand what was happening to them. They yearned for interaction with others who shared their experience.

They had prayed to receive the Holy Spirit in a powerful way, and their lives afterward reflected what they called "gifts of the Holy Spirit"—the phenomena mentioned by St. Paul in his First Letter to the Corinthians (chapters 12–14). They uttered prophecy. They spoke in tongues. They practiced faith healing. They looked, for all this, like Protestant Pentecostals, with whom they often found common cause—and with whom they sometimes formed ecumenical communities.

It was new, different, and exciting—a movement arriving at a time when Catholic worship offered little opportunity for novelty or spontaneity.

Charismatic Renewal traces its beginning to a retreat in Pittsburgh, Pennsylvania, in 1967. A prayer group from Duquesne University, whose membership included students and faculty, had been reading and discussing the book *The Cross and the Switchblade* by the Protestant Pentecostal pastor David Wilkerson. While on a retreat, the group prayed that they would receive the gifts described in that book and in the description of the first Pentecost in the biblical Acts of the Apostles.

Soon members were "slain in the Spirit"—they fell rigid to the floor. Some spoke in tongues. Others received the "gift of tears" and wept abundantly for joy.

Not long afterward, a prayer group at the University of Notre Dame underwent the same experience. And charismatic prayer spread, informally, from there. In 1967 charismatic Catholics held the first of what would become annual conferences at Notre Dame. Eighty-five people attended. But the numbers would triple or double from year to year, and in 1974 the event drew 30,000. Recordings of conference speakers, distributed on audiocassettes such as these, reached many more throughout the world. In 1974, there were an estimated 1,800 charismatic prayer groups worldwide with 350,000 members, including thousands among the clergy. It has experienced explosive growth in Latin America, Africa, and Asia.

Along the way the Charismatic Renewal experimented with new forms of community, with some breaking up acrimoniously and publicly.

The prayer groups encountered suspicion and misunderstanding in the movement's early years. But leaders worked closely with the hierarchy, beginning with Cardinal John Wright in Pittsburgh, and by 1971 had received recognition from Pope Paul VI. Over time the movement acquired an institutional form, with its own official or semi-official publications and gatherings. In 2013, the Catholic Charismatic Renewal reported 160 million members worldwide. But the influence of the Renewal extends far beyond those numbers. Indeed, its effect on music, worship, and Bible study in typical parishes cannot be measured. Catholic conferences, too, have proliferated and assumed the shape, if not always the style, of Notre Dame's early efforts.

Charismatic Catholics, today, serve in the upper reaches of the Church's hierarchy, and a Capuchin priest, Raniero Cantalamessa, has been the official preacher to the papal household since 1980.

For More

Alan Schreck. *A Mighty Current of Grace: The Story of the Catholic Charismatic Renewal.* Frederick, MD: Word Among Us, 2017.

Vinson Synan. *The Holiness-Pentecostal Tradition: Charismatic Movements in the Twentieth Century.* Grand Rapids, MI: Eerdmans, 1997.

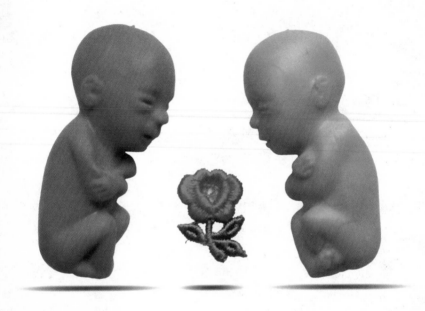

Educational aids of the pro-life movement. Items courtesy Helen Cindrich. Photo by Rosemary Aquilina.

95

Fetal Models

These fetal models, made of soft polymers, are remarkably lifelike—anatomically accurate in their rendering of a pre-born child at an early stage of gestation. The pro-life movement used these to educate the public and counter the disinformation of institutions that promoted abortion.

Abortion, according to its advocates, was simply a surgical procedure that removed a "blob of cells" from the body. It was, they maintained, no different from the extraction of a tooth or a tumor.

The pro-life movement, with mostly Catholic leadership, sought to change that perception and educate people about the obvious humanity of children at the fetal stage of human life. These models were one way in which "pro-lifers" did the job.

The Church has, since earliest times, strongly condemned abortion. Its doctrine is spelled out with clarity in the Christian documents of the first centuries. The *Didache* lists it among the characteristic practices of the "Way of Death." So does the first-century *Letter of Barnabas*; the second-century writings of Justin, Athenagoras, and Tertullian; and countless documents of the later centuries. The early Christians made no exceptions in their condemnation of the practice. Though they lived in a society where abortion and infanticide were legal and common, believers spoke up and took action to protect the most vulnerable human lives.

The modern pro-life movement coalesced as advocacy for abortion was increasing. In the wake of the Sexual Revolution, abortionists and activists seized the moment to organize and try to change laws restricting the practice in the United States. The National Association for Repeal of Abortion Laws (NARAL) was founded in 1969. In the uncertainty of the 1960s, its leaders found little effective resistance. Their rhetorical strategy (according to one of NARAL's three founders) was to dehumanize the unborn, frame the public discussion in terms of rights, freedom, and "choice"—and smear the Catholic Church as a retrograde institution that was anti-science and anti-woman. They saw the Catholic Church as their only effective opposition at that time.

NARAL saw only limited success with legislatures, at the state or national level. Most people, and most lawmakers, thought abortion should be at least restricted, if not illegal. But, by an end run around democratic process, abortion advocates succeeded. In 1973, the US Supreme Court, in its *Roe v. Wade* and *Doe v. Bolton* decisions, established abortion as a "right," effectively nullifying all restrictions in state law. And the abortion license spread rapidly through the rest of the world.

The pro-life movement mobilized. The first March for Life took place in Washington, DC, on the one-year anniversary of *Roe v. Wade*. Organized by a Catholic laywoman, Nellie Gray, the event drew around 20,000 people. It has continued to be an annual event, and estimated attendance has risen to more than half a million people annually. It is the largest annual protest in the nation's capital and has consistently been a peaceful witness.

Catholics at first dominated the pro-life movement. Abortion was seen as a "Catholic issue." In 1973, the largest evangelical organization in the country, the Southern Baptist Association, praised *Roe v. Wade* in its official publications.

But Catholics in the movement effectively reached out to other Christians and made the case for abortion as an urgent moral issue. Since 1979, the pro-life cause has been an increasingly ecumenical coalition. And the movement has, by necessity, risen to the defense of life at other stages— against the movement to legalize assisted suicide, euthanasia, and capital punishment. Beginning in 1983, Cardinal Joseph Bernardin of Chicago promoted a "consistent life ethic" and argued that these issues should constitute a "seamless garment" of concern for Christians.

Abortion advocates have come to dominate certain cultural institutions—government, medicine, higher education—but the peaceful witness and educational efforts seem to be succeeding. One founder of NARAL,

Bernard Nathanson, switched sides in the 1980s. Still identifying as an atheist, he came to believe that abortion was morally wrong. Eventually he asked to be baptized as a Catholic. At the turn of the century, a majority of younger Americans described themselves as more pro-life than pro-choice.

For More

Bernard Nathanson. *The Hand of God: A Journey from Death to Life by the Abortion Doctor Who Changed His Mind.* Washington, DC: Regnery, 2013.

Daniel K. Williams. *Defenders of the Unborn: The Pro-Life Movement before Roe v. Wade.* New York: Oxford University Press, 2016.

The site of Óscar Romero's martyrdom in San Salvador. Photo by ASSOCIATED PRESS / Luis Romero.

96
Altar *of* Sacrifice,
San Salvador

This is an altar of sacrifice—a standard feature in any Catholic church. It is the central furnishing in the church, the surface on which a priest offers Mass. What happens upon the altar at Mass is mystically united with the action of Jesus on the cross. The Lord's sacrifice is not repeated but re-presented in every time and place.

This particular altar is the focal point of the chapel of Divine Providence Hospital in San Salvador, the capital of El Salvador. At this altar, on March 24, 1980, Archbishop Óscar Romero died of gunshot wounds.

He had been archbishop in the capital since 1977 and, before that, an auxiliary bishop since 1970.

It was a difficult period in his country, a time of civil war. There was great economic inequality in El Salvador. Many people lived in abject poverty while a few held on to tremendous wealth. Many of the poor saw the nation's government as the protector of the wealthy. They had no hope for change. Some formed rebel groups, drawing funds from communist powers overseas. The rebels promoted the idea of class warfare—the Marxist notion of perpetual struggle between the poor and the rich. The government responded by brutal and sometimes indiscriminate repression.

Ordinary people often found themselves caught between two factions that were violent and unscrupulous.

Óscar Romero inherited a Church divided by bitterness, grief, and distrust. His flock included both poor and rich as the vast majority of

Salvadorans were Catholic. As auxiliary bishop and as archbishop, he tried to provide a quiet pastoral witness for peace.

Some Catholic clergy who worked among the poor also raised their voices in protest of social injustices. For this, they were harassed and threatened by the government. Yet they continued to do what they thought was right, sometimes leading very vocal public demonstrations. Some were close friends of Bishop Romero, though he took exception to their noisy approach.

Shortly after he was installed as archbishop, one of his friends, a Jesuit priest named Rutilio Grande, was assassinated by machine-gun fire as he walked to Mass. Two companions were also killed: an elderly man and a teenage boy. The government refused to investigate, and the fearful media would not cover the story.

Archbishop Romero was shaken when he saw Fr. Grande's body, and he was overwhelmed by a sense of duty, he said, "to follow the same path." He began to speak up against specific abuses by the government—threats, arrests, tortures, and murders. His diocesan newspaper told horrific stories that the secular press would not report. His radio sermons gained a large following and soon became the most trusted source of news in El Salvador.

The government retaliated against the Church. Dozens of priests were attacked, and six were killed. But Archbishop Romero continued raising his voice, and he gained an international following. He ignored the steady rumors of plots against his life. He urged Catholics who were in the military not to obey orders that were contrary to God's law.

For this he was gunned down consecrating the host on the altar while he celebrated Mass for the order of sisters who ran the hospital.

In death and in life he was controversial and often associated with liberation theology, a twentieth-century movement developed mostly in Latin America, which emphasized deliverance from political and economic oppression as an anticipation of ultimate salvation. The Vatican's Congregation for the Doctrine of the Faith issued a critical analysis of the movement in 1984, but St. John Paul II assimilated some of its key terms into his own social thought. In 2015, Óscar Romero was beatified as a martyr.

For More

Congregation for the Doctrine of Faith. *Instruction on Certain Aspects of the "Theology of Liberation."* Boston: St. Paul Editions, 1984.

Óscar Romero. *The Church Cannot Remain Silent: Unpublished Letters and Other Writings.* Maryknoll, NY: Orbis Books, 2016.

Satellite transmitters on the campus of the Eternal Word Television Network in Alabama. Photo by the authors.

97

Catholics *on* Television

These gigantic satellite transmitters rest on a hilltop in Irondale, Alabama. They belong to the Eternal Word Television Network (EWTN), a global network that broadcasts around the clock in English and Spanish. EWTN is by far the greatest success story in Catholic television.

It was founded in 1981 by Mother Angelica, a Poor Clare nun. She launched the network, by her own account, with two hundred dollars and twelve cloistered sisters. By 1985 EWTN was the fastest-growing cable network in the United States. Carried on 220 systems, it was seen in two million homes. In 1996 she added a full schedule of Spanish-language programming. Today, EWTN reaches every continent. It also broadcasts on satellite and shortwave radio and provides programming for many independent radio stations.

Mother Angelica enjoyed the most phenomenal success, but she was not the first to succeed at Catholic programming. As with the printing press and the radio, many Catholics, early on, saw the evangelistic potential in television and video. From 1952 to 1968, Bishop Fulton Sheen reached as many as ten million viewers a week through his series on network television. He also won an Emmy Award.

In the early 1980s Harry John, the Miller Beer heir, tried to establish an international Catholic television network to rival the work of Protestant televangelists. He spent tens of millions of dollars but never quite made it to the airwaves. The US bishops also tried, at various times, to establish a channel. They launched a for-profit venture, the Catholic

Telecommunications Network of America, the same year as Mother Angelica founded EWTN. But getting hundreds of bishops to agree on programming proved at first unwieldy and inefficient and finally impossible.

Catholic laypeople also found creative ways to evangelize with video. Dick Leach, a Chicago native and father of nine children, created a media empire best known for its production of children's programming in the 1990s. With his daughter-in-law Sheryl Leach, Dick introduced the character of Barney, a purple dinosaur who delivered positive messages sung to old, familiar melodies. The Leaches wanted to overcome a coarsening they saw in entertainment aimed at younger generations. Barney was their campaign to restore civility.

Their television show, *Barney and Friends*, aired on the Public Broadcasting System and won an Emmy Award. The family collaborated on another show, *Wishbone*, launched in 1995, about a dog that reimagined great works of literature. Episodes of *Wishbone* introduced young viewers to the stories of St. Joan of Arc and Our Lady of Guadalupe.

Some critics hold that the faith that built cathedrals is ill-suited to modern means of communication. Catholicism, they say, is a dinosaur.

But dinosaurs do seem to prosper in the new media.

For More

Raymond Arroyo. *Mother Angelica: The Remarkable Story of a Nun, Her Nerve, and a Network of Miracles.* New York: Image Books, 2007.

Fulton J. Sheen. *Treasure in Clay: The Autobiography of Fulton J. Sheen.* New York: Image Books, 1982.

Polish currency commemorating the papacy of Pope John Paul II. Photo by Fr. David Halaiko.

98

Banknotes, Poland, 2006

Through most of the twentieth century these banknotes could have been a metaphor for "never." When pigs fly . . . when Niagara falls . . . when the pope's face appears on Eastern European currency . . .

But the day came. On October 16, 2006, the National Bank of Poland issued this fifty-*zlotych* note to commemorate the twenty-eighth anniversary of Karol Wojtyła's election to the papacy. The pontiff had died in the previous year at the age of eighty-four. He appears on this note as a young man at the beginning of his pontificate—strong, vigorous, his hand upraised in blessing. The world map represents the sweep of his authority—and perhaps the travels of his peripatetic papacy. The reverse side renders an image from his inauguration in 1978: the young pope kissing the ring of the elderly Cardinal Stefan Wyszyński, the primate of Poland.

After occupation by the Nazis during World War II, Poland had been handed to the Soviets as the Allies divided up Europe as spoils of war. Young Karol Wojtyła was already enrolled in Krakow's underground seminary. Ordained a priest at twenty-six, he was a bishop at age thirty-eight and a cardinal-archbishop at forty-seven. He was beloved by his people and often spent time among them. Even as bishop, he would go to the Franciscan church every Saturday to wait in line to go to Confession.

Wojtyła held doctorates in theology and philosophy, was respected in both fields, and continued to publish serious academic writing through his years as bishop and archbishop. He contributed often to *The Yearbook of Phenomenological Research*, a prestigious international journal, and its editors once dedicated an entire edition to his book *The Acting Person*. Under a pseudonym he wrote poems and a play. Though very young at the Second Vatican Council, he contributed to the drafting of at least two documents.

When he arrived with his belongings in Rome in 1978, he was not merely a young archbishop of a major European city. He brought with him an amazing array of skills, qualities, and charisms. And he was athletic, handsome, and by all accounts holy. In his first encyclical letter as Pope John Paul II, he took aim at Communism, the seemingly invincible system that had been oppressing his people since 1945. "It is therefore difficult . . . to accept a position that gives only atheism the right of citizenship in public and social life, while believers are . . . barely tolerated or are treated as second-class citizens."

His first visit home to Poland, in 1979, drew vast crowds. He told them: "Be not afraid." They chanted: "We want God." They were emboldened. The trade union Solidarity grew in prominence and effectiveness. The government tried to discredit him by spreading false rumors, which were easily dismissed because of the integrity of the man's life. In their desperation, they murdered a priest associated with Solidarity, Fr. Jerzy Popiełuszko—but his martyrdom only made the people more passionate in their desire for justice.

Pope John Paul II worked closely with world leaders—not only with the enemies of Communism, like Ronald Reagan of the United States and Margaret Thatcher of Great Britain, but also with the Soviets themselves. He corresponded directly and effectively with Leonid Brezhnev, and probably succeeded in staving off a Russian invasion of Poland. Brezhnev's successor, Mikhail Gorbachev, believed that Pope John Paul II was history's single most "outstanding defender of the poor, the oppressed, the downtrodden." US President Reagan said it was John Paul's first visit to Poland that led him to conclude that religion was "the Soviets' Achilles' heel."

The unthinkable happened, beginning with the peaceful revolutions of 1989 and continuing into the early years of the next decade. The Soviet empire, once considered invincible, crumbled. The walls fell without violence.

John Paul's reign as pope was the second longest in modern history, and he was able to accomplish much. Even when hobbled by an assassination attempt and then Parkinson's disease, he kept producing—documents, speeches, canonizations, ecumenical outreach. His goal was the full implementation of the Second Vatican Council.

At his death, Catholics cried out "*Santo subito!*" ("Sainthood now!") and called him "John Paul the Great." A year later his face appeared on Polish currency. He was beatified six years after his death and declared a saint in another three years.

For More

Tad Szulc. *Pope John Paul II: The Biography*. New York: Simon and Schuster, 1996.

George Weigel. *Witness to Hope: The Biography of Pope John Paul II*. New York: Harper, 2005.

Hard-hat area and sanctuary at the cathedral in the Archdiocese of Seoul, South Korea.
Photo by Poranin Wichitworawong, Cha-am Phetchaburi, Thailand.

99

A Cathedral *in* Korea

Amid the billboards and business signs of Seoul, South Korea, rises the spire of Myeongdong Cathedral. The church is dedicated to the Virgin Mary under the title of the Immaculate Conception. The cornerstone of the building was laid in 1892. Pope Francis offered Mass at the cathedral in 2014. But renewal, renovation, and expansion are regular occurrences.

The Church in South Korea is growing. In 1920 there were only 300,000 Christians in Korea, but that number has grown in less than a century to around twelve million, almost a third of the country's population. According to a Pew Research Center report from 2014, from 1985 to 2005 Catholics grew as a share of the population from 5 percent to 11 percent. The largest Christian congregation in the world is in South Korea.

While churches in Europe and the United States are aging and closing up shop, the Church in the "Global South" can hardly contain its growth. The growth of Catholics in South Korea is even across all age groups.

The Church's map has undergone an overhaul since 1910. In that year, 65 percent of the world's Catholics lived in Europe, 24 percent in Latin America and the Caribbean, 5 percent in North America, and 5 percent in Asia and the Pacific. In sub-Saharan Africa and in the Middle East, Catholics accounted for less than 1 percent of the population.

Today, sub-Saharan Africa claims 16 percent of the world's Catholics—and Europe just 24 percent. Latin America and the Caribbean account for 39 percent, Asia and the Pacific 12 percent, and North America 8 percent. The Middle East has held steady at 1 percent.

The proportions have vastly changed, and that is changing history—the way it's lived and the way it's written. For the last five centuries, the

Church's story has been written as Europe's story, mostly. That is unlikely to be the case in the next generation.

Research seems to indicate that Catholics in the Global South differ significantly from their co-religionists in the North. Europeans and North Americans are more likely to believe that the Church cannot survive in its current state—and that it will need to change in order to survive. The historian Philip Jenkins, in his book *The Next Christendom*, remarked:

> Viewed from Cambridge or Amsterdam, such views may make excellent sense, but in the context of global Christianity, this kind of liberalism looks distinctly dated. It would not be easy to convince a congregation in Seoul or Nairobi that Christianity is dying, when their main concern is building a worship facility big enough for the 10,000 or 20,000 members they have gained over the past few years. And these new converts are mostly teenagers and young adults, very few with white hair. Nor can these churches be easily told that, in order to reach a mass audience, they must bring their message more into accord with (Western) secular authorities.

Many Christians in the South, moreover, are proving their faith amid severe challenges. In many places, Catholics are a persecuted minority, whose growth is seen as a provocation and threat. More than 200 million Christians in some sixty countries live with some form of restriction on their faith.

The moral authority of such believers cannot be denied or diminished. The Global South has, in the last generation, become more influential and visible in the universal Church. Africa and India were both, very recently, considered mission territories. Today they are sending missionaries to the secularized North. In 2013 the cardinals elected the first non-European pope in many centuries.

The spires of churches rise today, as always, as signs—signs of faith competing for public attention, signs of hope for the future, and sometimes signs of contradiction.

For More

John L. Allen Jr. *The Global War on Christians: Dispatches from the Front Lines of Anti-Christian Persecution.* New York: Image, 2013.

Philip Jenkins. *The Next Christendom: The Coming of Global Christianity.* New York: Oxford University Press, 2002.

What pilgrims leave behind: small details of their story. Photo by Fr. Gaurav Shroff.

100

Pilgrim Offerings

These are the things that pilgrims leave behind—some of the coins from their native land, some of the coins from the country they're visiting, and there's a devotional bracelet, too. Some of it is dropped intentionally, some accidentally. It will be there to be discovered; perhaps someone will use it to piece together the story of an episode, an era, a character, or a movement in history.

The Second Vatican Council repeatedly referred to the Church as the people of God "on earthly pilgrimage" toward the heavenly city. Christians are wayfarers, a pilgrim Church on earth.

And pilgrimage is marked by surprise. Read the fourth- and fifth-century accounts of Helena, Egeria, the Bordeaux Pilgrim, and Paula as they made their individual ways to the Holy Land. They encountered surprises along the way. They made detours. They experienced unexpected graces and blessings.

The Church on earth is always in motion. Catholic doctrine and devotion are always developing. And every age presents particular challenges, which require a creative response.

The Church in the Middle Ages looked different from the Church of the Apostolic Fathers. Those early bishops could not have predicted the concerns, joys, hopes, art, literary forms, and architecture of their distant descendants. Nor could they have foreseen what would happen when distant cultures draw together or collide.

The Church is on pilgrimage and so is each member. That is vividly true in the lives, today, of refugees. An unprecedented number of Christians are today on the move—fleeing persecution in their homelands, living temporarily in camps, hoping to survive, and hoping to find another home. As an anonymous apologist in the second century put it: "For them every foreign country is a motherland, and every motherland is a foreign country" (*Letter to Diognetus*).

These modern travelers follow the footsteps of many before them—those who fled or were exiled from Jerusalem in AD 70, from Egypt in 642, from Constantinople in 1453, and from Armenia in 1917.

Tomorrow is a new chapter in our same old story.

> Now those who were scattered because of the persecution that arose over Stephen traveled as far as Phoenicia and Cyprus and Antioch, speaking the word to none except Jews. But there were some of them, men of Cyprus and Cyrene, who on coming to Antioch spoke to the Greeks also, preaching the Lord Jesus. And the hand of the Lord was with them, and a great number that believed turned to the Lord. (Acts 11:19–21)

Mileage will vary. The routes will be different. But the Pilgrim Church will move upon the earth—move Godward—and take the world with it.

For More

Mike Aquilina. *Yours Is the Church: How Catholicism Shapes Our World.* Ann Arbor, MI: Servant Books, 2012.

Rodney Stark. *The Triumph of Faith: Why the World Is More Religious than Ever.* Wilmington, DE: ISI Books, 2015.

Acknowledgments

This book would never have seen print without the heroic generosity of three men: Fr. Richard Kunst, the curator at PapalArtifacts.com; Fr. Gaurav Shroff of the Archdiocese of Atlanta; and Dr. James Papandrea of Garrett-Evangelical Theological Seminary. We cannot thank them enough.

So many people, in fact, showed us far more kindness than we deserved. We extend heartfelt thanks to them, one and all: Michael Andaloro, Rosemary Aquilina, Tom Brouns (tazmpictures), Susan Brown, Laurie Burgess, Fr. Jason Charron, Helen Cindrich, Robert Corzine, Paul Crawford, Mario and Christina Dickerson, Hilary Douwes, Robert Fernandez, Natalia Finegan, Patrick Finegan, Regis Flaherty, Ricardo André Frantz, Tom Grady, Jane Greer, Fr. Frederick Gruber, Mark Gruber, Raymond Gruby, Marc Hagen, Fr. David Halaiko, Fr. Bernard Healy, Colin Hepburn, Elizabeth Hogan, Hayley Jackson, Derris Jeffcoat, Matthew Leonard, Alyssa Lewis, Jim Luptak, John Marino, Gerald Martin, Brandon McGinley, Linda Mertz, Richard Miesel, Gregory Orfalea, Joseph Pearce, Julieta Flores Robbins, Thomas A. Robinson, Chris Sassouni, David Scott, Fr. Richard Simon, Silvia Corral Simpson, Carl Sommer, Lori Stewart, Joe Sweeney, Jon Sweeney, Michael Szatkowski, Gabrielle Tucci, Rafael Piña Valdez, Cardinal Donald Wuerl, Mark Zimmerman, and the good folks at Art Resource.

All photos in this book are used with kind permission of their owners or authorized agents. Credits appear with each image.

We did not want to weigh the book down with notes. So most sources are cited within the text; most others can be tracked down by a simple Web search (or in the books recommended in each chapter). If you're still stumped, please contact the authors in care of the publisher.

Index

Mike Aquilina is a Catholic author, popular speaker, poet, and songwriter who serves as the executive vice president of the St. Paul Center for Biblical Theology.

Aquilina earned a bachelor's degree in English/writing (Phi Beta Kappa) from Penn State University in 1985. He is the author or editor of more than fifty books, including *The Fathers of the Church*, *The Mass of the Early Christians*, and *Angels of God*. He contributed work on early Christianity to the *Encyclopedia of Catholic Social Thought*. Aquilina has cohosted ten series on EWTN and hosted two documentaries. In 2015, Aquilina wrote the companion volume to the NBC miniseries *A.D.: The Bible Continues*, and in 2016, he wrote the companion volume to the MGM remake of the movie *Ben-Hur*.

He has published hundreds of articles, essays, and reviews in periodicals such as *First Things*, *Crisis*, *National Catholic Register*, *The Priest*, *Columbia*, and *Our Sunday Visitor*. He is a frequent guest on TV and radio, including a weekly appearance on the *Son Rise Morning Show*.

Aquilina previously served as editor of *New Covenant: A Magazine of Catholic Spirituality*, *The Pittsburgh Catholic*, and Black Box Corp. He also worked as editorial director at the Barash Group. He has received honors from the Catholic Press Association, including "Best Magazine" for *New Covenant* during his editorship.

He lives in the Pittsburgh, Pennsylvania, area with his wife, Terri. They have six children.

Grace Aquilina is a freelance editor who lives in Pittsburgh, Pennsylvania.